ALSO BY n+1

Happiness

Happiness

TEN YEARS OF n+1

SELECTED BY THE EDITORS OF *n+1* MAGAZINE

ff

FABER AND FABER, INC.

AN AFFILIATE OF FARRAR, STRAUS AND GIROUX

NEW YORK

Faber and Faber, Inc.
An affiliate of Farrar, Straus and Giroux
18 West 18th Street, New York 10011

Selection copyright © 2014 by n+1 Foundation
All rights reserved
Printed in the United States of America
First edition, 2014

Owing to limitations of space, all acknowledgments for permission to reprint
previously published material can be found on pages 367–368.

Library of Congress Cataloging-in-Publication Data
Happiness : ten years of n+1 / selected by the editors of n+1. — First
edition.
    pages   cm
    ISBN 978-0-86547-822-0 (paperback) — ISBN 978-0-374-71237-2
(ebook)
    1. United State—Civilization—21st century.   I. N+1 Foundation
(New York, New York)   II. N+1.

E169.12.H365 2014
973.93—dc23

                                                        2014004043

Designed by Jonathan D. Lippincott

Faber and Faber, Inc., books may be purchased for educational, business,
or promotional use. For information on bulk purchases, please contact the Macmillan
Corporate and Premium Sales Department at 1-800-221-7945, extension 5442,
or write to specialmarkets@macmillan.com.

www.fsgbooks.com
www.twitter.com/fsgbooks • www.facebook.com/fsgbooks

1   3   5   7   9   10   8   6   4   2

CONTENTS

CONTENTS

INTRODUCTION

by Mary Karr

A proper introduction oughta circle the collection like a hostess at a cocktail party, saying a little something nice about everybody. But propriety is not my forte, nor is it the *n+1ers'*.

They're intellectual outlaws of the first order. They zigzag across the cultural landscape (both highfalutin and pop), scouting for beauty among the young, the unpublished, and unheard of. Hand to heart, I swear the best literary writing in English blooms inside each issue. If they had a sandwich board, I'd wear it; if they had a flag, I'd wave it.

Not so at first blush.

On a cold morning in 2003 in my Hell's Kitchen apartment, twenty-eight-year-old Keith Gessen—former fictioner in the Syracuse MFA program, where I teach—showed up with two of his pals to talk about founding a literary mag.

Gessen was a Russian Jew who had, as far as I could tell, spent most of his time at Syracuse playing hockey. Bespectacled Mark Greif was dark, lumbering, and in the muddy midst of a PhD at Yale. Slim Benjamin Kunkel was laboring on his soon-to-be-big-deal novel *Indecision*. He was quieter and almost too blondly pretty to look at head-on.

Over bagels, they chatted about the decline of lit crit, *The New Republic* taking potshots at youngsters, the cult of *McSweeney's*, how online journalism was leaning in the glib direction of *Salon* and *Slate*. Their mag would fix all that. *n+1*, they were calling it.

My judgment was swift as a swinging blade. Boneheaded idea! Publishing itself was circling the drain—hadn't even the august *Lingua Franca* just bitten it? And *Partisan Review*—after seventy years! Those heroes couldn't drum up the requisite dough to pump out pages—how did these yahoos expect to? Waste of time. *Nyet*, no, nevah.

Then I wrote them a check.

And their vision started to grow on me. They wanted sprawling, ambitious articles you couldn't squash into single sound bites. They were the antivenin to the elevator pitch. They wanted to establish themselves as curious *thinkers*, not pious *knowers*.

[Serious] writing about culture has become the exclusive province of bullies, reactionaries, and Englishmen.

(Issue One)

The moral responsibility is not to be intelligent. It's to think. An attribute, self-satisfied and fixed, gets confused with an action, thinking, which revalues old ideas as well as defends them. Thought adds something new to the world; simple intelligence wields hardened truth like a bludgeon.

(Issue One)

As they bundled into coats, I offered the ultimate gift—my own writing! I would deign to permit the likes of them to publish, say, an essay by *moi*. Which idea they failed to fall on like wolves. Were they studying their feet? Shifting their eyes from mine? Ultimately, they demurred.

"You're too well-known," Keith said.

Shocking, this. Many (most?) little mags court the established scrivener, maybe even publish medium-shitty work by said writer so as to flaunt her name in the contents. These *n+1*ers sought quality from the ranks of the invisible. The sheer quality of the work would magnetically draw readers to the unknown. That they believed this made them possibly the dumbest young literary humans I'd met in a while.

Soon I was at the Pink Pony at a benefit hosted by none other than *The New York Review of Books*'s Barbara Epstein. The other editors—Marco Roth, Allison Lorentzen, Chad Harbach—wowed me much as the first phalanx had. Money was being scraped up. Gessen was sleeping on the sofa of the neoghetto office downtown, and contributors were being paid off in beer.

Still, I gnawed my thumbnail before the first issues burst into print to solid acclaim.

The editors took on lesser mags without being snarky. They opposed the war in Iraq—this was in 2004, when such an opinion was not yet mandatory in New York—and they were willing to stand up to the people who cheered for it.

Mark Greif's "Against Exercise" still hangs among the brightest stars in my nonfiction constellation. In an age when food and body worship have become near-religious among our educated classes, Greif denigrates the whole practice by making it worthy of Kafka's penal colony.

Best of all, *n+1* ponied up with the promised luminary unknowns—those Susan Sontags– and George Orwells–to-be emerging like sirens from the fog of oblivion into print.

Elif Batuman took on Isaac Babel with a voice I got a girl crush on right off. Batuman had the wise charm of Hannah Arendt—if Arendt wore a red rubber nose and floppy shoes.

The "millennium" edition of Tolstoy fills a hundred volumes and weighs as much as a newborn beluga whale . . .

Comparing Tostoy's works to Babel's is like comparing a long road to a pocket watch.

Batuman has long since been "discovered" by *The New Yorker* et al. A lot of their writers have. And a magazine that began as white/Jewish and very male has become less white, and a lot less male.

Ten years in, I still find the most rereadable writing—Coleridge's old test was rereading—in *n+1*.

There are only two things wrong with this assemblage.

One, it's not big enough. Where's Nikil Saval's history of the office, or Carla Blumenkranz's history of the website Gawker? Where's Elizabeth Gumport on feminism, privacy, and Chris Kraus; Christopher Glazek's attack on the prison-industrial complex; or Dayna Tortorici's hilarious (unsigned) editorial denouncing the online "rage machine"? The anthologist has stinted. A proper anthology should weigh as much as—in Batuman's metaphor—a big-mouthed bass at least.

And two: after ten years, this magazine remains too much of a damn secret. The editors have proved pretty good at editing; at promoting this thing, they're as clueless as they were in 2003. The concocters of this fantastic literary endeavor still have to hustle to grind out issues. Contributors are paid, but barely.

This brave, hard-won offering to the world needs many more people reading it. They will be those who believe in alchemy—that adding the fresh mystery of beautiful, relevant writing (n) to the lone reader (1) is to forge a coin of untold value, precious, imperishable.

Happiness

THE INTELLECTUAL SITUATION
(HAPPINESS)

The Editors

A history of happiness is a funny thing, since, for a long time, happiness was viewed as merely the absence of history. No one lived for happiness the way we do today. In an individual life, it would have been a lack of catastrophic events. As the goal of an era, or civilization, it would have meant stasis, absolutely nothing happening. If you did hit the blank-time jackpot of happiness, the best thing to do was drop dead.

Then came modernity. "Periods of happiness are blank pages in history," Hegel declared—summarizing the ancient view—and proceeded to spill ink all over them. The more optimistic savants of the era began writing happiness directly into history, into life. They made happiness the goal of civilization, and of the individual living in civilization.

The young Saint-Just was probably exaggerating for rhetorical effect when he declared, in 1792, "Happiness is a new idea in Europe." But he wasn't wrong. He should have looked across the ocean, too. From the American and French Revolutions forward, engineers of happiness came into firm control. Ideas like "the pursuit of happiness" and the "greatest happiness for the greatest number" migrated from the academies and drawing rooms of eighteenth-century thinkers to the Continental Congress and the National Assembly. While cheerful Bentham doodled plans for his perfect prison, gloomy Carlyle recognized utility and its pleasures as the "idols of the age."

The principle of happiness was going to provide the key to a Newtonian science of the human. Traders and treasurers were thrilled: self-interest would put greed and morality together with a big fat smile. Definitions of happiness were called for and experts stepped forward to provide them. The invading authorities are still with us: economists, political scientists, and brain doctors.

Not everyone in the nineteenth century went down the long slide to happiness, endlessly. Novelists said again and again they would never represent happiness. Tolstoy's opening line about all happy families being the same is the best known, but Balzac, too, said, "Le Bonheur n'a pas d'histoire," happiness has no story. The novel's only actual version of happiness—marriage—came to seem, toward the end of the century, something of a dark joke. After all that trouble, went the joke, you marry Gilbert Osmond. Those who tried to get away from the marriage plot by seeking their own happiness—Tess of the D'Urbervilles, Emma Bovary, Anna Karenina—got just what they didn't deserve. The novel didn't make you any promises. Quite the opposite: it could have scared you off of life. But somehow its congenital unhappiness actually made you want to live.

And the philosophical tradition, too, secreted an antitoxin, in its own form of institutionalized unhappiness—critique. From Marx, Nietzsche, and Freud, to the Western Marxism of the twentieth century, the unhappy consciousness of a certain kind of philosopher gave you the only hope comparable to that of the novel. Where the novel was personal and individual, critique was historical and social. Adorno: "The splinter in your eye is the best magnifying glass."

But it looks today like the happiness doctors have won. Totalitarian states enforced happiness through love of force, worship of terror, submergence in the mass. Liberal democracy was more easygoing about it, and that proved wiser. Pills keep us cheerful; sex is healthy exercise; violent light entertainment passes the time. Aldous Huxley wrote a letter to George Orwell right after *1984* appeared, in which he praised the Big Brother vision but had to say he thought his own prediction of the future would be a lot closer to the truth. Not a boot stomping on your face for all eternity, but a society in which preferring unhappiness—because you didn't want happiness by ersatz means—would be the totally unintelligible thing. We are told the terrorists hate our freedoms—but who was freer than those guys, riding around Afghanistan in pickup trucks with Kalashnikovs? It's not our freedoms we're going to bring the peoples of the world. No, we're going to bring them our *happiness*.

(2005)

TORTURE AND PARENTING

Marco Roth

After E. and I smoked a cigarette each on the patio steps, we went back inside and began to drink beer in great gulps. We set up the backgammon board and played with a combination of intensity and absent-mindedness, forced to count out intervals we once had memorized. Jessye Norman's voice soared to sing the last line of the third of Strauss's *Four Last Songs*, "Tief und Tausendfach zu Leben," but through it all, upstairs in her darkened nursery, our six-month-old daughter cried, and through it all we heard her.

Do not think that we were being horrible, indifferent parents. We were trying very hard the whole time to be good and dutiful ones. We were practicing what the army of child sleep specialists calls "extinction," letting our daughter learn to settle herself to sleep on her own. There are many ways of extinguishing your child: "graduated extinction," or Ferberizing, as well as extensive cuddling and prolonged breast-feeding (not really practicable for working mothers), and probably some other method involving elaborate Wiccan rituals. Ferberizing allows you to sit with your child while she cries, talk to her or stroke her hair, everything but pick her up, and to do these soothings at intervals gradually longer and longer. Behind Ferber is the sound idea that your child needs to know you are there in order to settle herself to sleep. Behind the outright extinguishers, or whatever you want to call them, is the no less sound theory that your child wants to be cuddled to sleep and nothing else will do, so you might as well teach her that though you are there before she's about to sleep, and when she wakes up with a genuine hunger, you are not there while she tries to sleep.

No agreement can be found among parents, and the books, for all their appearance of scientific scrupulousness, play to different fears. "Nobody knows the effects of leaving your child alone to cry," writes Elizabeth Pantley, author of *The No-Cry Sleep Solution*, in a way that leads you to think these effects could only be terrible. T. Berry Brazelton, the parenting industry's Dr. Phil, warns that you should never reward your child for crying. We steered between the Scylla and Charybdis of good advice by consulting our friends with children. One of them, who'd read a Ferber book and then went the other way with his daughter, said, "I can't imagine letting her know you're there and not giving her what she wants. Why torture her?"

That argument was enough for us. We couldn't bear to think that the sound of our voices could become a source of pain to our child. The other benefit of extinction was its apparent speed. In the case of our friend's daughter, she'd cried forty-five minutes the first night, thirty minutes the next, twenty the following, then five, and after that only a few whimpers of exhaustion. It was a cold, hard, and ruthlessly efficient way of doing the cold, hard, ruthless, and needful thing of placing an infant on a sleep cycle in tune with the rhythms of life in a job-holding society. All the books agree that establishing a routine and pattern is important, and, in the manner of all self-help books, the primary instrument of both Ferber and non-Ferber is the schedule work sheet in which you note down all the times your child sleeps, and for how long. You become, in short, your own home sleep psychologist. Parents need routines, too, and clocking in obsessively can be one of them.

Of course E. and I thought that these work sheets were a trick, something to do to make us feel like caring, conscientious parents as we began the process of abandoning our child to a world with no cuddling on demand. To leave your child to cry, for even a minute, goes against every instinct and social response. Not to rush and pick her up requires an immense act of will. We could do no right, but we feared that we could also do wrong. So we chose to do our duty and to feel bad about it. E. bore down and set up routines: an evening meal, a bath, a time for quiet holding and singing and reading of stories and play, and then, at the appointed hour, off to bed, good-nights said in a tone of false assurance (another commandment of sleep therapists: do not convey your own anxiety to your child!), the lights out, the crying beginning from the time her head is laid in the crib and her arms reach up. And so we shut the door and snuck downstairs to do the things we do when we feel bad.

That first night, as we diced and went for the second beer at the half-hour mark, unbidden into my mind came the thought that we were behaving exactly like the guilty torturers of history and legend, propping each other up as we went about the unthinkable. Strauss's songs blended into both a compensation for human suffering and suffering's soundtrack; a momentary understanding flickered of why those *kommandants* listened to their Mozart and Bach.

We were not torturers, of course, or *kapos*, despite the workings of my guilty imagination. What separated us from them— besides our soft Persian rugs and baby blankets in rustic patterns, as against their barbed wire and wood pallets—was, of course, intention. Everything we do with our daughter is governed by love, and we wish her to become a full and free individual, capable of love in her own right. Intention, however, is a thin defense. Love has never prevented people from mistreating their children: "This hurts me more than it hurts you!" And indeed—for here is the thing—the Bush administration has relied very heavily on the excuse of good intentions in its bid to make torture acceptable to Americans. Alberto Gonzales's government memo of 2002, adopted by the Justice Department, defines torture only as an intention to inflict pain. It doesn't matter what you do to the person before you, as long as you really want the truth, or to save lives, or to save someone's soul. You can rip out fingernails to get what you want, and as long as what you want is not to hurt your subject, you are not engaged in torture, at least not according to the impeccable mind of our attorney general.

Metaphors are not arguments; they are collisions in a mental environment. Perhaps it was our friend's remark that first suggested an association between certain varieties of "extinction" and torture. Or perhaps it was simply being alive and a reader of the news in today's America. If you don't know that America now engages in torture and sends people to countries that also torture, someone has done a very good job indeed of putting you to sleep. If you don't know that our attorney general is an apologist for torture and our defense secretary an enthusiastic proponent of it, you are sleeping soundly. The fact that Americans are torturers saturates the atmosphere, even our modest trinity house in Philadelphia, and the modest peaceable lives most of us lead. The metaphor cannot help being false and exaggerated in some ways, as in the Sylvia Plath poem "Daddy" (known in our family as "Shall I compare thee to an SS officer?"), but the metaphor also contains the traces of an actual resemblance, however distorted.

If parenting, even responsible parenting, made me feel like a torturer, it wasn't exactly because I'm melodramatic or overwrought but because the official torturers now conceive of themselves in the same terms as the parenting manuals. They, too, are technicians of the naked human personality. The "Human Resource Exploitation Manual," a formerly classified government document used to instruct "anticommunist" Latin American security forces in the bad old 1980s, puts the theory of torture in terms that any reader of *Healthy Sleep Habits, Happy Child* can easily understand. The aim of torture, here called "questioning," is "to induce regression in the subject," i.e., to shatter that person's identity by returning him to a state of infantile dependence on his captors. For this, violence itself is actually deemed inefficient and unnecessary (not to mention risky and unpopular once the news gets out). For some of us, the scandal of Abu Ghraib and the sadomasochistic sexual tortures of Guantanamo Bay (fake menstrual blood, simulated sex, et cetera) is less about our horror at torture than the broken taboos, the lack of restraint on display, in comparison to the refined techniques once taught in the School of the Americas.

Far more effective, the torture theorists say, is to shatter the routines that make us adults without physical violence. Sleep deprivation becomes the favored tactic, accompanied by such macabre tricks as putting clocks forward or back randomly, making sure that the prisoner cannot tell day from night, irregular feeding, temporary starvation, random extremes of temperature, loud music constantly, and, of course, random responses from the captors, either rage or bizarre affection, always absurd and unmotivated. (It's allowed, for instance, to reward uncooperative behavior, the better to induce false hopes in the subject.) Beatings might play an occasional role in hastening regression, but please don't get carried away. In short, the torturer becomes the bad parent, whose job it is to destroy the entire work of childhood in a matter of days and weeks. Obtaining information is but a side effect of the paramount project: turning adults into unhappy children.

A notion shared by the popular psychologists of torture and infants: the core self is a paltry thing, composed mainly of certain habits and persistent associations. Just as this self can only be constructed through cycles and work sheet–plotted routinization, so it can be destroyed by deroutinization. At least since the Scottish Enlightenment, people have recognized that habits and chains of association make up a strong part of individual identity, but it would be a twisted view of humans that made our habits both the necessary and sufficient condition of our individual life. People survive torture. Personalities even survive torture, their individuality racked and maimed, like their bodies, but still legible. Winston Smith, by the tables of the "Chestnut Tree," is a creature haunted by an ungraspable sense of shame and guilt at his self-betrayal as much as he is the model reformed citizen of Airstrip One. Torture isn't immoral because the individual fails to survive, but precisely because the individual does survive in a region of the mind no longer accessible to the person.

The parallels between parenting and torture, unwittingly created by behavioral psychologists in both camps, suddenly intersect and cross over. We rebel at leaving our child to cry, because something about it violates our humanity. We may want our child to get a head start on competition in the global economy or, quite simply, to fall asleep so we can catch up on sleep ourselves, but there is more to parents and children than the establishment of safe routines. Our children may develop healthy sleep habits, and we, too, will be able to get up for work again without ten cups of coffee, but the desires of children and their parents for love—not information—will always exceed the circumscribed hours of wakefulness and the model of efficiency.

When we put our children to sleep, even with the best intentions, we begin to instruct them in a fine art of self-limitation we practice on ourselves, an art that's just a step away from self-mutilation. But would it be so monstrous to let ourselves go completely? When Marcel sneaks downstairs at the beginning of *Swann's Way*, he is sent back to bed. When he returns again to beg another good-night kiss from his mother, he is caught by his father and inexplicably given the very thing he wants and more: his mother gets to sleep with him. "See, we're not torturers," his father says.

But for Marcel, this inexplicable pardon, a reverse of Abraham's sacrifice of Isaac, as he puts it, confirms his exile from a community of healthy, disciplined children—a generation that will be mowed down in the First World War. "My sadness was no longer a punishable offense, but an involuntary illness . . . for which I was no longer responsible." Sadness, like memory, is involuntary, and yet the involuntary spasms, those things that cannot be controlled, make Marcel into Marcel and not Saint-Loup. Another name for his sadness is (unsatisfied) love.

Parents, it seems, inevitably feel like torturers. But do those masters of regression, our new model torturers, feel like parents? If we extend the idea of Stockholm syndrome (the victim's feeling of love for his torturer) to the torturers, the answer seems to be yes. But an empirical proof that the feeling goes both ways will have to wait. Defense Department psychologists may be taking notes as they debrief, but the public won't see these documents anytime soon, and our journalists, elsewhere so eager to extort confessions from child abusers, have not gone in search of retired torturers.

Also, English-speaking torturers may soon be in short supply. Our new favored method of extraordinary rendition brings new meaning to the term "nanny state." Just as many affluent American parents hire women from poorer countries to look after their children and do much of the dirty work of parenting, so we now send our prisoners of war to states whose torturers cling to old-fashioned "spare the rod, spoil the prisoner" mentalities.

Prisoners and children. We have reached another metaphorical crossroads. Our executive branch and their lockstep followers in Congress would argue that their harsh measures are justified, not only because these people are our enemies, but because they have chosen to sin. They are no longer children but adults with free will. To fight America is to fight God, Democracy, History, and Freedom all at once, and to such sinners belongs outer darkness. "Who could be more impious than one who'd dare to sorrow at the judgment God decrees?" Virgil rebukes Dante as he sheds a tear for the eviscerated, boiled, and forked souls in the *Inferno*. America the perfect makes no mistakes. But those who accept that George Bush is God's regent on earth should also accept that this makes W. everybody's surrogate daddy while he stands in for the big daddy in the sky. The word is paternalism. If America truly has dominion over all men and women and the beasts of the field in a neofeudal order, all of us are America's children. Is it all right to torture children? Just ask the president, or rather his wife. Her favorite scene in world literature, she once said, is Dostoevsky's "Grand Inquisitor" from *The Brothers Karamazov.* The professional interpreters in our press have been at work on this delicious admission that allows us to construct the twisted history of our ruling family. Who knows if Laura ever talked about Dostoevsky with George? Do our parents talk to each other? What do they say? Did they notice that the scene begins when Ivan Karamazov asks his brother if he would torture a child if it meant ensuring happiness for the rest of the world? We know our president's answer would be an enthusiastic thumbs-up, as long as it's someone else's thumb.

(2005)

AFTERNOON OF
THE SEX CHILDREN

Mark Greif

Not long ago I took part in one of the conversations you're not
supposed to have. It turned on whether Vladimir Nabokov, author of *Lolita*, really desired underage girls. The usual arguments
came out: Nabokov was a master of personae, and Humbert Humbert a game to him. Kinbote, analogous narrator of *Pale Fire*,
didn't make you think Nabokov loved boys. The late novels were
Nabokov's allegories of the seductions of aestheticism, which
transfigures the forbidden into the beautiful; or moral paintings
of our acceptance of crime, when crime is presented alluringly. So
love of the wrong object becomes a metaphor for art, ethics, personality, and so forth.

I was reluctant to say that I felt these explanations were inadequate and even in bad faith. The trouble with *Lolita* is plainly
its ability to describe what a sexual twelve-year-old looks like.
What her dress is like when it brushes her knees, what her toes
are like with painted nails, how the color sits on the plump bow
of her lips—the phrase for this is that it is "too real"; that's the
scandal. It continues to be the scandal fifty years after publication, and it will be a scandal whenever any adult acknowledges

the capacity to upend his vision and see a child, protected larval stage of the organism, as a sexual object. The girl is still a child, only now she is a sex child. Yet this makes me feel Nabokov was not a pedophile, but something he is not credited with being—a social critic.

You, too, see it, or should. The trend of these fifty years has been to make us see sexual youth where it doesn't exist, and ignore it as it does. Adults project the sex of children in lust, or examine children sexually with magnifying glasses to make sure they don't appeal to us. But these lenses became burning glasses. The hips of Betty Grable melted and disappeared. The breasts of Marilyn Monroe ran off and were replaced with silicone. The geography of fashion created new erogenous zones—pelvic midriff, rear cleavage—for dieters starving off their secondary sex characteristics, and for young teens, in the convergence of the exerciser and the pubescent child. The waif and the pixie became ideal. Mama and daughter look the same again before the bedroom mirror—not dressed up in Mama's pearls and heels, this time, but in children's wear. The dream belongs to sixteen, or to those who can starve themselves to sixteen.

The critic Philip Fisher used to note that *Lolita*, tightly plotted as it is, repeats one scene twice. Humbert spies a lit window far opposite. Because he longs to see a nymphet, he sees one. The wave of arousal returns, its tide dampening him up to his knees. As he nears the climax, the form is refocused as an adult woman or man. Disgusting! But this is a simple inversion of a characteristic experience of our time. A man will see a distant form, in low-cut top and low-slung jeans, and think he is on the trail of eroticism; draw near, and identify a child. Revolting! The defenses against it continue the problem. The more a whole nation inspects the sex characteristics of children to make sure it is not becoming aroused by childishness, and slyly hunts around to make sure its most untrustworthy members are not being so aroused, the more it risks creating a sexual fascination with the child. However you gaze, to accept the fantasy, or to assure yourself you see nothing, you join in an abomination.

We live in the afternoon of the sex children; Nabokov just saw the dawn.

Now children from junior high to high school to college live in the most perfect sex environment devised by contemporary society—or so adults believe. Now they are inmates in great sex colonies where they wheel in circles holding hands with their pants down. Henry Darger, emblematic artist of our time with his girl armies, made for our sensibilities what Gauguin's Tahitian beauties were to the French nineteenth-century bourgeoisie—repositories of true, voluptuous, savage inner nature.

Yet in public we want to believe that children are not prepared for sex as we are, do not understand it, and have a special, fragile, glassy truth inside them that will be endangered by premature use—as if the pearls of highest value for us, our chase after sex, our truth of "sexuality," should not also be the treasure for them.

It took the whole history of postwar American culture to make the sex child. It required a merging of old prurient fantasies, dating from the Victorians and Progressives, with the actual sexual liberation of children after midcentury. You needed the expansion of the commercial market for children—selling to kids with sex as everything is sold with sex. You needed the bad faith of Madison Avenue advertisers and Seventh Avenue fashion writers. You needed the sinister prudery of Orange County evangelicalism and the paraliterature of child sex that arises in antipedophilia crusades (*Treacherous Love*; *It Happened to Nancy*)— erotica purveyed to middle-school libraries. You needed the internet.

Victorian child-loving is only loosely the background for our current preoccupation with the pedophile and the sexual child. With Lewis Carroll and Alice, John Ruskin and Rose La Touche, the fantastic young bride and her gauzy innocence, we know we are in the realm of adult prurience. It is *child sexual liberation* that transforms the current moment. We can no longer say it is only fantasy that exists about the sex lives of children. Or, rather— maybe this is the better way to say it—children have been insistently invited into our fantasy, too, and when they grow up they'll furnish the adult continuity of this same madness.

Is it necessary to say that the majority of the sex children we see and desire are not legally children? The representatives of the sex child in our entertainment culture are often eighteen to twenty-one—legal adults. The root of their significance is that their sexual value points backward, to the status of the child, and not forward to the adult. So there is Britney, famous at the age of eighteen for a grind video to "Oops, I Did It Again" ("I'm not that innocent"), and Paris, nineteen years old in her amateur porn DVD (*1 Night in Paris*); alumnae of the Mickey Mouse Club like Christina—licking her lips at twenty on the *Rolling Stone* cover, miniskirt pulled open above the headline "Guess What Christina Wants"; and Lindsay, veteran of Disney children's films, whose breast size, extreme dieting, and accidental self-exposures on the red carpet are the stuff of *Entertainment Tonight*. It's important that these are not adult "stars" in the way of Nicole Kidman or Julia Roberts; not called beautiful, rarely featured in adult films. Instead they furnish the core of entertainment news to two distinct audiences: children nine to fourteen, who enjoy their music and films on these works' own terms, and adults who regard them— well, as what?*

Oddly, those of us who face these questions now have been sex children ourselves; we come after the great divide. You would think we'd remember. Our sex was handed to us, liberated, when we appeared in the world. We managed to feel like rebels with all the other twelve-year-olds, deluded, but not to be blamed for that. A great tween gang of sexual ruffians, trolling the basement TV for scrambled porn, tangling on couches, coming up for air in clouds of musk, shirts on backward; what did we learn? Having lived in the phantasm evidently does not diminish the phantasm. One still looks at those kids enviously; that is one of the mysteries to be solved. It is as if crossing the divide to adulthood entailed a great self-blinding in the act of seeing what is not, precisely, there; and forgetting what one oneself experienced. If we turn to the sex children as avidly as anyone, it must be because they are *doing something for us, too,* as participants in this society and as individuals. And the supplement will not be found in their childhood at all, but in the overall system of adult life.

---

*The entertainment does not seem to be only for adult men. It's a difficult question whether there is strict symmetry by gender, so that boys should also become sex objects for adult women, and adult male fashion regress to youth. In the private realm, schoolteachers keep being revealed as molesters when they get pregnant by their seventh-graders; so that is one kind of appeal. And in the popular culture, Abercrombie & Fitch names a certain iconography of high school muscle-bound male toplessness, teen depilation, and wrestling as signs of eros—an eroticism drawn from gay men's pleasure in the college boy and teen, repurposed for heterosexuality. But it does seem the popular culture is still just testing the waters to find the extent of adult women's desire. This is the meaning of the aphasic silences, for example, around Demi's Ashton and Gabi's lawn-boy lover on *Desperate Housewives*. The logic of our society should ultimately even out private fantasies between the genders. But perhaps because there is always so great a capacity for fantasy and pleasure in self-display— not just in pursuit of one's opposite number—for now adult women's investment in the sex children, at least in public, remains largely oriented to youthful girls.

•

The lure of a permanent childhood in America partly comes from the overwhelming feeling that one hasn't yet achieved one's true youth, because true youth would be defined by freedom so total that no one can attain it. Presumably even the spring break kids, rutting, tanning, boozing with abandon, know there is a more perfect spring break beyond the horizon. Without a powerful aspiration to become adult, without some separate value that downplays childhood for sharper freedoms in age and maturity, the feeling of dissatisfaction can proceed indefinitely, in the midst of marriage, child rearing, retirement, unto death.

The college years—of all times—stand out as the apex of sex childhood. Even if college is routinized and undemanding, it is still inevitably residential, and therefore the place to perfect one's life as a sex child. You move away from home into a setting where you are with other children—strangers all. You must be patient for four years just to get a degree. So there can be little to do but fornicate. Certainly from the wider culture, of MTV and rumor, you know four years is all you will get. The semester provides an interruption between institutionalized sex jubilees: spring break, or just the weekends. The frat-house party assumes a gothic significance, not only for prurient adults but for the collegians themselves who report, on Monday, their decadence.

As a college student today, you always know what things *could* be like. The "Girls Gone Wild" cameras show a world where at this very moment someone is spontaneously lifting her shirt for a logoed hat. You might think the whole thing was a put-on except that everyone seems so earnest. The most earnest write sex columns ("Sex and the Elm City") in which the elite and joyless of Yale aspire to be like the déclassé and uninhibited of Florida State. The new full-scale campus sex magazines (e.g., Boston University's *Boink* [2005] and Harvard's *H Bomb* [2004]) seek truth in naked self-photography and accounts of sex with strangers as if each incident were God's revelation on Sinai. The lesson each time is that sleeping with strangers or being photographed naked lets the authors know themselves better. Many of these institutions are driven by women. Perhaps they, even more than young men, feel an urgency to know themselves while they can—since America curses them with a premonition of disappointment: when flesh sags, freedom will wane.

From college to high school, high school to junior high, the age of sex childhood recedes and descends. "The Sexual Revolution Hits Junior High," says my newspaper, reporting as news what is not new. Twice a year *Newsweek* and *Time* vaunt the New Virginity. No one believes in the New Virginity. According to polls of those who stick with it, their abstinence is fortified with large measures of fellatio. Eighty percent of people have intercourse in their teens, says the Centers for Disease Control. (Why the Centers for Disease Control keep records of sexual normalcy, unsmilingly pathologized as an "epidemic," is its own question.) My newspaper tells me that menstruation starts for girls today at eleven, or as early as nine. No one knows why.

Yet the early reality of sex childhood is its restrictive practical dimension. It exists only in the context of the large institutions that dominate children's lives, the schools. In these prisonlike closed worlds of finite numbers of children, with no visible status but the wealth they bring in from outside (worn as clothes) and the dominance they can achieve in the activities of school days (friend making, gossiping, academic and athletic success), sex has a different meaning than in adult licentiousness or collegiate glory. Sex appeal is demanded long before sex, and when sex arrives, it appears within ordinary romantic relationships. New sexual acts are only substitutes for any earlier generation's acts, as you'd expect. Where petting was, there shall fellatio be.

It will simply never be the case that children can treat sex with the free-floating fantasy and brutality that adults can, because we adults are atomized in our dealings with others as children in school are not. If I do something rotten on a blind date, I never need to see the only witness again. A child does something rotten, and his date is sitting next to him in homeroom. The adult world sends down its sexual norms, which cannot blossom in a closed institution (though alarmists say they originate there), but which the children tuck away to fulfill just as soon as they can. Children are the beneficiaries of a culture that declares in all its television, jokes, talk, and advertising that if sex isn't the most significant thing in existence, it is the one element never missing from any activity that is fun. They are watchers, silent, with open eyes, and they grow in the blue light.

So much for the decadent reality of childhood.

But adults then look back from exile and see wrongly, thinking the children are free, because we've hemmed them in with images of a transitory future freedom. Never mind that we ourselves led carnal lives that would make old men weep. Those lives hardly counted: inevitably we were caught in actual human relationships with particular people, in a matrix of leaden rules and personal ties. Envy of one's sexual successors is now a recurrent feature of our portion of modernity. Philip Larkin:

When I see a couple of kids,
And guess he's fucking her and she's

Taking pills or wearing a diaphragm,
I know this is paradise

Everyone old has dreamed of all their lives—
. . . everyone young going down the long slide

To happiness, endlessly. I wonder if
Anyone looked at me, forty years back,
And thought, *That'll be the life* . . .
                                    He
And his lot will all go down the long slide
Like free bloody birds.

                                    ("High Windows")

Larkin's solace in the poem was high windows and the icy blue; in real life, an enormous collection of pornography.

The dirty magazines and their supposedly legitimate counterparts in fact play a significant role in the system of sex childhood. In Larkin's life, the poetry of longing went hand in hand with the fulfillments of porn, and all of us share in this interchange at a more banal level. The colloquialisms "men's magazines" and "women's magazines" generally seem to name two very different sets of publications. "Women's magazines" are instructional— how to display oneself, how to serve men, and nowadays (maybe always) how to steal sexual and emotional pleasure from men, outwitting them, while getting erotic and affective satisfactions, too, in the preparations for your self-display. "Men's magazines," for their part, are pornographic—how to look at women, how to fantasize about women, how to enjoy and dominate, and what one becomes while fantasizing this domination. The two genres are distinct, but continuous.

The women's advice and fashion magazines, *Cosmopolitan*, *Glamour*, *Elle*, *Vogue*, hold a permanent mandate for an erotic youthfulness, though not literal sexual youth. They provide shortcuts to staying young for old and young alike: how to keep your skin young, how to keep your muscles young, how to keep your ideas young, how to feel perpetually young, how to siphon vitality from elsewhere to be "young" even if you're not, literally, young, and how to use your youth if you are. You learn early what you'll lose late, and get accustomed to denying the aging that you might never have minded as much without this help.

Men's magazines fix readers' desires in the range of women's shapes and bodies and modes of seduction and subordination—fragmenting the market by body part and sex act and level of explicitness, but also by age. Pornography has a special investment in youth. The college girl is a central feature of *Playboy* in its "Girls of the Big Ten" pictorials; *Hustler* has a relentless Barely Legal franchise in magazines and videos, aped by *Just 18* and *Finally Legal* and all the bargain titles behind the convenience-store counter. In the demimonde of the internet, an even more central category of all online pornography is "teen." Of course, it is profoundly illegal in the United States to photograph anyone under eighteen sexually; in what is called 2257 compliance, producers of pornography must keep public legal records proving that every model is eighteen or older.

Technically, therefore, there are only two ages, eighteen and nineteen, at which "teen" models can be actual teens. Nor do the models ever seem to be sexually immature; child pornography doesn't seem to be what the sites are for. Rather, putative teen models are made *situationally* immature—portrayed with symbols of the student life, the classroom, the cheerleading squad, the college dorm, the family home, the babysitting, the first job; not the husband, not the child, not the real estate brokerage or board-room or bank office, never adult life.*

Thus a society that finds it illegal to exploit anyone beneath the age of legal majority is at the same time interested in the simulation of youth—often by people who are sexually mature but still only on the cusp of adulthood. And in its legitimate publications, as in its vice, it encourages a more general, socially compulsory female urgency to provision youth across the life span, and a male rush to take it.

Though the young person has never been old, the old person once was young. When you look up the age ladder, you look at strangers; when you look down the age ladder, you are always looking at versions of yourself. As an adult, it depends entirely on your conception of yourself whether those fantastic younger incarnations will seem long left behind or all-too-continuous with who you are now. And this conception of yourself depends, in turn, on the culture's attitudes to adulthood and childhood, age and youth. This is where the trouble arises. For in a culture to which sex furnishes the first true experiences, it makes a kind of sense to return to the ages at which sex was first used to pursue experience and one was supposedly in a privileged position to find it. Now we begin to talk, not about our sex per se, but about a fundamental change in our notion of freedom, and what our lives are a competition for.†

---

*Feminist critiques of pornography rooted in an idea of male violence and revenge against the threat of women's liberation might have predicted a different outcome in our age of equality: wider representations of the literal humiliation or subordination of adult women in power. What they did not anticipate was a turn to sexualized youth. Though the two lines of critique are not at all incompatible (i.e., youth still may be a way of denying adult equality), one sees now that feminist critiques of youth and aging are proving to be more significant historically than the MacKinnon-Dworkin line of pornography criticism.

†I want to acknowledge two popular lines of thought that insist on the attraction to sexually mature children as natural not social, contravening my account. One is the commonsense

We must begin to talk directly about the change that was well begun in Nabokov's day and is well advanced in ours, the transformation that created the world in which we are both freed and enslaved. That was sexual liberation.

historical argument that until recently sexually mature children of the middle teen years *were* adults, because human beings used to marry in their teens. Natasha, the dream of Russian womanhood in *War and Peace*, one of the greatest novels of the nineteenth century, set in that century's early years, is fourteen when she becomes the object of her first suitors' attention—and admirable suitors, too: hussars in the czar's army, and a count. Her girlishness is treated matter-of-factly by those who are drawn to it as an appealing aspect of her personality, and it is considered realistically by her parents, who are concerned she may be too immature yet to leave home and run a household. In the United States, as the historian Philip Jenkins has summarized, the standard age of sexual consent was ten years old until the 1890s, when it was raised to sixteen or eighteen depending on the state.

The other argument is one occasionally offered explicitly, but much more often implicitly, in the field of evolutionary psychology. Evolutionary psychology explains behavioral dispositions in modern human beings by the optimal strategies for passing on genes, through patterns hardwired into our brains by our evolutionary past and the continuing reproductive demands of the present. "Youth is a critical cue," writes evolutionary psychologist David M. Buss in the standard book on the subject of sex, "since women's reproductive value declines steadily with increasing age after twenty. By the age of forty, a woman's reproductive capacity is low, and by fifty it is close to zero" (*The Evolution of Desire*). The desire for children from the moment of visible pubescence (say, twelve today) to the maximum age before reproductive decline (age twenty) may therefore be the best means for passing on genes. This inclination would be set beneath the level of consciousness, as men's desire is targeted to females who are fertile, healthy, and poised for the longest period of childbearing possible before the decline sets in. On evolutionary-biological presuppositions, it ought to be the case that human males today and yesterday, and in every society, should be maximally attracted to newly postpubescent girls unless it be determined statistically that there is some ramping-up of reproductive success in the years after menarche—in which case, certainly, no later than fourteen or fifteen.

Neither the historical nor the biological argument seems to meet the problem of the sex child as we now know it, because I think neither captures our current experience of desire, in which the sex children come in only secondarily, through some kind of mediation of fancy; in our real lives adults feel the sexual appeal of other adults. Unless sexual desire is wholly unconscious, not plastic and social, and the social level entirely a screen or delusion—a very complex delusion to cover biological determinism—then with the sex children it's my sense that we are dealing primarily with the sexual appeal of youth rather than the actual determinative sexual attractiveness of *youths*. It would be something like a desire for the sex child's incipience, the child's taste of first majority before the rules clamp down: youth as eternal becoming, in eternal novelty of experience. Apart from such fancies, the appeal of sexually mature children seems to me particularly weak, not strong. But I understand that introspection is not science and I am aware this may not satisfy partisans of the "natural" views.

•

Liberation implies freedom to do what you have already been doing or have meant to do. It unbars what is native to you, free in cost and freely your possession, and removes the iron weight of social interdiction. Even in the great phase of full human liberation which extended from the 1960s to the present day, however, what has passed as liberation has often been *liberalization*. (Marcuse used this distinction.) Liberalization makes for a free traffic in goods formerly regulated and interdicted, creating markets in what you already possess for free. It has a way of making your possessions no longer native to you at the very moment that they're freed for your enjoyment. Ultimately you no longer know *how* to possess them, correctly, unless you are following new rules which emerge to dominate the traffic in these goods.

In sexual liberation, major achievements included the end of shame and illegality in sex outside of marriage (throughout the twentieth century); the disentangling of sex from reproduction (completed with the introduction of the oral contraceptive pill in 1960); the feminist reorganization of intercourse around the female orgasm and female pleasure (closer to 1970); and the beginning of a destigmatization of same-sex sexuality (1970 to the present). The underlying notion in all these reforms was to remove social penalties from what people were doing anyway.

But a test of liberation, as distinct from liberalization, must be whether you have also been freed to be free *from* sex, too—to ignore it, or to be asexual, without consequent social opprobrium or imputation of deficiency. If truly liberated, you should engage in sex or not as you please, and have it be a matter of indifference to you; you should recognize your own sex, or not, whenever and however you please. We ought to see social categories of asexuals who are free to have no sex just as others are free to have endless spectacular sex, and not feel for them either suspicion or pity. One of the cruel betrayals of sexual liberation, in liberalization, was the illusion that a person can only be free if he holds sex as all-important and exposes it endlessly to others—providing it, proving it, enjoying it.

This was a new kind of unfreedom. In hindsight, the betrayal of sexual liberation was a mistake the liberators seemed fated to make. Because moralists had said for so many centuries, "Sex must be controlled, because it is so powerful and important," sexual liberators were seduced into saying, in opposition, "Sex must be *liberated*, because it is so powerful and important." But in fact a better liberation would have occurred if reformers had freed sex not by its centrality to life, but by its triviality. They could have said: "Sex is a biological function—and for that reason no grounds to persecute anyone. It is *truthless*—you must not bring force to bear on people for the basic, biological, and private; you may not persecute them on grounds so accidental. You must leave them alone, neither forcing them to deny their sex nor to bring it into the light."

This misformulation of liberation only became as damaging as it did because another force turned out to have great use for the idea that sex is the bearer of the richest experiences: commerce. The field of sex was initially very difficult to liberate against a set of rival norms which had structured it for centuries: priority of the family, religious prohibitions, restraint of biology. Once liberation reached a point of adequate success, however, sex was unconscionably easy to "liberate" further, as commerce discovered it had a new means of entry into private life and threw its weight behind the new values. What in fact was occurring was liberalization by forces of commercial transaction, as they entered to expand and coordinate the new field of exchange. Left-wing ideas of free love, the nonsinfulness of the body, women's equality of dignity, intelligence, and capability, had been hard-pressed to find adequate standing before—and they are still in trouble, constantly worn away. Whereas incitement to sex, ubiquitous sexual display, sinfulness redefined as the unconditioned, unexercised, and unaroused body, and a new shamefulness for anyone who manifests a nonsexuality or, worst of all, willful sexlessness—that was easy.

Opposition to this is not only supposed to be old-fashioned but also joyless and puritanical—in fact, ugly. Sex talk is so much a part of daily glamour and the assurance of being a progressive person that one hates to renounce it; but one has to see that in general it is commercial sex talk that's reactionary, and opposition that's progressive. Liberalization has succeeded in hanging an aesthetic ugliness upon all discussions of liberation, except the purely ornamental celebrations of "the Woodstock generation" one sees on TV. Original liberators are ogres in the aesthetic symbolism of liberalization. They don't shave their legs! They're content to be fat! They have no fun. To say that a bodily impulse is something all of us have, and no regimentation or expertise or purchases can make one have it any more, *is* to become filthy and disgusting. It is to be nonproductive waste in an economy of markets, something nonsalable. It is not the repression of sex that opposes liberation (just as Foucault alerted us), but "inciting" sex as we know it—whatever puts sex into motion, draws it into *publicity*, apart from the legitimate relations between the private (the place of bodily safety) and the public (the sphere of equality).

The question remains why liberalization turned back to gorge itself on youth.

How should a system convince people that they do not

possess their sex properly? Teach them that in their possession it is shapeless and unconditioned. Only once it has been modified, layered with experts, honeycombed with norms, overlaid with pictorial representations and sold back to them, can it fulfill itself as what its possessors "always wanted." Breasts starved away by dieting will be reacquired in breast implant surgery— to attain the original free good, once destroyed, now re-created unnaturally.

How to convince them that what appears plentiful and free— even those goods which, in fact, are universally distributed—is scarce? Extend the reach of these new norms that cannot be met without outside intervention. Youth becomes a primary norm in the competition for sex. The surprise in this is not that youth would be desirable—it has always had its charm—but that you would think youth ought to be competitively *ineffective*, since it is universally distributed at the start of life. Yet youth is naturally evanescent, in fact vanishing every single day that one lives. It can be made the fundamental experience of a vanishing commodity, the ur-experience of obsolescence. Plus, it was everyone's universal possession at one time; and so artful means to keep it seem justified by a "natural" outcome, what you already were; and youth can be requalified physically as an aspect of memory, for every single consumer, in minutiae of appearance that you alone know (looking at yourself every day in a mirror, you alone know the history of your face and body) even while other people don't. We still pretend we are most interested in beauty, and it covers our interest in youth. Beauty is too much someone else's good luck; we accept that it is unequally distributed. Youth is more effective precisely because it is something all of us are always losing.

From the desire to repossess what has been lost (or was never truly taken advantage of) comes, in the end, the ceaseless extension of competition. It is easily encouraged. It doesn't require anything nefarious or self-conscious, certainly not top-down control, though it's sometimes convenient to speak of the process metaphorically, as a field of control. All it requires is a culture in which instruments of commentary and talk (news, talk shows, advice magazines) are accompanied and paid for by advertisers of aesthetic and aestheticizable products—everything from skin cream to Viagra to cars. This is supremely prosaic; but this is it. Once people can be convinced that they need to remain young for others to desire them, and that there are so many instrumentalities with which they can remain young; once they can be encouraged to suspect that youth is a particularly real and justifiable criterion for desire, then the competition will accelerate by the interchange of all these talkers: the professional commentators and product vendors and the needy audiences and ordinary people. Norms will not be set in advance, but are created constantly between the doubting individual and the knowing culture; or between the suddenly inventive individual and the "adaptive" and trend-spotting culture; a dialectic ultimately reproduced *inside* individuals who doubt ("I'm growing old") but seek know-how ("I'll be young")—in the channeling of desire in the bedroom, in conversation, in the marketplace.

For our object lessons and examples, it becomes advantageous for those searching for sexually desirable youthfulness to follow the trail to those who actually have youth. Thus young people in all forms of representation—advertising, celebrity following, advice literature, day-to-day talk and myth—augment the competitive system of youth whether or not they are the "target market" of any particular campaign.

And yet the young are off-limits sexually, by law and morality and, more visibly, because of institutions that instruct and protect them. An adult simply will not get his or her hands on a college student—in large part because that student is in a closed institution. Professors have increasingly learned to stay away from students by threat of firing and public shaming. An adult should never wind up in sexual contact with a high school student unless conscience is gone and jail holds no fear; but neither will he run into many of them. The real-world disastrous exceptions of abuse, as we well know, come from those inside the institutions which instruct and protect the child: teachers, priests, babysitters, and, far and away most frequently, parents and family members. This criminal subset has an ambiguous relation to the wider fascination. For society as a whole, gazing at those youths who are sexually mature but restricted from the market institutionally or legally, sex children become that most perfect of grounds for competition, a fantastic commodity unattainable in its pure form.

Hence the final double bind of social preoccupation with the sex children in a commercial society regimented by a vain pursuit of absolute freedom. On one side, the young become fascinating because they have in its most complete form the youth that we demand for ourselves, for our own competitive advantage. They are the biologically superrich whose assets we wish to burgle because we feel they don't know the treasures they keep; they stand accidentally at the peak of the competitive pyramid. *Desire for sex childhood is thus a completion of the competitive system.* On the other side, the sex child as an individual is the only figure in this order who is thought to be free from competition; who holds sex as still a natural good, undiminished, a capability, purely potential—not something ever scarcer and jeopardized by our unattractiveness and our aging. For sex children, sex remains a new experience of freedom and truth that retains its promise to shape a better self. The kids are not innocent of carnality, but they are innocent of competition. *Desire for sex childhood thus becomes a wish for freedom from the system.* The sex child can be a utopia personified, even as she props up the brutal dystopia to which her youth furnishes the competitive principle.

As I attempted the first draft of this essay, the news was filled with reports about a twenty-two-year-old North Dakota college student, Dru Sjodin, who was abducted and murdered as she left her retail job at Victoria's Secret. Police arrested a fifty-year-old "Level Three sex offender" who had been identified in the mall parking lot though he lived thirty miles away in Minnesota. The man had Sjodin's blood in his car; police couldn't find the girl. But the news kept showing a college glamour picture, comparing her to other abducted youths, and dwelling on her workplace with its lingerie.

At the time, I thought: We can expect this to keep happening as long as sex with the sex children is our society's most treasured, fantasized consumer good. There was something inevitable about a murderer going to the mall to abduct a sex child— though under the circumstances it seemed terrible to say so. The whole tragedy was too depressing. So I stopped writing.

During the second attempt, I reached the clinical literature on child molestation. Some of it is tolerable. This includes the accounts of abused children who enter therapy and meet child psychologists who then record their cures in a whole hopeful literature on the side of healing. What is mostly intolerable, on the other hand, is the literature about child molesters. There are valuable contributions to criminology and psychology on the library shelves, which outline the problems of pedophilia and sexual abuse and molestation, often with in-depth interviews. I couldn't read very much of them. Sorry as I felt for these men, it seemed clear to me they should be destroyed. But this was really insane, and went against my other beliefs. So I began to consider: What is the meaning of abomination today, in a nonreligious age? It must be that there are points of cultural juncture at which phenomena are produced that, though explicable, are *indefensible* in the terms of any of the structures which produce or analyze them. You don't want to appeal to trauma, rehabilitation, socialization, or biological inclination. You can't just run away from the phenomena, and yet they can't be brought into the other terms of social analysis without an unacceptable derangement of values. This explains the impasse in which the annihilative impulse takes hold. So I stopped a second time.

In an increasingly dark mood, I came to the darkest way to frame the enigma of the sex children. A fraction of young people are extraordinarily highly valued, emulated, desired, examined, broadcast, lusted after, attended to in our society. These legal ex-children are attended to specifically as repositories of fresh sexuality, not, say, of intellect or even beauty. As their age goes up to seventeen, eighteen, and nineteen, the culture very quickly awards them its summit of sexual value. Yet as their age goes down from some indefinite point, to sixteen, fifteen, fourteen, and so on, the sexual appeal of childhood quickly reaches our culture's zone of absolute evil. Worse than the murderer, worse than the adult rapist of adults, and even worse than the person who physically and emotionally abuses children, is the person who sexually tampers with a child in any degree—who can then never be reintegrated into society except as a sex offender—or is simply the author of monstrous thoughts, a cyberstalker netted in police stings in chat rooms, or found downloading underage images to his hard drive. This is the "pedophile," whether or not he acts. Since the two zones—maximum *value* of sex, and maximum *evil* for sex—are right next to each other, shouldn't we wonder if there's some structural relation in society between our supergood and absolute evil?

The most direct explanation is that we may be witnessing two disparate systems as they come into conflict at just one point. System A would be the sexual valuation of youth, spurred by the liberalization of sex and its attachment to youth in a competitive economy. System B would be adult morality, the moral impulse to shield beings who need protection from sexual tampering and attention—because of the cruel nonreciprocity inflicted on a young child who doesn't yet have sexual desire (in true pedophilia, molestation of those beneath pubescence); the equally cruel coercion of those old enough to desire but not to have an adult's power to consent or to see how their actions will look to a future self (molestation of adolescents); and the deep betrayal, in all acts of sexual abuse, of the order of society and of its future, in something like a society-level version of the taboo on incest. Now, System A (sexual value, commerce) possesses a major flaw in its tendency to drive sexual attention down the age scale relentlessly— even to those legal children who hold sex in its newest and most inaccessible form. System B would fight this tendency, trying to provide necessary restraints; but perhaps it becomes most destructively punitive just where it refuses to disavow System A entirely. By otherwise accepting the sexual value of youthfulness, in other words—with such threatening possible side effects— morality would have to narrow itself vengefully upon the single point of visible contradiction, and overpunish whomever pursues too much youth, or does so too literally.

What's really striking to anyone who watches the news is, of course, the *intensity* of punitive violence where the two systems clash. From the point of view of morality, the overpunishment of the pedophile and the sex offender (barred from living anonymously, unrehabilitable, hounded from town to town, unable to return to society) makes perfect sense, because of the extreme moral reprehensibility of abusing a child—combined with a dubious contemporary doctrine that *desires* can never be rehabilitated. It would also make sense, however, if we feared that the ruthlessness of this interdiction of pedophilia helped rationalize or reinforce the interests which confer extreme sexual value on youth just a bit up the ladder. *One fears our cultural preoccupation with pedophilia is not really about valuing childhood but about overvaluing child sex.* It would be as if the culture understood it must be so ruthless to stop tampering with real children, just because it is working so hard to keep afloat the extreme commercial valuation of youth and its concrete manifestations in the slightly older sex child. Does the culture react so vehemently at just this point because were the screen of morality to collapse, the real situation would have to be confessed—the child's extreme uninterest in adults; the child's sexual "liberation" as a subeffect of our own false liberation; the brutalization of life at all levels by sexual incitement?

One further step into the darkness has to complete the critique. The most pitiful and recondite form of pedophilia is sexual attachment to children below the age of sexual maturity—true pedophilia, which seems so utterly unmotivated, a matter of strict pathology. But a certain amount of the permanent persistence of child molesting as a phenomenon must not come from a fixed psychic category but from the misdirecting of sexual impulse to young people who temporarily fill a place of temptation or fascination—especially in desire for teens who are sexually mature, but whom an adult may still do a profound wrong by addressing sexually. It seems likely that an incessant overvaluing of the sex of the young will *train* some people toward wrong objects. This should swell the numbers of the class of incipient or intermittent wrongdoers who might no longer see a bright line between right and wrong—because social discourse has made that beam wobble, then scintillate, attract, and confuse.

If this is so, such immoral attention is not just a matter of a "loosening" of morality, but the combination of liberalization (*not* liberation) with a blinkered form of cultural interdiction. The pedophilic sensibility of the culture is strengthened. Thus we may produce the obsession we claim to resent; the new pedophile would become a product of our system of values.

One rehabilitative solution would be to try to extinguish the worship of youth. Childhood is precisely the period when you can't do what you like. You are unformed and dumb. It is the time of first experiences; but first experiences can be read either as engravings from which all further iterations are struck and decline in clarity, or as defective and insufficient premonitions of a reality that will only develop in adulthood. We know the beauty of the young, which it is traditional to admire—their unlined features, their unworn flesh—but we also can know that the beauty of children is the beauty of another, merely incipient form of life, and nothing to emulate. One view of the young body is as an ideal. The other is as an unpressed blank.

A second solution would be the trivialization of sex altogether. This is much harder, because every aspect of the culture is so much against it, counterliberators and prudes included. Aldous Huxley warned of a world in which we'd arrange sexual intercourse

as we make dates for coffee, with the same politeness and obliga-
tion. That now seems like an impossibly beautiful idyll. At least
coffee dates share out assets pacifically. You meet for coffee with
people you don't really want to see, and people who don't want to
see you agree to meet you, and yet everyone manages to get something out of it. If only sex could be like coffee! But sex has not
proved adaptable to this and probably never will, despite the recent
overcoming of a heretofore limiting condition—the inability to
control physical arousal at will. The new pharmacopoeia of tumes-
cence drugs will soon give way, according to reports of current
clinical trials, to libido drugs that act directly on the brain rather
than the vascular system—and for both men and women. I'm
still not optimistic they will produce a revolution in etiquette.

The reason it seems a sex of pure politeness and equal access
does not work is that the constant preparation to imagine any
and every other person as a sexual object (something our culture
already encourages) proves to be ruthlessly egocentric and antiso-
cial, making every other living body a tool for self-pleasure or gain.
At times I wonder if we are witnessing a sexualization of the life
process itself, in which all pleasure is canalized into the sexual,
and the function of warm, living flesh in any form is to allow us
access to autoerotism through the circuit of an other. This is
echoed at the intellectual level in the discourse of "self-discovery."
The real underlying question of sexual encounter today may not
be "What is he like in bed?" (heard often enough, and said without shame) but "What am I like in bed?" (never spoken). That is
to say, at the deepest level, one says: "Whom do I discover myself
to be in sex?"—so that sex becomes the special province of self-
discovery.

Meanwhile, the more traditional way of trivializing sex, by
subordinating it to overwhelming romantic love, has diminished

as an option as the focus on self-discovery has increasingly devitalized full romantic love. Self-discovery puts a reflecting wall between the self and attention to the other, so that all energy supposedly exerted in fascination, attraction, and love just bounces back, even when it appears to go out as love for the other. When self-discovery is combined with the notion of a continually new or renewed self, and this newness is associated with literal or metaphorical youth—well, then you simply have a segment of the affluent first world at the present moment.

This means the trivialization of sex and the denigration of youth will have to start with an act of willful revaluation. It will require preferring the values of adulthood: intellect over enthusiasm, autonomy over adventure, elegance over vitality, sophistication over innocence—and, perhaps, a pursuit of the confirmation or repetition of experience rather than experiences of novelty.

The trivialization of sex and the denigration of childhood can still be put on the agenda of a humane civilization. However, I think it's basically too late for us. Perhaps I simply mean that I know it is too late for me. If you kick at these things, you are kicking at the heart of certain systems; if you deny yourself the lure of sex, for example, or the superiority of youth, you feel you will perish from starvation. But if I can't save myself or my children, probably, I still might help my grandchildren. The only hope would be, wherever possible, to deny ourselves in our fatuousness and build a barricade, penning us inside, quarantining this epoch which we must learn to name and disparage.

Let the future, at least, know that we were fools. Make our era distinct and closed so that the future can see something to move beyond. Record our testament, that this was a juvenile phase in liberation which must give way to a spiritual adulthood! Turn back to adults; see in the wrinkles at the side of the eye that catch the cobalt, the lines of laughter in the face, the prolific flesh, those subtle clothes of adulthood, the desire-inspiring repositories of *wisdom* and *experience*. Know that what we wish to be nourished upon is age and accomplishment, not emptiness and newness. Then, in sophisticated and depraved sexuality, rather than youth's innocence and the fake blush of truth, let our remaining impulses run in the sex of the old for the old—until they run out. Make a model for a better era. Once more, my moderns—in a superior decadence, in adult darkness rather than juvenile light—rise to the occasion! One effort more if you wish to be called liberators.

(2006)

DIANA ABBOTT: A LESSON

Benjamin Kunkel

She is waking up for the second time today. The first time was at 7:30, to National Public Radio, with its earnest recitation of the latest calamities, so that Daniel could be launched on his day and stand a chance of beating the rush-hour traffic to Westwood, and now Diana Abbott (who starts at the sound of alarm clocks, ambulance sirens, even telephones; for whom a peal from her new cell phone can be as startling as a call in the middle of the night) is waking up in the way she likes, slowly and late, to no buzzer or newscast. A few notes of inquisitive birdsong, species unknown, ride atop the fade and swell of traffic noise.

Diana slides out of bed naked, feeling as if she has learned something about Coetzee in her sleep. She steps into her underwear and wonders what it is.

In preparation for a book review she must write—1,100 words, for one of the big Sunday supplements—she has steeped herself again in the work of J. M. Coetzee, the South African novelist, and he has gotten under her skin. It is almost as natural to her as the sight of her own body in the closet-door mirror that the first thought to cross her mind today should be of Coetzee. Coetzee, she notes, hooking on her bra, rarely writes of women with bodies like hers, smooth and young and as yet unhurt. What Coetzee writes about is pain; and so there is, for instance—the instance that comes first to mind—Mrs. Curren in *Age of Iron*, dying of cancer in late middle age as, for the first time in her life, she begins to understand the cruelty of apartheid. (That is how a book reviewer might put it.) Before, Mrs. Curren had only acknowledged this cruelty; now she somewhat understands it. Through the narrow rite of her own pain she is initiated into the enormous tribulation of the others. That is the Coetzee pattern, that is what he does especially to the educated and comfortable among his characters, that is the sadism he characteristically performs on behalf of compassion. Were Diana to treat this theme in an essay she would discuss in particular the novels *Waiting for the Barbarians* and *Disgrace*.

Diana rotates her skirt into place, looking down at her young pale ankles, recalling the description of Mrs. Curren's legs as "mottled, blue-veined, stuck out like sticks before me." Perhaps in her review Diana will mention that Mrs. Curren from *Age of Iron* shares initials with Elizabeth Costello, eponymous character of the book under review, and that these two ECs have other traits in common as well, being distraught, solitary, and not long for this world: a pair of uncomforting grandmas, dispensing unwelcome thoughts in place of hugs and sweets. That would be a clever comparison, and would demonstrate that Diana, as always, has done her homework. For the moment, however, she is more interested in this matter of the sympathy, mingled with distaste, that Coetzee clearly feels for aging female flesh. It is there in *Elizabeth Costello* just as it is in the early book *In the Heart of the Country*, where his narrator (or narratrix) writes: "I blush for my own thin smell, the smell of an unused woman, sharp with hysteria, like onions, like urine."

For this, Diana thinks, is another thing about Coetzee: his fastidiousness turns easily into repugnance. He pays such strict attention to pain, including the pain of growing old, and then shivers with disgust at all the generations of people and animals suffering so indiscreetly before him. Coetzee apparently dislikes such displays; his own agonies he would apparently prefer to keep to himself (and yet he is a writer).

Diana has dressed neatly in a ribbed white tank top and a slate-colored A-line skirt made of some silky confection of rayon and other industrial materials, as if she will be meeting someone for lunch. In fact she has no plan for the day except to sit at her desk and knock out this review. Then, at around seven o'clock, Daniel will come home, God willing (Diana does not believe in God, but it made an impression on her as a girl that her maternal grandparents never anticipated the fulfillment of their travel plans without appending this proviso of His will), and when Daniel comes home they will cook dinner together and open a bottle of wine. They will kiss each other and review their separate days. Perhaps it is not too early to begin planning in detail the wedding they have set for June. Soon they will have to. But it makes Diana anxious to specify her wishes.

She shakes a circular patty of vegetarian sausage out of its frosty envelope, into a slick of extra-virgin olive oil in the nonstick pan; she stoops slightly and adjusts the flame. She opens the refrigerator, produces half a bell pepper and a quarter of an onion from their plastic bags, and begins dicing them on her cutting board. On the first page of the first volume of Coetzee's memoirs, *Boyhood*, Mrs. Coetzee is seen employing a paring knife to cut out "the horny shells" from under the tongues of the family hens, the better to increase their fertility. "The hens shriek and struggle, their eyes bulging. He"—Coetzee writes of his former self in the third person—"shudders and turns away."

How strange that she and Coetzee have become so intimate when she isn't even sure of his name. Is it "cut-zee-uh" or more like "coat-zee"? Coat-zee, she says to herself, considering this wrong but also less pretentious. She ought, after all, to be careful: she seemed pretentious and literary enough in New York, and now she lives in L.A. in the Marina del Rey section, inside an enormous apartment complex bearing the theme-park name of Mariner's Village. She doubts whether her and Daniel's L.A. friends will want to hear about an author whom they are required to call cut-zee-uh. Their interest might be piqued if she were to mention that a screenplay has been adapted from *Waiting for the Barbarians*, Coetzee's great novel about imperialism, about—again in the short-hand of the reviewer—knowing or not knowing what is being done to the enemies of your government. But according to Daniel the screenplay was drawn up years ago and is going nowhere. "The barbarians aren't very popular these days," Daniel has informed her, as though Diana has hardly stuck her head out into the world and does not know.

Daniel works in Westwood for a medium-size production company. For the time being he is making enough money that he suffers Diana to stay at home, rising late, trying to write, and occasionally depositing into their joint account a check of several hundred dollars for a book review published in some prestigious outlet. As for the psychological superstructure sponsored by this economic base, you might say that Daniel absorbs Diana's anxiety and other outsize moods, while Diana prods Daniel out of his mere decency and competence into a liveliness he might not otherwise experience. And of course there is much more than that going on. But she respects their happiness enough not to investigate its sources.

Diana sits down sidesaddle on a cushion to the side of their lacquered red square of a Japanese-type table. She begins cutting up her sausage at right angles, spearing veggie gobbets on her fork along with chunks of pepper and onion.

Elizabeth Costello is not, to her mind, one of Coetzee's great books, for reasons she hopes she can explain in the words allotted to her. Still, she recalls how important Elizabeth Costello the character was to her when Diana first encountered her. Coetzee's conceit was undeniably clever: invited to give a pair of lectures at Princeton, he instead presented his audience with two short stories or vignettes in which a famous novelist—an Australian woman named Elizabeth Costello—surprises her collegiate audience by lecturing them on animal rights. The new book not only incorporates the text of those two stories or scenes (published in 1999 as *The Lives of Animals*); it also elaborates upon their formal tactic, assembling a novel of sorts out of a series of chapters in which the noted writer Elizabeth Costello is one way or another compelled to deliver a speech or make a statement, just as often happens to the world-famous Coetzee (however small his renown among thirtyish film-industry people in the city of Los Angeles). Parts of Costello's imaginary documents are then transcribed and reproduced by Coetzee. In this way the words of the fictional author, like the words of any real author, are woven in and out of the overbearing context of her life, responded to half adequately, half coherently, by a host of colleagues, admirers, family members, and other strangers, and meanwhile affirmed or undermined by Costello's own memories and unspoken reservations.

In the end these eight "lessons," as the chapters are called, would seem to be Coetzee's attempt to renovate by way of novelistic technique the ancient form of the Platonic dialogue. And the best thing about the book, to Diana's mind, is the bare idea of it: to demonstrate what we all know and often forget, namely, that the arguments set forth in papers or speeches (or hinted at in book reviews) are not so much the products of pure reason as they are allegories of our circumstances, the confessions of our flesh young or old.

Diana supposes that she had perceived all that in 1999, reading *The Lives of Animals* in her room in the tiny place on Elizabeth Street that she shared with Stephanie and Sharmila, and then in the morning going off to work, part of the girl-army of editorial assistants, for a huge publisher in midtown. But at the time what mattered to her was only this: that the writer she so much admired had apparently come out, albeit in drag and under an assumed name, in favor of ethical vegetarianism. For in her lecture Elizabeth Costello plainly if somewhat hysterically condemns "what is being done to animals at this moment in production facilities (I hesitate to call them farms any longer), in abattoirs, in trawlers, in laboratories, all over the world"—those are the words the sense of which, if not the exact order, Diana now recalls—and then creates an awkward scene at the dinner reception afterward, where only three people dare order the fish instead of the nut rissole. It made sense that Coetzee, with his ear, like that of the Magistrate in *Waiting for the Barbarians*, "tuned to the pitch of human pain," should also have begun to listen to the mute or muffled cries of animals, since physical pain cannot be very different between humans and animals, whatever else may be. Nevertheless Coetzee's concern for animals had surprised Diana, had pleased her, had seemed to give her company.

In 1999 her friends, with their minuscule New York apartments and their ten-dollar cocktails, with their purchases of expensive shoes when their paychecks arrived, followed by a diet of breakfast cereal at the end of the month ("that time of the month," witty Stephanie called it), had developed a gloss of metropolitan toughness which Diana seemed unable to acquire. The strange nature of this toughness was to demonstrate that you were having a good time in the city, that you did not apologize for or feel embarrassed by your pleasures. And Diana, too, had drunk her share of vodka gimlets; had slept with enough guys to form an indie-rock band or two; and had sunk several paychecks into such fancy vegan shoes that you couldn't tell the difference from leather. It was absurd: one night out at dinner in her vegan slingbacks, and cuddled up the next pajama-clad with J. M. Coetzee. Nor when she met Daniel and fell rapidly, gratefully in love with him, did he solve her contradiction. What he did was look on with sympathy, with—if she is required to define that look—a mixture of condescension and admiration such as one shows toward the superior sensitivities of a gifted child.

Diana has never been tough. Her prose, even in her journal, may be cool, hard, and rather formal, masculine as she thinks of it; and she was once a good athlete. But in truth, or rather in life, she remains at twenty-eight a girly sort of girl, with a sweet tooth, a soft heart, a perhaps old-fashioned modesty. Her voice is soft and full of succor; she shrinks from on-screen violence; and she is to an almost farcical degree a cooer at babies and a lover of animals. Recently she persuaded Daniel to let her adopt a cat from the shelter, and now this morning reverie of hers (extended perhaps to unrealistic lengths, but not withal so improbable in a woman like Diana Abbott) is interrupted by the cat himself, Jeremy they call him, as he rolls his brindled length against her calf, flicks his tail once, twice, and looks straight into her eyes.

"Oh, Jeremy, what am I doing with myself?" The cat regards her with unnerving feline frankness until she covers his head with her hand, scratching him between the ears. Jeremy's purr conveys acknowledgment rather than delight; it is his style to receive all affection as being merely his due. "You have no memory of your life before here," she tells the blasé creature. "You don't remember how the other cats live."

Diana gets up to rinse her dishes and deposit them in the sink, the cat following her to the kitchen and sitting eloquently before his bowl. Diana bends down to serve him a scoop, wondering what is in such food: chicken? pork? But she is not curious enough to read the table of contents—or the list of ingredients, rather.

"Shamekilling": that is Joyce's word, in *Ulysses*, for the eyes of a cat, and it is true, Joyce is right, there is no shame in Jeremy's eyes, nothing complicates his appetite, nothing interrupts his selfishness.

Diana stands up and looks out the window. Today is another sparkling October day toward the end of the long California summer, the exact term for which must not be "summer"; and suddenly she feels, in the bright lull of this early hour, that even for a long-faced miserabilist like J. M. Coetzee, life must be better than he lets on. Indeed she feels, also of a sudden, that she will write an excellent book review, the considered work, appreciative yet critical, of someone who has gone so deeply into the author's work as to emerge on the other side.

Why, after all, must Coetzee be such a gloom-monger? For if he desires to draw attention to suffering, doesn't the apprehension of such become the more acute when full allowance is made for the possibility of happiness? Or might it be that John Maxwell Coetzee, like so many men, is simply afraid of life? Might it even be that he writes about postmenopausal women not so much out of sympathy as out of preference, because no more messy life can emerge from between their knobby sticklike legs? Might it even perhaps be that his ostentatious compassion for the injured and excluded conceals a lament over his own life and its mysterious spoilage?

The computer pipes and burbles with reviving electronic life. Settling into her chair Diana tries to at least start the day sitting up straight. It used to be that she wrote wearing yoga pants and one or another of Daniel's soft old T-shirts. That was until she began to suspect that disorder in dress encouraged bad posture and abetted sloppy thinking. Now she dresses for work as if it is work and she a real person, hired and official, with established outlines and a definite point of view.

Diana has double-clicked the Word icon and created a new document. She looks out the dazzled window, like an actress awaiting a line prompting; but there is nothing to see except the waxy elliptic leaves of a eucalyptus tree and the pastel camouflage of its patchy bark.

"Like her creator," Diana bravely types, "the South African novelist J. M. Coetzee, Elizabeth Costello is a world-famous writer much in demand on the lecture circuit."

She stops—a dud. What is wanted by readers of the *Sunday Book World* is a hook, a grabber, and that sentence is not it. As usual Diana wishes she could get all the facts out of the way and proceed straightaway to the good stuff, the flashing ideas, the nourished glow of the interpretation. She wishes she could somehow establish in one fell swoop the method of the book, and survey in a sentence its difficult-to-summarize contents. Before the "lessons" were gathered into a book they were published piecemeal over the course of five years, and perhaps this accounts for why *Elizabeth Costello* is somewhat diffuse in its effect, lacking the cumulative impact of the best novels.

Admittedly many of the chapters are interesting in themselves. For instance in Lesson 2: "The Novel in Africa," Elizabeth Costello and a washed-up Nigerian novelist named Emmanuel Egudu are lecturing the pale-skinned liberal clients of a Scandinavian cruise line on the subject of African fiction. Egudu offers a canned hymn to African oral culture (evidently it is important to Coetzee not to patronize or prettify his black characters), while our EC, ever the contrarian, complains that there is "no African novel worth speaking of" because there is no substantial African readership: writers from countries on other continents write primarily for their compatriots, whereas Africans must write for Europeans and Americans and therefore "perform" their Africanness instead of merely speaking from it. Whether correct or not—Diana has not read enough African fiction to judge—the argument is cogent. Yet Coetzee makes one wonder whether Costello's quarrel with Egudu does not owe something to the fact that he, at one time her lover, has remained a lady's man, virile and charming in his dashiki, while her sex life is now well behind her.

In another "lesson," the fictional Costello prepares a lecture on the real-life novelist Paul West, condemning his scenes of torture as in some sense complicitous with the obscenity they depict. (Readers of *Waiting for the Barbarians*, unable to forget the scenes of torture in that novel, will note Coetzee's implicit self-critique.) Naturally Costello is discomfited to learn that Paul West himself has been invited to Amsterdam to deliver a talk from the same lectern as herself. And yet, true to form, she goes ahead with her prepared remarks. Not the sort of woman to admit to liking anything, Elizabeth Costello does seem to enjoy making people uncomfortable. As her son remarks in Lesson 1, "She is by no means a comforting writer"—just as people often say of Coetzee.

The twist of irony comes at the end of the chapter, when Coetzee gives us Costello in a bathroom stall, thinking that there are privacies the novelist should not trespass against.

Yes, it would be nice to give an idea of all this without taking up too many of the 1,100 words, and to point out with similar brevity some of the book's more obvious implications. For instance, the problems of Africa are gone over among wealthy retirees visiting Antarctica on a ship called *Northern Lights*; the nature of animals is interrogated in that least junglelike of settings, the university; and the renowned writer arrives to discuss radical evil not in Sarajevo or Kigali but in orderly and placid, social-democratic Amsterdam. How hospitable and comfortable are the fora for the speaking of unwelcome and uncomfortable thoughts! Elizabeth Costello's consistent failure to be collegial would seem a buried protest against intellectual collegiality as such—as if the disturbing writers and the difficult thinkers have agreed in advance that their disputes do not count, that on the deepest level they all get along. It must trouble Coetzee that such a disagreeable writer as himself is everywhere celebrated and given prizes.

But that is not the way to commence a book review, neither with a barrage of information nor with a résumé of its themes. Diana has been prepared to complain that Elizabeth Costello—cold, brusque, abstracted—is not credibly a woman, is too much like J. M. Coetzee in a skirt. But what of Diana herself? What of her voice as a critic? If we are to take into account the circumstances of the author, as Coetzee implies we should, then we must note that Diana's own case is that of a young woman whom it is only frank to call pretty, and who ought, therefore, to know how to seduce readers, to tempt them, to lead them on. Diana is not some girl gone wild; she ought, when it comes to revealing information, to know better than to tear off all seven veils at once.

(But of course she does not know how to seduce people—she has always been the one seduced.)

Diana deletes the stupid sentence she has written. She reaches back to gather her dark blond hair into a ponytail. She sits up straight, squares her shoulders, and tries again.

"J. M. Coetzee writes thin books, but they almost stack up into a new literary culture. You can almost imagine an alternate universe, several inches to the side of our own, in which Coetzee's stringent practices are the prevailing norms. In our universe, literary modernism established the vagaries of consciousness as the great subject of the novel. Coetzee, on the other hand, writes about the body and pain. And in our universe," Diana continues, "memoirists write of themselves in terms of I and me. Imagine if instead we did what Coetzee does in his two volumes of memoir, *Boyhood* and *Youth*, and wrote about ourselves in the third-person singular, in a voice poised somewhere between unavoidable narcissism (I am looking at myself) and necessary indifference (I am only one third person among the others, one *he* in a world of *hes* and *shes*)."

She wants to suggest that we might likewise imagine a world in which *Elizabeth Costello* is not the only book of its kind, a world in which moral-philosophical debates are frequently conducted by fictional characters whose lives illustrate or dispute the relevant ideas. But mustn't she then explain how what Coetzee is doing amounts to the novelization of the essay rather than the old-fashioned novel of ideas? And where does she get off talking confidently of "the old-fashioned novel of ideas" when she hasn't read Thomas Mann? She ought to have studied more of the classics, the canon. Had she done so, she might not write in such a stiff old-fashioned way, trying to sound as if she has been properly educated.

Diana holds down the delete key until there is nothing on-screen but the throbbing cursor. What does she think about Coetzee, or about anything? What course was she enrolled in when they were teaching people how to think?

Bored, disappointed with herself, bored with being disappointed with herself, she flips open *Life & Times of Michael K.* It is her favorite Coetzee. Set in a South Africa of civil war and concentration camps, one that happily never came to pass a second time, the novel concerns the "coloured" Michael K's desire to live free of categorization and control, hiding out from the world in a hole in the ground and sustaining himself as well as he can, a pitiably simpleminded person, on his pumpkin patch and whatever the earth will provide.

"He returned to eating insects. Since time was poured out upon him in such an unending stream, there were whole mornings he could spend on his belly over an ant-nest picking out the larvae one by one with a grass-stalk and putting them in his mouth. Or he would peel back the bark from the dead trees looking for beetle grubs . . ."

So even gentle Michael K is not quite a vegetarian. Diana skips ahead: "He also ate roots. He had no fear of being poisoned, for he seemed to know the difference between a benign bitterness and a malign one, as though he had once been an animal and the knowledge of good and bad plants had not died in his soul."

How beautiful and severe, as the whole book is! Coetzee's writing is no longer so good as that. In *Elizabeth Costello* many of the images seem drawn from a kind of Esperanto of metaphor (e.g., "the Nazi forest of horrors"), and Coetzee's purse-lipped tone and general attitude of strictness, much praised by the critics, do not prevent him from indulging in the more-than-occasional prefab phrase (e.g., "a mood of bottomless dejection"). There is an irritable and petulant scrupulousness about Costello that has been imported from other recent books of Coetzee's, and that rests in fact on empty scruples, a pretended strictness: "But she cannot believe it is a true smile"—looking at Emmanuel Egudu—"cannot believe it comes from the heart, if that is where smiles come from." Except that no one believes smiles come from the heart, we all know it is merely an idiom. A discipline of vigilance has become a habit of grumpiness, a stance has relaxed into a pose, and the prose reveals as much.

It was different in Coetzee's first books, where the harshness, the steeliness, the unforgiving quality—what all the critics refer to under different names—seemed the natural by-product of his honesty. Now the severity is sometimes in place of honesty. Diana recalls the thoughts of Elizabeth Costello's son on being taken to bed by one of his mother's academic admirers: "*Research*: will that be her name for it afterwards? *Using a secondary source?*" This seems to bespeak the author's cynicism more than it does the real concerns of the character in question. In *Michael K* the clear-eyed description of a few acts of kindness indicated how rare a thing was kindness in that world. Capable of perceiving charity, Coetzee could therefore perceive how little of it there was. These days Diana has doubts about the accuracy of Coetzee's perceptions, just as she would with any habitual complainer. It doesn't help matters that all characters in *Elizabeth Costello* speak in more or less the same voice.

If one wants to fix a date, Coetzee's prose began to slacken in 1994, with *The Master of Petersburg*, a novel about Dostoevsky. (Diana dislikes this trend of novelists writing about their literary forebears, borrowing the prestige of other writers to make use of as their own.) She recalls a sentence about a woman with whom Dostoevsky is conducting an affair: "She is in his arms like Jeanne d'Arc in the flames: the spirit wrestling against its bonds while the body burns away." The reference to Saint Joan is superfluous, therefore pretentious, and the rest of the short sentence sprawls, as far as is possible in its narrow bed, with religious hyperbole and bookish cliché. It reveals that Coetzee has paid visits to the church and the library; it does not persuade Diana that he knows anything of a woman's thoughts in bed.

It is curious that depictions of women having sex (the one doing research, the other perishing in secondhand metaphorical flames) should occasion such bad writing on Coetzee's part. Yet Coetzee can be a bad writer about plenty of things: "a chill down his spine"; "each man is an island"; "But it is too late now, the damage is done"; "Now he is in a fight for his life." Diana has read through the recent book *Youth*, striking out portions of his sentences as if she were his editor. And in *Youth*, too, he has his younger self think idiotic thoughts: "Are all Englishwomen so beautiful when their clothes are off, he wonders." A young man who has ridden the Tube does not plausibly wonder this. And the refusal to attribute to his younger self an original thought or a charitable impulse is a failure of realism. Sometime in the nineties Coetzee, as stylist and psychologist, slipped, and even *Disgrace*, the best of the later books (with the chill of David Lurie's impending extinction blowing through it), is uneven in these respects.

An explanation may be proposed: forced to take note exclusively of pain, Coetzee's sensibility rebelled at the task, growing somewhat dull and vague so that his awareness of suffering would not have to remain so sharp, so precise. Hence the clichés, the grumpiness, and other defenses against insight. Or else it may be, more simply, that Coetzee, like Costello, is now old and tired.

Diana wishes she could just quote at length from *Michael K* and leave it at that. Coetzee wrote so well about what is elemental— the need for food, warmth, safety, freedom—that when she first read him she felt as if her life had been hiding in plain sight and she had only now seen it. As for the lives of others, his books did more than her subscriptions to a left-wing weekly or her half-hearted inquiry into Buddhism to rebuke the frivolity of her Manhattan existence, to remind her that the world was an economy of pain.

And there was something more: Coetzee seemed so dubious about the possibilities of language-as-communication, preferring instead to consider words as a species of music (cf. *Disgrace* and *Foe* for articulations of this properly Viconian idea), that Diana wondered whether she should not give up writing. After finding out, two years after meeting Daniel, that he would support her, she had wondered whether she should not simply content herself with the animal sufficiency of their life together, and abandon writing. Really: Why write? Speak of the darkest matters, and still you have only produced a decoration for a comfortable room. Adorno said it long ago, when domiciled in L.A., even Kafka's books have become so much furniture.

Diana finds herself thinking again what she has thought before: she should be an activist, not a writer. The thought is never serious. Still, she does not see that it avails anything to write high-brow book chat. Her reviews communicate nothing, convince people of nothing. They are a talented girl's brittle recital, more or less pleasant on the ear. Sometimes people offer that she writes well; never do they say she has induced them to think.

So what should she write in her valedictory book review? "At his best J. M. Coetzee's writing reminds us—or me, I should say me—that there is very little that animals, human or otherwise, require, and that many of them nevertheless go without. That is the nature of our world, it makes me distraught, and in his best books I commune with my distress. *Waiting for the Barbarians, Life & Times of Michael K,* and *Age of Iron* are novels that seared me and salved me, I can't say how, when I lived as a slush-pile Lolita in booming Nolita in the late 1990s. (What is my tone here?) Also I love *In the Heart of the Country,* which I suppose a reviewer would describe as a metafictional novel narrated by an aging white virgin in a remote corner of South Africa. It's the best book I know about hysteria and also one of the best metafictions, nor is this a coincidence: metafiction is hysteria, it's a feeling that you have not made contact with the world, that you do not know your dimensions, that you don't know what sound you will make on contact with the—

"But then you will ask"—Diana is surprised at what she is typing—"why become more intimate with reality when (à la Mrs. Curren and the Magistrate, also David Lurie in *Disgrace*) the touch of the world equals pain? The people who make our world—*Ils sont dans le vrai,* Flaubert re: workmen on the street—are people who suffer. Never mind under what conditions my skirt has been made or my food grown, a girl in the Philippines may have gone blind soldering the circuits inside the computer on which I write these wild words. Yet why share her fate even so far as to know about it? That is what Daniel asks when I am like this: why"

Diana breaks off her text, highlights it, presses delete. It is a lucky thing that she is not a blogger—people would think she was nuts.

It has become depressingly plain that she is not going to write another word this morning. It might improve her mood to masturbate or smoke a cigarette, but these are precisely the decadent activities she fears that nonwriters suspect writers of indulging in all day, and therefore she, at one time an occasional smoker and semiregular masturbator, no longer indulges herself in either way on weekdays.

There is always, however, when laziness requires an object, the internet.

Diana closes her blank document and visits nytimes.com. She feels a pang of guilt at sticking with *The New York Times* when really she should embrace her new California life and read the L.A. paper. Nevertheless it is the paper of record she has turned to, and the paper of record which tells her in summaries of to-day's stories that the U.S. military practices how to shoot down hijacked commercial airliners as often as three to four times a week; that the New York Public Library's exhibit *Russia Engages the World* contains rich cultural artifacts from Russia's imperial-ist past; that preliminary findings support the claims of critics that President Bush used dubious intelligence to justify his deci-sion to go to war; that Israel intends to build about six hundred new homes in three large West Bank settlements; that North Korea has raised the stakes by saying that it is making atomic bombs from plutonium it has reprocessed from eight thousand spent fuel rods; that Steven B. Markovitz, a former trader at Millennium Partners, has pleaded guilty to after-hours trading in mutual fund shares; and that—but what is this?—the Swedish Academy has awarded the South African novelist J. M. Coetzee the Nobel Prize in Literature for his bleak examination of the human condition.

Diana remembers at once. This is what she learned in her sleep, what she heard on NPR. Coetzee has won the Nobel Prize. For-gotten, repeated, and remembered, the news somehow returns her to zero, erasing the morning, deleting her few sentences were they not already gone, and Diana laughs to herself at her ineffec-tuality and at the parlous state of the world.

•

"See you later," she has said to Jeremy, who followed her to the door, curious perhaps about this break in her routine. Now she is driving down Lincoln toward the beach she likes. J. M. Coetzee has won the Nobel Prize so Diana Abbott is taking the day off. Is that illogical? Well, she never took a course in logic.

She had wanted to write a piece about Coetzee. She does not much want to write something about a Nobelist. (The term itself sounds like a South American mispronunciation of "novelist.") Now if Diana praises Coetzee it will seem she is only adding her voice to the right-thinking chorus; and if she pans *Elizabeth Costello* it will look like mere contrarianism. And who will care either way? Perhaps she should confine her views on books to her journal. A writer is most valuable, anyway, when he feels like a private possession, when you feel that you are the only one taking him to bed. As of today Coetzee belongs to everyone, to that human condition he is alleged to depict.

Diana is waiting at the light, windows down, as a disheveled middle-aged woman—hair matted, face the color of fired clay, white Athena College T-shirt falling off one shoulder in helpless imitation of a certain early-eighties style—wheels her possessions across the street, remonstrating with herself over something in an impatient tone of voice. How could anyone who has set foot outside her apartment believe in a shared human condition? And speaking of humanity hasn't Coetzee himself said, accepting the Jerusalem Prize in 1987, that his writing and that of other South Africans constitutes "a less than fully human literature, unnaturally preoccupied with power and the torsions of power"? Perhaps L.A. adds no barriers to a fully human literature, but Diana is by no means certain.

The light turns green and Diana resumes driving to the beach through the spooked sunlight of the West Side. A midnight-colored sports car has left her in the metaphorical dust.

How clean the air is out here, washed by the breezes off the ocean. One would not suspect the smog banked at one's back, or guess at the prices of the real estate, so humble do the low-slung stores and dwellings look in the presence of the sea.

Perhaps in Coetzee's case especially, prizes and acclaim draw attention to his flaws. There is a desire for praise at the heart of his work; you see it in the memoirs. There is a wish to be congratulated on having such high standards, on judging oneself and one's fellows so severely. Isn't that the melancholic's chief consolation, to be considered too good for this world? Surely this is one reason why the melancholic turns to writing. He—or she—is proud of her distress and cannot help but display it. It may be that Coetzee's famous aversion to publicity is thus something of an overcompensation, the exaggerated self-effacement of the hopelessly vain. An unfair speculation, quite out-of-bounds in a review, but it may be accurate. Diana after all is a vain and a shy person both.

Diana looks behind her, changes lanes. She bears right onto Avenida del Rey, drives a distance along the shore, noses into a parking space. She gets out of the car, taking her cell phone and sunglasses with her. The VW Jetta responds with an obedient electronic chirrup as she locks its doors by remote. And then she is taking off her sandals, placing them in her once hip Kate Spade bag, and walking barefoot through the sand.

"I will take off my shoes and crunch through the seasand," says that hysterical narrator in *In the Heart of the Country*, "wondering at the millions of tiny deaths that have gone to make it up." Diana often experiences things by way of allusions, which may be hardly to experience them at all.

Belatedness is the term for this situation. The novelists and poets, naturalists of our inner life, have by now tagged and sorted most of the species therein. Coetzee at least has risen to the occasion, dealing squarely with the problem of his belatedness and addressing his precursors directly. He is at his best when most insolent. *Life & Times of Michael K* alludes of course to Kafka's Joseph K. But in an interview Coetzee declared that he saw no reason why Kafka should hold a patent on the letter. And while *Waiting for the Barbarians* may be a lengthy paraphrase of Cavafy's poem by the same title, it is also clearly the superior work of art, making the poem seem an anticipatory gloss on the novel. Coetzee is less successful in *The Master of Petersburg*, which seems a weak homage to Dostoevsky rather than a victory at the master's game.

Diana is walking southeast along the sparsely populated Playa del Rey. Its visitors this afternoon would appear to be homeless people, a few truant teenagers, and at least one prosperous man—the dark-haired one with the trotting dogs—in the prime of his life, mysteriously free for the afternoon. The sunlight lies across her neck like nothing so much as Bengay.

Obviously the problem of belatedness afflicts Coetzee still. In the final lesson of *Elizabeth Costello* our heroine is called before a mysterious border-town tribunal which demands a "statement" from her before they will let her pass through—to peace, to death, one is not sure. "The wall, the gate, the sentry, are straight out of Kafka. So is the demand for a confession, so is the courtroom with the dozing bailiff and the panel of old men in their crows' robes pretending to pay attention while she thrashes in the toils of her own words." Trapped in a parody of Kafka, Elizabeth Costello must nevertheless produce a statement in earnest. Clichéd her predicament may be, but it is her predicament all the same. And so it is for Diana herself to the nth degree. The writers arriving before her already arrived late; they became a troupe of allusionists and pasticheurs. How late are you, then, when you show up after the late? There is far too much literary history for Diana ever to master it, and far too much for her ever to escape from it; it is her fate never quite to be either sophisticated or naïve.

Diana runs down to the water through the squishy sheen of the wet sand, into the cool sizzle of the surf. It feels so much later than two o'clock in the afternoon. That is what she gets for moving to California, where the world has already been at its business all day, getting and spending, murdering and creating, handing out sentences and handing out prizes, before the sun has peeked over the Santa Monica Mountains and the local NPR affiliate begun to broadcast its reports.

Diana is kicking through the surf, feeling guilty and exhilarated like a truant.

Really everyone who wins the Nobel Prize does seem overrated. Is this the best anyone can do? you wonder. Note to self, she thinks: Don't win Nobel Prize. So far there is little danger. Three months ago she sent out her best short story to five publications; the result to date is two perfunctory rejections. Meanwhile she is at work on a novel—that is what she tells Daniel and her parents. It would be truer to say that the idea of the novel simply follows her wherever she goes. It is one of her skills to be able to describe how other novelists sound. But she doesn't for the life of her know what her own fiction should sound like; that is the missing timbre for which she is constantly listening, the unknown tune to which her ears are pricked up. How much easier it would be to write a pastiche of Coetzee! But that is not how to do it. The way to write is not as if you have just learned the craft, at the school of the masters; the way to write is as if you have somehow always known how.

Diana is knee-deep in the Pacific. What is she feeling, as the dissolving wreaths of foam slide past her, to make her laugh and almost cry? She laughs, she almost cries, it is better than *Elizabeth Costello*. She feels violently partitioned among her moods. Young and null, healthy and decadent, hopeful and in despair, what is up with her? It feels so early in her life—earlier than it actually is—and at the same time so late in the day, much later than a clock would admit.

After this review is completed maybe she won't read Coetzee anymore. She admires him too much, maybe understands him too well. And maybe he isn't good enough! This is what Diana is always doing, what too many women do: she gives herself over to someone else's perspective and loses her own.

Why should she have allowed her sensibility to align so neatly with Coetzee's or have felt that he somehow speaks for her? She is not from South Africa but from America, a more happily mongrelized location. Her father, moreover, is nothing like the no-account bully Coetzee describes in *Boyhood*, and her mother is not much like Coetzee's was—baffled, needy, and defeated. Were Diana Abbott to write a memoir, the first memory presented would not be that of a mother going at the family hens with a knife. (Can Coetzee's interest in animal rights be traced to such a memory? Did little John Coetzee guess so early that our comforters and protectors have attained their position at the expense of other life? And will Diana herself become a mother, as Daniel believes she will?) In *Girlhood*, Diana Abbott would instead describe her mother coming to sit down, with her enormous grown-up person's weight, on the little girl's bed, and rubbing her daughter's back in the nightly ritual. Why was nighttime so much itchier than the day, Diana had wanted to know. And her mother—this is one of Diana's first memories—had told her that it is only when we are lying still at night that we notice all our itches. Intended as comfort, in the way of all explanations, the answer had disturbed Diana, and for several years it bothered her—on the way to school, or at school, or being driven home—that she must have itches to scratch that were going unattended, that the itches were constantly there, suffering, as it were, by themselves.

But that has nothing to do with Coetzee. And why should it? Why should she identify at all with this unsmiling man and traffic in his few cold themes of pain and power? Except for when her right ring finger was shattered by a hurtling lacrosse ball and had to be amputated above the knuckle, Diana has hardly been acquainted with intense physical pain. As for the maldistribution of power in the world, it has not polluted all of her pleasures, especially not her sexual pleasures, as seems to be the case with Coetzee, for whom sex would appear never to be a win-win situation. Life is good, in large part, at most times, for her and Daniel and their families. In the win-win stratum of American society to which they belong, life is substantially good, and next summer they will be married. And if now she is crying—not weeping, certainly not bawling, merely crying a little as she stands in the surf—it is not because anything bad has happened. But there is a chilling line spoken by the Queen in *Richard III* that Diana often thinks of: "I fear our happiness is at the height."

Suddenly—sometimes things do happen suddenly, as in books—Diana arrives at a new understanding. Knee-deep in the water, she seems to cringe as if in anticipation of a blow, but she does not in fact cringe, she keeps wading forward, and no blow comes, only the slack tide smacking between her thighs and wetting the hem of her skirt. She is a morbid young woman; that much she has known. But here is the new thing: she understands it now as the special morbidity—the special curiosity about pain, the special fear of pain—of someone who has not intensely suffered or witnessed others doing so. The thought fills her with such strange shame that she turns away from the ocean.

Standing there on the beach is the dark-haired man with the two dogs, looking at her. She waves to him and smiles, embarrassed by her tears. Clark Kent waves broadly back. He has the thickened look of the former athlete who now makes lots of money. He also looks mischievous and pleased, as if he has been caught ogling by a woman who doesn't mind.

Diana turns back to the water and wades a distance farther from the shore, a mystery to herself and no doubt her onlooker both.

She is wondering what she will do with the rest of the day, whether she will ever turn in her review, when her cell phone starts to ring. She very nearly screams back at the ringing phone. Instead she fishes the clamshell-style device from her bag, not unfolding it to see the incoming number, not answering the call, instead holding the phone crying in her palm. Chances are it is Daniel calling from work or her mother reporting on her latest checkup; few others have this number yet. But Diana doesn't want to hear either good news or bad, doesn't want to make any plans whatever, doesn't want to hear at present that she is loved. In the melodramatic gesture of a fictional character, richly if obscurely symbolic, Diana—a real person, never mind her surprise at this fact—takes the shrilling phone and throws it as far she can out into the water, where it disappears with hardly a splash. How will I explain this to Daniel? she wonders, and in the same moment, furious at him for his banality and mental vagueness, doubts whether she will marry him.

She marches back to the beach, out of the water. Diana's robust onlooker is still watching her, while one of his dogs looks for a sign of permission to run in search of the hurled object. "Was that a cell phone you just threw in there?" the man asks.

"Yes." She means to sound defiant; instead she sounds abashed. She smiles her best all-purpose smile.

"That was some throw." He betrays no awareness that she is crying—which causes Diana to recall that she is wearing sunglasses. So is he. "You've got a good arm on you," the man says, whether flirtatiously, condescendingly, admiringly, humorously, or only to make conversation. "You don't throw like a girl."

"I throw like a fucking quarterback," Diana says through tears, and walks past, not stopping. Boys used to tell her this in wonder, and grown-ups that she was never at a loss for words.

(2005)

GUT-LEVEL LEGISLATION, OR, REDISTRIBUTION

Mark Greif

One of the lessons of starting a magazine today is that if you pay any attention to politics you will collect a class of detractors, who demand immediately to know What and Wherefore and Whether and How. Are you to be filed next to *Mother Jones* and *Z* and *The American Spectator* in the back row, or with *The Nation* and *The Weekly Standard* and *The American Prospect* up front? Is it possible you have not endorsed a candidate, or adopted a party? Within the party, a position? If not a position, an issue? The notion that politics could be served by thinking about problems and principles, rather than rehearsing strategy, leaves them not so much bemused as furious.

The furious political detractors need "responsibility," which in their hands is a fiction of power. If you question the world from an armchair, it offends them deeply. If you believe you run the world from it, it exalts them—because you have bought into the fiction that justifies their elitism. These commentators who have no access to a legislative agenda and really no more exalted basis for political action than that of their ordinary citizenship (but they do not believe they are ordinary citizens) bleat and growl and put themselves on record for various initiatives of Congress over which they have no influence and upon which they will have no effect. To be on record is to be "politically responsible" in that false sense. No rebuke is made to the process of opinionating itself—this ritual of fomenting an opinion on everything, and so justifying the excited self-stimulation of a class of unelected arbiters who don't respect the citizens within themselves.

"What do you stand for! What will you do!" Legislatively? Are you kidding? Well, there is something one can do, without succumbing to the pundits: for the day when the Congress rolls up to our doorsteps and asks for our legislative initiatives, maybe it is up to every citizen to know what is in his heart and have his true bills and resolutions ready. Call it "political surrealism"— the practice of asking for what is at present impossible, in order to get at last, by indirection or implausible directness, the principles that would underlie the world we'd want rather than the one we have.

§ *Principle*: The purpose of government is to share out money so that there are no poor citizens—therefore no one for whom we must feel guilty because of the arbitrariness of fate. The purpose of life is to free individuals for *individualism.* Individualism is the project of making your own life as appealing as you can, as remarkable as you like, without the encumbrances of an unequal society, which renders your successes undeserved. Government is the outside corrective that leaves us free for life.

§ *Legislative Initiative No. 1*: Add a tax bracket of 100 percent to cut off individual income at a fixed ceiling, allowing any individual to bring home a maximum of $100,000 a year from all sources and no more.

§ *Legislative Initiative No. 2*: Give every citizen a total of $10,000 a year from the government revenues, paid as a monthly award, in recognition of being an adult in the United States.

The redistribution of wealth can be unnerving whenever it comes up, and most unnerving to those who have the least wealth, because they have worked hardest for every dollar and can't afford to lose it.

But redistribution comes in two steps, and when you look at the steps it's not so unnerving. The first step was already accomplished last century. It was the permanent establishment of a graduated income tax, one of the greatest triumphs of civilization. A consensus was built to grade taxation to equalize the relative pain of taxation for each income earner. A little money is as useful to a person with little money overall as a larger sum is useful to a person with lots of money—and so, for equal citizenship, they carry an equal burden. Tax them proportionately the same, and everyone pays the same stake for government with the same degree of sacrifice.

The second step is our task in *this* century. It is an active redistribution to help dissolve the two portions of society whose existence is antithetical to democracy and civilization, and which harm the members of each of these classes: the obscenely poor and the absurdly rich. Each group must be helped. That means not only ending poverty, but ending absurd wealth. Obscene poverty doesn't motivate the poor or please the rest of us; it makes the poor desperate, criminal, and unhappy. Absurd wealth doesn't help the rich or motivate the rest of us; it makes the rich (for the most part good, decent, hardworking, and talented people) into selfish guilty parties, responsible for social evil. It is cruel to rig our system to create these extremes, and cast fellow citizens into the two sewers that border the national road. For all of us, both superwealth and superpoverty make achievement trivial and un- real, and finally destroy the American principles of hard work and just deserts. Luckily, eradicating one (individual super- wealth) might help eradicate the other (superpoverty).

True property is that which is proper to you: what you mix your hands into (Locke), what is characteristic of you and no one else, and would change state in anyone else's possession. It is your clothes, your domicile, the things you touch and use, the land you personally walk. Property is the proprium, a possession that be- comes like a characteristic; it starts as if it could belong to anyone, and comes to be what differentiates you. If it wears the mark of your feet and the smudge of your fingertips, your scent and your private atmosphere, then there is indeed something special and inviolable about property, even when it has come into your hands inequitably, by inheritance or a surfeit of income. The diamond worn at the throat every evening must share a certain protection, under the law, with the torn cloak that keeps some shivering per- son warm.

This is distinct, however, from all wealth which is not capa- ble of being used in the ordinary necessities of a life or even the ordinary luxuries. From any wealth that cannot be touched or worn or walked every day by its possessor, that neither comes from nor enables the mixing-in of hands but always and inevita- bly exists as a kind of notional accumulation of numbers, the protection of the proprium withdraws. When you have more houses than you or loved ones can live in; more cars than you can drive; more income in a year than can be spent on what you or your family can actually use, even uselessly use; then we are not speaking of property anymore, not the proprium, but of the inappropriate and alien—that which one gathers to oneself through the accident of social arrangements, exploiting them willfully or accidentally, and not through the private and the personal.

Thus the rationale for restricting *income*. Inequality will always exist, but in itself it is something different. One has to recognize that while the proprium may be passed down in nonmonetary forms, too—in the peculiarities of your genetics from your parents; in the heirloom, dwelling, tool, or decoration which wears the traces of hands and breath—income always comes as a consequence of arrangements of the community, via the shared space of trade, the discussion and rules, the systems of investment, and all the voluntary associations of society, of which the largest association is government.

A rich person—continuing to draw $100,000 a year in income—stays rich, but puts part of it into his own home and bank account and part into the needs and luxuries he may actually use. This sum will be converted reasonably into the *proper*, the personal, without any absurdity. A superrich person, however, who takes in $1 million, $10 million, or $100 million, will not and can never spend it on any sane vision of the necessities of life, at least not without a parasitic order in which normal goods (a home, a dinner) are overpriced (by the existence of those who will compete to pay for them) and other goods are made to be abnormal and bloated (like the multiacre mansion). The social system allocates the extra $9.9 million mistakenly. Reallocated, it would do much more benefit in a guaranteed citizens' income for many individuals in households with total incomes both above and below the median (now about $45,000 per household). But this is without—and this is very important—doing any harm to the formerly superrich person; if anything, it may do him a great benefit.

(And it should also be without any person or office to decide to whom money should be allocated. The goal is an automatic mechanism and universal good, not a form of control. Everyone must be given an equal sum, the $10,000, to help him be free. And that must include the rich top earner of $100,000—to keep him free, too, with the opportunity, through all the years of his adulthood, to *change* his life.)

The threat from those who oppose this line of thought is that, without "incentives," people will stop working. The worst-case scenario is that tens of thousands of people who hold jobs in finance, corporate management, and the professions (not to mention professional sports and acting) will quit their jobs and end their careers because they did not truly want to be bankers, lawyers, CEOs, actors, ballplayers, et cetera. They were only doing it for the money! Actually, they wanted to be high school teachers, social workers, general practitioners, stay-at-home parents, or criminals and layabouts.

Far from this being a tragedy, this would be the greatest single triumph of human emancipation in a century. A small portion of the rich and unhappy would be freed at last from the slavery of jobs that aren't their life's work—and all of us would be freed from an insane system.

If there is anyone working a job who would stop doing that job should his income—and all his richest compatriots' incomes—drop to $100,000 a year, *he should not be doing that job.* He should *never* have been doing that job—for his own life's sake. It's just not a life, to do work you don't want to do when you have other choices and can think of something better (and have a $10,000 cushion to supplement a different choice of life). If no one would choose to do this job for a mere $100,000 a year, if all would pursue something else more humanly valuable; if, say, there would no longer be anyone willing to be a trader, a captain of industry, an actor, or an athlete for that kind of money—then the job should not exist.

The supposed collapse of the economy without unlimited income levels is one of the most suspicious aspects of commonplace economic psychology. Ask yourself, for once, if you believe it. Does the inventor just not bother to invent anymore if inventions still benefit larger collectivities—a company, a society—but do not lead to a jump in his or any other inventor's already satisfactory personal income? Do the professions really collapse if doctors and lawyers work for life and justice and $100,000, rather than $1 million? Will the arts and entertainment collapse if the actors, writers, and producers work for glory and $100,000? Do ballplayers go into some other line and stop playing? If you're panicking because you can't imagine a ceiling of $100,000, well, make it $150,000. Our whole system is predicated on the erroneous idea that individuals are likely to hate the work they have chosen but overwhelmingly love money. Presumably the opposite should be true. Even the really successful trader *must* love his work in some way—he enjoys the competition, temporarily measured in money, and the action and strategy and game of thought and organization, which are his life's calling. And all this glory could be pursued in a society in which he only took home $100,000 from this sport of kings—and he, and all of us, might be better off.

•

"But how can you ask other people to lower their salaries, without giving your life to charity, first? Isn't it hypocrisy to call for change for everyone without turning over your own income?" Morality is not saved by any individual's efforts to do charity, a pocketful here, a handful there. Charity is the vice of unequal systems. (I'm only repeating Wilde's "The Soul of Man Under Socialism.") We shouldn't have to weigh whether our money would do more good in a destitute person's pocket, or our time do more good if we ladled soup to the hungry, or our study do more good if it taught reading to the illiterate. It always, always would. Because it is hard to give up your money, however, when not everyone else does, and hard to give up your time when not everyone else does—and nearly impossible when you have less time, and less money, than the visibly rich and comfortable—and frankly, because it's not often a good idea to give up your true calling or your life at all, our giving is limited and fitful. It can never make a large-scale difference.

Not only decency, justice, and community but nobility, excellence, and individualism can come about only by redistribution, not charity, in a society organized against drastic monetary inequality in the first place. It would be a good society in the broadest sense, one in which life was worth living, because the good life (as a life of morality, and as a life of justified luxury) could be pursued without contradiction.

The essence of individualism is *morally relevant* inequality. The misuse of inequality occurs when it comes to be based on wealth rather than ability; on birth rather than talent; on positioning rather than genius; on alienable money (which could belong to anyone) rather than action and works (which can only be done by you). These distortions spell the end of a society of individualists. Money inequality creates a single system which corrals every person and places him above or beneath another, in a single file stretching from hell to the moon. These so-called "individualists" will then be led, by the common standard of the dollar, to common interests, common desires, and little that's *individual* at all.

Some say, the more the rich are rich, the better off will everyone be. But really the Dick Cheneys of this world are obese because they're eating everybody else's dinner. Trickle-down economics is an alimentary philosophy: the more the rich eat, the more crusts they stuff in their maws, the more they create for the benefit of all the rest of us underneath them. Even if it worked, one could not forget that what they pass on to us is predigested, already traveling through their stomachs and fattening them first, giving excess nutriment to the undeserving. Their monuments, too, which we do marvel at, are composed of waste. Why gain the world as excrement? Why should we not take it in its morally original form—if money need not pass through the rich to reach us?

§ *Legislative Initiative No. 3.* It makes most sense to have a president and vice president who will forswear wealth permanently. A man who rules for the demos need not come from the demos. But he ought to enter it; he ought to become one of the people he is responsible most for helping—that means the rest of us.

Worst-case scenario two, if we prioritize human satisfaction instead of productivity, is de-development. For centuries, it has been at the back of the Western mind that technological development might reach a point at which a democratic community would want to stop, or change direction. So the Erewhonians, in Butler's utopia, broke their machines.

It's finally become possible to take a better view: not unlimited laissez-faire hubris, and not irrational machine-breaking, either. In a country where some portions of development have gone further than anybody would like, because of everyone's discrete private actions (as in the liquidation of landscape and the lower atmosphere), while other portions (as in medical insurance and preventive care) have not gone far enough, then *intentional de-development* might be the best thing that can occur. The eradication of diseases is not something you would like to see end; nor would you want to lose the food supply, transportation, and good order of the law and defense. On the other hand, more cell phones and wireless, an expanded total entertainment environment, more computerization for consumer tracking, greater concentrations of capital and better exploitation of "inefficiencies" in the trading of securities, the final throes of extraction and gas-guzzling and—to hell with it. I'd rather live in a more equal world at a slower pace.

(2006)

THE INTELLECTUAL SITUATION
(DEATH IS NOT THE END)

The Editors

Was theory a gigantic hoax? On the contrary. It was the only salvation, for a twenty-year period, from two colossal abdications by American thinkers and writers. From about 1975 to 1995, through a historical accident, a lot of American thinking and mental living got done by people who were French, and by young Americans who followed the French.

The two grand abdications: one occurred in academic philosophy departments, the other in American fiction. In philosophy, from the 1930s on, a revolutionary group had been fighting inside universities to overcome the "tradition." This insurgency, at first called "logical positivism" or "logical empiricism," then simply "analytic philosophy," was the best thing going. The original idea was that logical analysis of language would show which philosophical problems might be solved, and which eradicated because they were not phrasable in clear, logical language. That meant wiping out most of what Hegel had left us, and Europe still understood, as philosophy—including history, being, death, recognition, love. Still brand-new in the 1930s (Carnap, Russell, Ayer) when trying to develop its ideal logical language, it had only just become institutional in the analytic pragmatism of the 1950s and 1960s (Quine), in time to be cranked up again in the 1970s (Kripke), saved from termination by the reintroduction of naïve assumptions rejected at the start.

They weren't wrong, the positivists—you didn't have to get very far into academic Idealism to see it was so much soft-boiled egg. The tragedy of analytic philosophy was the fact that it *won* so decisively in U.S. philosophy departments—annihilating its traditionalist competition—at just the wrong time. It triumphed in the sixties, when the actual convulsions of U.S. society called for a renewed treatment of love, freedom, the other, politics, and history—"pseudo-problems" turned intensely real. It was nice to have John Searle so understanding of SDS at Berkeley, and Hilary Putnam chanting Maoist slogans at Harvard; but the kids in Paris had Foucault.

In fiction, nothing is so clear-cut. But the overall problem will be familiar. During the same midcentury decades when analytic philosophy vanquished all comers, the novel was exalted in American culture as having a near-scriptural power of assessment and prophecy. (Bellow on Chicago: "Terrible dumbness covered it, like a judgment that would never find its word." But there in *Augie March* he had the words.) By the 1940s and 1950s, when newly professional critics ruled both the small literary journals and the universities, American greatness became a closed system. Because the critics had just solidified two different canons at the same time—an Old Testament of the American Renaissance (Emerson, Hawthorne, Melville, Whitman), and a New Testament of American modernism (James, Eliot, Hemingway, Faulkner)—they didn't need to step outside it. It was type and antitype, the 1920s speaking to the 1850s and vice versa, accomplishing all things, and contemporary postwar writers were left out in the cold. The demands on new novelists, for a "Great American Novel" in the vein of these gospels, became too great to meet. The astonishing thing was that artists still occasionally delivered, as Ellison and Bellow each did once—but they were an end, not a beginning.

By the midsixties something crippling was happening to fiction, still quite hard to explain: articulate writers blamed the sheer craziness of American life (Roth) or the "exhaustion" of forms (Barth). There was the pressure of criticism, which could lead even a dyed-in-the-wool critic like Sontag to declare herself "Against Interpretation"; others pointed to academic writing programs and the group therapy of the workshop. In short order, 1968 arrived, and the chaotic seventies, an era which received—in place of *Germinal* or *Sentimental Education* or *The Possessed*, or even *The Grapes of Wrath*!—Thomas Pynchon's *Gravity's Rainbow* and William Gaddis's *JR*. One was a symbolico-enyclopedic epic unembarrassed beside Joyce, the other (in a mode stolen from the minor English modernist Henry Green, alternating dead-to-rights dialogue with brief descriptive passages of hallucinated brilliance, and elevated by Gaddis to demented majesty) a novel concerning nothing less than American capitalism. But in retrospect these books appear marginal where the "Great American Novel" was supposed to be central, heroic sighs of depletion instead of inaugural hymns.

Terry Eagleton once pointed out that the French theorists preserved the modernist tradition in literature when fiction writers did not. Verbose, allusive, experimental, but always to a purpose—declaring that certain thoughts could only be had in certain kinds of words—yes, that was theory. But the more significant thing is that theory took over the *thinking* function of fiction as well as the stylistic: it treated social theory in the way the novel always had, more for liberatory power than strict fidelity to scholarship, and offered wild suspicion as the route to personal enlightenment. It did the novelistic job of a whole period: it produced the works, at once literary and intellectual, that came to terms with the immediate aftermath of the sixties.

Many of the classics of the era opened with feats of prose that American novels of the 1970s and 1980s rarely even attempted. Lévi-Strauss could describe a sunset in *Tristes Tropiques* for longer than a sun takes to set. Foucault did fourteen pages on a single painting, Velázquez's *Las Meninas*. Then there was the drive and audacity of the *History of Sexuality*, Volume 1: "For a long time, the story goes, we supported a Victorian regime"—with the Proustian *longtemps*, thrown off, with such brio, in a work of history! You could walk away from a book like that able to understand nearly everything in the newspaper, on the street, in a brand-new way. Ah, so the discourses of sex and health, not repressed but proliferated, sustain the illusory modern "truth" of the self! It helped that the concepts of theory were so complicated that only a nineteen-year-old could understand them.

Where, frankly, were you going to get your diagnosis of society—from Bret Easton Ellis's *American Psycho*? Lyotard did it better in *Libidinal Economy*, and was much scarier—without pornographic bloodshed. A civilization that may have punished less, but punished better, administering its surveillance from inside one's own mind (*Discipline and Punish*), or replaced the real with a mediatized world of simulations (*Simulacra and Simulation*), or had an economic incentive to reconfigure disparate knowledge as commensurable "information" (*The Postmodern Condition*)—well, that was very clearly the world we lived in. Whereas the itsy-bitsy stories of sad revelations in *The Best American Short Stories 1989*—that was some trivial bullshit.

The best and most exciting novels of the same period, the ones that made you think the notion of a "Great American Novel" hadn't been misconceived all along, were openly responding to theorists. Don DeLillo's *White Noise* brought in a theorist as a character. Pat Barker's *Regeneration* trilogy (okay, she's British), and especially *The Eye in the Door*, triumphed as a controlled experiment in the application of feminist theory to stories (of World War I) a whole nation took for granted.

Theory is only something that could "die" in the last five years because it was an import from a country, France, that had discontinued the model, while the most visible American inheritors were exegetes and epigones, translators and disciples—therefore mediocre. Theory's death was also literal. Hardly any of the old heroes are alive. The exceptions are Baudrillard (alive, but cynical), Habermas (old and healthy, but German), and, incredibly, Claude Lévi-Strauss. Might Althusser be alive, imprisoned? No, dead. Pan-European successor candidates, the likes of Žižek, Badiou, Ferry, Virilio, Agamben, Negri, Vattimo, Sloterdijk, Luhmann, Kittler, seem somehow, well, *small* by comparison. Optical illusion? No, they really are smaller. Or up to something different.

The big mistake right now would be to fail to keep faith with what theory once meant to us. You hear a great collective sigh of relief from people who don't have to read "that stuff" anymore— the ones who never read it in the first place. But who will insult these people now, expose their life as self-deception, their media as obstacles to truth, their conventional wisdom as ideology? It will be unbearable to live with such people if they aren't regularly insulted.

And all of us who spent our formative years on a critique of the sign can't only have gone into advertising. So theory will return in unexpected ways. *The Corrections*, a monumental renewal of the critical social novel, spent its first hundred pages in the skin of a teacher of theory. Chip ended up the house-husband of a successful doctor; Franzen himself took up the bigger task, and made something properly novelistic of phenomena that he, too, like Chip, like all of us, had looked to theory to explain.

Theory is dead, and long live theory. The designated mourners have tenure, anyway, so they'll be around a bit. As for the rest of us, an opening has emerged, in the novel and in intellect. What to do with it?

(2005)

BABEL IN CALIFORNIA

Elif Batuman

When the Russian Academy of Sciences puts together an author's collected works, they aren't aiming for something you can put in a suitcase and run away with. The "millennium" edition of Tolstoy fills a hundred volumes and weighs as much as a newborn beluga whale. (I brought my bathroom scale to the library and weighed it, ten volumes at a time.) Dostoevsky comes in thirty volumes, Turgenev in twenty-eight, Pushkin in seventeen. Even Lermontov, a lyric poet killed in a duel at age twenty-six, has four volumes. It's different in France, where definitive editions are printed on "Bible paper." The Bibliothèque de la Pléiade manages to fit Balzac's entire *Human Comedy* in twelve volumes, and his remaining writings in two volumes, for a combined total weight of eighteen pounds.

The collected works of Isaac Babel fill only two small volumes. Comparing Tolstoy's works to Babel's is like comparing a long road to a pocket watch. Babel's best-loved works all fit in the first volume: the Odessa, Childhood, and Petersburg cycles; *Red Cavalry*; and the 1920 diary, on which *Red Cavalry* is based. The compactness makes itself felt all the more acutely, since Babel's oeuvre is

known to be incomplete. When the NKVD came to his dacha in
1939, Babel's first words were, "They didn't let me finish." The
secret police seized and confiscated nine folders from the dacha,
and fifteen from Babel's Moscow apartment. They seized and confiscated Babel himself, on charges of spying for France and even
Austria. Neither manuscripts nor writer were seen again.

In the next years, Babel's published works were removed from
circulation. His name was erased from encyclopedias and film
credits. Rumors circulated—Babel was in a special camp for writers, he was writing for the camp newspaper—but nobody knew
for sure if he was dead or alive. In 1954, the year after Stalin's death,
Babel was officially exonerated, and the dossier of his criminal
case was made public. Inside was just one page: a certificate at-
testing to his death, under unknown circumstances, on March 17,
1941. Like Sherlock Holmes in "The Adventure of the Final Problem," Babel had vanished, leaving behind a single sheet of paper.

Nobody really knows why Babel was arrested when he was. He
had made powerful enemies early in his career with the publication of the *Red Cavalry* stories, which immortalize the botched
Russo-Polish military campaign of 1920. In 1924, Commander
Semyon Budyonny of the First Cavalry publicly accused Babel of
"counterrevolutionary lies" and character assassination. In later
years, as Budyonny rose in the Party system, from marshal of the
Soviet Union to first deputy commissar for defense and Hero of
the Soviet Union, Babel found himself on increasingly thin ice—
especially after the death of his protector, Maxim Gorky, in 1936.
Nonetheless, he survived the height of the Great Purge in 1937–38,
and was arrested only in 1939, when World War II was just around
the corner and Stalin presumably had bigger fish to fry. What
tipped the scale?

The Nazi-Soviet pact might have played a role: because of

Babel's close ties with the French Left, his continued existence was necessary to maintain Soviet-French diplomatic relations—which became a moot point once Stalin sided with Hitler. Some evidence suggests that Babel was arrested in preparation for one last show trial that was to accuse the entire intellectual elite, from the film legend Sergei Eisenstein to the polar explorer Otto Schmidt, but which was called off in September when Hitler invaded Poland.

Some scholars attribute Babel's arrest to his bizarre relationship with the former people's commissar Nikolai Yezhov: Babel had had an affair in the 1920s with Evgeniya Gladun-Khayutina, Yezhov's future wife, and it was said that, even in the 1930s, Babel would visit the couple at home, where they would all play ninepins and listen to Yezhov tell gruesome stories about the gulag. When Lavrenty "Stalin's Butcher" Beria came to power in 1938, he made a point of exterminating anyone who had ever had anything to do with Yezhov.

Others insist that Babel was arrested "for no reason at all," and that to say otherwise is to commit the sin of attributing logic to the totalitarian machine.

When Babel's box in the KGB archives was declassified in the 1990s, it became known that the warrant for his arrest had been issued thirty-five days after the fact. Following seventy-two hours of continuous interrogation and probably torture, Babel had signed a confession testifying that he had been recruited into a spy network in 1927 by Ilya Ehrenburg and for years systematically supplied André Malraux with the secrets of Soviet aviation—the last detail apparently borrowed from Babel's late screenplay, *Number 4 Staraya Square* (1939), which chronicles the byzantine intrigues among scientists in a plant devoted to the construction of Soviet dirigibles.

"I am innocent. I have never been a spy," Babel says in the transcript of his twenty-minute "trial," which took place in Beria's chambers. "I accused myself falsely. I was forced to make false accusations against myself and others . . . I am asking for only one thing—let me finish my work." Babel was executed by firing squad in the basement of the Lubyanka on January 26, 1940, and his body was dumped in a communal grave. Nineteen forty, not 1941: even the death certificate had been a lie.

The first time I read Isaac Babel was in a college creative writing class. The instructor was a sympathetic Jewish novelist with a Jesus-like beard, an affinity for Russian literature, and a melancholy sense of humor, such that one afternoon he even "realized" the truth of human mortality, right there in the classroom. He pointed at each of us around the seminar table: "*You're* going to die. And *you're* going to die. And *you're* going to die." I still remember the expression on the face of one of my classmates, a genial scion of the Kennedy family who always wrote the same story, about a busy corporate lawyer who neglected his wife. The expression was confused.

In this class we were assigned to read "My First Goose," the story of a Jewish intellectual's first night at a new Red Army billet during the 1920 campaign. Immediately upon his arrival, his new comrades, illiterate Cossacks, greet him by throwing his suitcase in the street. The intellectual, noticing a goose waddling around the billet, steps on its neck, impales it on a saber, and orders the landlady to cook it for his dinner. The Cossacks then accept him as one of their own and make room for him at the fireside, where he reads them one of Lenin's speeches from a recent issue of *Pravda*.

When I first read this story in college, it made absolutely no sense to me. Why did he have to kill that goose? What was so great about sitting around a campfire, reading Lenin? Among the stories we read in that class, Chekhov's "Lady with Lapdog" moved me much more deeply. I especially remember the passage about how everyone has two lives—one open and visible, full of work, convention, responsibilities, jokes, and the other "running its course in secret"—and how easy it is for circumstances to line up so that everything you hold most important, interesting, and meaningful is somehow in the second life, the secret one. In fact, this theme of a second, secret life is extremely important to Babel, but I didn't figure that out until later.

The second time I read Babel was in graduate school, for a seminar on literary biography. I read the 1920 diary and the entire *Red Cavalry* cycle in one sitting, on a rainy Saturday in February, while baking a Black Forest cake. As Babel immortalized for posterity the military embarrassment of the botched 1920 Russo-Polish campaign, so he immortalized for me the culinary embarrassment of this cake, which came out of the oven looking like an old hat and which, after I had optimistically treated it with half a two-dollar bottle of kirschwasser, produced the final pan-sensory impression of an old hat soaked in cough syrup.

There are certain books that one remembers together with the material circumstances of reading: how long it took, the time of year, the color of the cover. Often, it's the material circumstances themselves that make you remember a book that way—but sometimes it's the other way around. I'm sure that my memory of that afternoon—the smell of rain and baking chocolate, the depressing apartment with its inflatable sofa, the sliding glass door that overlooked rainy palm trees and a Safeway parking lot—is due to the precious, almost-lost quality of Babel's 1920 diary.

The diary starts on page fifty-five—Babel lost the first fifty-four pages. Three days later, another twenty-one pages go missing—a month's worth of entries. "Slept badly, thinking of the manuscripts," Babel writes. "Dejection, loss of energy, I know I will get over it, but when?" For the next couple of days, despite all his efforts, everything reminds him of the lost pages: "A peasant (Parfenty Melnik, the one who did his military service in Elisavetpol) complains that his horse is swollen with milk, they took away her foal, sadness, the manuscripts, the manuscripts . . ."

The diary isn't about war, but about a writer during a war—about a writer voraciously experiencing war as a source of material. Viktor Shklovsky, who invented the theory that literary subject material is always secondary to literary form, was a great admirer of Babel. "He wasn't alienated from life," Shklovsky wrote. "But it always seemed to me that Babel, when he went to bed every night, appended his signature to the day he had just lived, as if it were a story." Babel wasn't alienated from life—to the contrary, he sought it out—but he was incapable of living it otherwise than as the material for literature.

The epigraph to the 1920 diary could be the famous phrase from the beginning of *Don Quixote*: "since I'm always reading, even scraps of paper I find in the street . . ." In Brody, in the aftermath of a pogrom, while looking for oats to feed his horse, Babel stumbles upon a German bookstore: "marvelous uncut books, albums . . . a chrestomathy, the history of all the Boleslaws . . . Tetmajer, new translations, a pile of new Polish national literature, textbooks. I rummage like a madman, I run around." In a looted Polish estate, in a drawing room where horses are standing on the carpet, he discovers a chest of "extremely precious books": "the constitution approved by the Sejm at the beginning of the 18th century, old folios from the times of Nicholas I, the Polish code of laws, precious bindings, Polish manuscripts of the 16th century, writings of monks, old French novels . . . French novels on little tables, many French and Polish books about child care, smashed intimate feminine accessories, remnants of butter in a butter dish—newlyweds?" In an abandoned Polish castle, he finds "French letters dated 1820, *nôtre petit héros achève 7 semaines.* My God, who wrote it, when . . ."

These materials are assimilated and expanded upon in the *Red Cavalry* stories, for example in "Berestechko," whose narrator also finds a French letter in a Polish castle: "Paul, mon bien aimé, on dit que l'empereur Napoléon est mort, est-ce vrai? Moi, je me sens bien, les couches ont été faciles . . ." From the phrase *"nôtre petit héros achève 7 semaines,"* Babel conjures the full precariousness of time, a point as delicately positioned in human history as a seven-week-old child, or a false rumor of Napoleon's death.

Reading the whole *Red Cavalry* cycle after the diary, I understood "My First Goose." I understood how important it was that the suitcase thrown in the street by the Cossacks was full of manuscripts and newspapers. I understood what it meant for Babel to read Lenin aloud to the Cossacks. It was the first hostile encounter of writing with life itself. "My First Goose," like much of *Red Cavalry*, is about the price Babel paid for his literary material. Osip Mandelstam once asked Babel why he went out of his way to socialize with agents of the secret police, with people like Yezhov: "Was it a desire to see what it was like in the exclusive store where the merchandise was death? Did he just want to touch it with his fingers? 'No,' Babel replied, 'I don't want to touch it with my fingers—I just like to have a sniff and see what it smells like.'" But, of course, he had to touch it with his fingers.

He had to shed blood with his own hands, if only that of a goose. Without that blood, *Red Cavalry* could never have been written. "It sometimes happens that I don't spare myself and spend an hour kicking the enemy, or sometimes more than an hour," observes one of Babel's narrators, a Cossack swineherd turned Red Army general. "I want to understand life, to learn what it really is."

The imperative to understand life and describe it provides an urgent, moving refrain in the 1920 diary.

"Describe the orderlies—the divisional chief of staff and the others—Cherkashin, Tarasov."

"Describe Matyazh, Misha. *Muzhiks*, I want to penetrate their souls."

Whenever Babel meets anyone, he has to fathom what he is. Always "what," not "who."

"What is Mikhail Karlovich?" "What is Zholnarkevich? A Pole? His feelings?"

"What are our soldiers?" "What are Cossacks?" "What is Bolshevism?"

"What is Kiperman? Describe his trousers."

"Describe the work of a war correspondent, what is a war correspondent?" (At the time he wrote this sentence, Babel himself was technically a war correspondent.)

Sometimes he seems to beg the question, asking, of somebody called Vinokurov: "What is this gluttonous, pitiful, tall youth, with his soft voice, droopy soul, and sharp mind?"

"What is Grishchuk? Submissiveness, endless silence, boundless indolence. Fifty *versts* from home, hasn't been home in six years, doesn't run."

"I go into the mill. What is a water mill? Describe."

"Describe the forest."

"Two emaciated horses, describe the horses."

"Describe the air, the soldiers."

"Describe the bazaar, baskets of cherries, the inside of the tavern."

"Describe this unendurable rain."

"Describe 'rapid fire.' "

"Describe the wounded."

"The intolerable desire to sleep—describe."

"Absolutely must describe limping Gubanov, scourge of the regiment."

"Describe Bakhturov, Ivan Ivanovich, and Petro."

"The castle of Count Raciborski. A seventy-year-old man and his ninety-year-old mother. People say it was always just the two of them, that they're crazy. Describe."

Babel's "describe" in his diaries shares a certain melancholy quality with Watson's mention of those of Sherlock Holmes's cases that do not appear in his annals: "the case of the Darlington substitution scandal," the "singular affair of the aluminum crutch," "the mystery of the Giant Rat of Sumatra . . . for which the world is not yet prepared." All the stories that will never be told—all the writers who were not allowed to finish! It's much more comforting to think that, in their way, the promises have already been executed—that perhaps Babel has already sufficiently described limping Gubanov, scourge of the regiment, and that the mystery of the Giant Rat of Sumatra is, after all, already the mystery of the Giant Rat of Sumatra. Babel does return to the Raciborskis in *Red Cavalry*: "A ninety-year-old countess and her son had lived in the castle. She had tormented him for not having given the dying clan any heirs, and—the *muzhiks* told me this—she used to beat him with the coachman's whip." But even with the Zolaesque note of hereditary vitiation, the Turgenevian kinkiness of the coachman's whip, and the hinted Soviet rhetoric of a knightly Poland "gone berserk" (a phrase from Babel's own propaganda work), the "description" is still just two sentences.

One of the most chilling relics to emerge from Babel's KGB dossier was the pair of mug shots taken upon his arrest in 1939.

Photographed in profile, Babel gazes into the distance, chin raised, with an expression of pained resoluteness. Photographed face-on, however, he seems to be looking at something quite close to him. He seems to be looking at someone whom he knows to be on the verge of committing a terrible action. Of these images, a German historian once observed: "Both show the writer without his glasses and with one black eye, medically speaking a *monocle haematoma*, evidence of the violence used against him."

I felt sorry for the German historian. I understood that it was the inadequacy of "without his glasses and with one black eye" that drove him to use a phrase so absurd as "medically speaking a *monocle haematoma*." The absence of glasses is unspeakably violent. You need long words, Latin words, to describe it. Babel was never photographed without his glasses. He never wrote without them, either. His narrator always has, to quote a popular line from the Odessa stories, "spectacles on his nose and autumn in his heart." Another famous line, spoken by Babel's narrator to a nearsighted comrade at a beautiful Finnish winter resort: "I beg you, Alexander Fyodorovich, buy a pair of glasses!"

In "My First Goose," the Cossack divisional commander yells at the Jewish intellectual: "They send you over without asking— and here you'll get killed just for wearing glasses! So, you think you can live with us?" The glasses represent precisely Babel's determination to live with them, to watch their every move, with an attention bordering on love—to see everything and write it all down. "Everything about Babel gave an impression of all-consuming curiosity," Nadezhda Mandelstam once wrote: "the way he held his head, his mouth and chin, and particularly his eyes. It is not often that one sees such undisguised curiosity in the eyes of a grown-up. I had the feeling that Babel's main driving force was the unbridled curiosity with which he scrutinized life and people." That's what they took away when they replaced his glasses with the *monocle haematoma*.

I had been persuaded to sign up for the biography seminar by one of my classmates, Matej, who knew the professor. "He's a textbook Jewish intellectual from New York," Matej said excitedly, as if describing some rare woodland creature. (Matej was a textbook Catholic intellectual from Zagreb.) "When he talks about Isaac Babel, he gets so excited that he starts to stutter. But it's not the annoying kind of stutter that obstructs understanding. It's an endearing stutter that makes you feel sympathy and affection."

At the end of the term, Matej and I had agreed to collaborate on a presentation about Babel. We met one cold, gray afternoon at a dirty metal table outside the library, where we compared notes, drank coffee, and went through nearly an entire pack of Matej's Winston Lights, which, I learned, he ordered in bulk from an Indian reservation. We settled on a general angle right away, but when it came to details, we didn't see eye to eye on anything. For nearly an hour we argued about a single sentence in "The Tachanka Theory": a story about the transformation of warfare by the *tachanka*, a wagon with a machine gun attached to the back.

Once it is armed with *tachanki*, Babel writes, a Ukrainian village ceases to be a military target, because the guns can be buried under haystacks.

When it started to rain, Matej and I decided to go into the library to look up the Russian original of the sentence we disagreed about: "These hidden points—suggested, but not directly perceived—yield in their sum a construction of the new Ukrainian village: savage, rebellious, and self-seeking." Even once we had the Russian text, though, we still disagreed about the meaning of "hidden points." Rereading this story now, I can't see what we could have been debating for so long, but I remember Matej saying irritably, "You're making it sound as if he's just adding things up, like he's some kind of double-entry bookkeeper."

"That's exactly right," I snapped. "He *is* a double-entry bookkeeper!"

We concluded that we would never agree on anything, because I was a materialist, whereas he had a fundamentally religious view of history. Finally we parted ways, Matej to write about Babel's replacement of old gods with a new mythology, and I to write about Babel as a bookkeeper.

"How good it is," writes Mandelstam, "that I managed to love not the priestly flame of the icon lamp but the little red flame of literary spite!" I don't know if Matej wrote his presentation in the priestly flame of the icon lamp, but I think it was literary spite that made me want to prove that Babel "was really" a bookkeeper. But, to my own surprise, it actually turned out to be true: not only did accountants and clerks keep turning up in Babel's stories, but Babel himself had been educated at the Kiev Commercial Institute, where he received top marks in general accounting. I was particularly struck by the story "Pan Apolek,"

in which the Polish protagonist calls the narrator "Mr. Clerk"—
"*pan pisar'*" in the original. *Pan* is Polish for "sir" or "Mr.," and
pisar' is a Russian word for "clerk." In Polish, however, *pisarz* means
not "clerk," but "writer." Pan Apolek was trying to call the narrator "Mr. Writer," but the writer in the Red Cavalry turned into
a clerk.

I ended up writing about the double-entry relationship in
Babel's work between literature and lived experience, centering
on "Pan Apolek" (the story of a village church painter who en-
dows biblical figures with the faces of his fellow villagers: a
double entry of preexisting artistic form with observations from
life). The seminar presentation went well, and I expanded upon
it a few months later at a Slavic colloquium, where it caught the
interest of the department Babel expert, Grisha Freidin. Freidin
said he would help me revise the paper for publication—"Why
would you study the gospel with anyone but St. Peter?" he
demanded—and offered me a job doing research for his new critical biography of Babel.

The title of the book was fluctuating at that time between
A Jew on Horseback and *The Other Babel*. I was fascinated by
the idea of *The Other Babel*, namely, that Babel wasn't who we
thought he was, or who said he was: he was some *other person*. His
"Autobiography"—a document barely one and a half pages long—
is full of untruths, such as his claim to have worked for the Cheka
starting in October 1917, two months before the Cheka was
founded, or to have fought on "the Romanian front." "Now you
might think 'the Romanian front' is a joke," Freidin said. "Well,
it's not, it seems it really did exist. But Babel was never there."

Babel's undocumented life was likewise full of mysteries—
chief among them, why he had returned to Moscow from Paris
in 1933, after having spent nearly all of 1932 struggling to get

permission to go abroad. Stranger still, why, in 1935, just when the purges were starting, did Babel begin making plans to bring his mother, sister, wife, and daughter from Brussels and Paris back to the Soviet Union?

As my first research assignment, I went to the Hoover Archives to look up the Russian émigré newspapers in Paris from 1934 and 1935, starting with the assassination of Sergei Kirov, to see how much Babel's family would have known about the purges. The newspapers hadn't been transferred to microfilm, and the originals, which had been bound in enormous, tombstone-size books, couldn't be photocopied because of the fragility of the paper. I sat in a corner with my laptop, typing out the lists of people who had been shot or sent to Siberia, typing the headlines about Kirov, and other headlines like "Who Burned the Reichstag?" and "Bonnie and Clyde Shot Dead." Hours slipped by and the next thing I knew, all the lights went out. When I got up, I realized that the entire library was not only dark but also deserted and locked. I banged on the locked doors for a while with no result, then felt my way through the dark to a hallway with administrative offices, where I was happy to discover a tiny Russian woman reading a microfiche and eating lasagna from a tiny plastic box. She seemed surprised to see me, and even more surprised when I asked for directions on how to leave the building.

" 'Get out'?" she echoed, as if referring to the exotic custom of an unknown people. "Ah, I do not know."

"Oh," I said. "But how are *you* going to get out?"

"Me? Well, it is . . ." She glanced away, evasively. "But I show you something." She got up from her desk, took a flashlight from a drawer, and went back into the hallway, motioning me to follow. We came to an emergency door with a big sign: ALARM WILL SOUND.

"It is not locked," she said. "But behind you, it will lock."

The alarm did not sound. I went down several flights of steps and out another fire door, and found myself in the yellow late-afternoon sunlight, standing in a concrete well below ground level. At the main entrance to Hoover Tower, just around the corner, two Chinese women wearing enormous straw hats were rapping on the door. I unlocked my bicycle and slowly rode home. I had no idea why Babel wanted his family to come back to the Soviet Union in 1935.

That month, Freidin began organizing an international Babel conference, to be held at Stanford, and I started working on an accompanying exhibit of literary materials from the Hoover Archives.

The contents of the hundred-plus boxes on Babel turned out to be extremely diverse, a bit like one of those looted Polish manors: copies of *Red Cavalry* in Spanish and Hebrew; "original watercolors" of the Polish conflict, executed circa 1970; a *Big Book of Jewish Humor*, circa 1990; an issue of the avant-garde journal *LEF*, edited by Mayakovsky; *The Way They Were*, a book of child-hood photographs of famous people, in alphabetical order, with a bookmark to the page where fourteen-year-old Babel in a sailor suit was facing a teenage Joan Baez. There was a book on the Cavalry Army designed by Alexander Rodchenko, with a photo-graph of Commander Budyonny's mother, Melaniya Nikitichna, standing outside a hut, squinting at the camera, bearing in her arms a baby goose. ("Budyonny's first goose," observed Freidin, "and Budyonny's trousers." The trousers were hanging on a clothesline in the background.)

I had also been instructed to choose two propaganda posters from 1920, one Polish and one Soviet. The exhibit coordinator took me into a labyrinthine basement, where a new collection was being indexed. On top of a bank of filing cabinets lay various posters from 1920 representing Russia as the Whore of Babylon, or as the Four Horsemen of the Apocalypse, on horses with Lenin and Trotsky heads; one showed Christ's body lying in the post-Apocalyptic rubble—"This Is How All of Poland Will Look, Once Conquered by the Bolsheviks"—bringing to mind Babel's diary entry about "the looting of an old church": "how many counts and serfs, magnificent Italian art, rosy Paters rocking the infant Jesus, Rembrandt . . . It's very clear, the old gods are being destroyed."

"I'm sorry we don't have any Russian propaganda posters," the coordinator said. "I'm afraid it's a bit one-sided."

"But look," I said, noticing some Cyrillic script in the stack. "Here is one in Russian." I drew out an enormous poster showing a slavering bulldog wearing a king's crown: "Majestic Poland: Last Dog of the Entente."

"Oh, sure," said the coordinator, "there are posters *in* Russian, but they aren't pro-Bolshevik. These are all Polish posters."

I stared at the poster, wondering why Polish people had chosen that terrifying, wild-eyed dog as a representation of "Majestic Poland." Then I spotted a second poster in Russian, with a picture of a round little capitalist with a mustache and a derby hat—like the Monopoly man, but holding a whip.

" 'The Polish masters want to turn the Russian peasants into slaves,' " I read aloud. I suggested it was difficult to interpret this as a pro-Polish poster.

The coordinator nodded enthusiastically: "Yes, these posters are full of ambiguous imagery."

Back upstairs in the reading room, I put on my gloves—everyone in the archive had to wear white cotton gloves, like at

Alice's mad tea party—and turned to a box of 1920 Polish war memorabilia. My eye was caught by a single yellowed sheet of paper with a printed Polish text signed by Commander in Chief Józef Piłsudski, July 3, 1920, beginning with the phrase *"Obywatele Rzeczpospolitej!"* I recognized the phrase from Babel's diary entry of July 15. He had found a copy of this very proclamation on the ground in Belyov: "'We will remember you, everything will be for you, Soldiers of the *Rzeczpospolita!*' Touching, sad, without the steel of Bolshevik slogans . . . no words like *order, ideals,* and *living in freedom.*"

In *Red Cavalry,* the narrator discovers this same proclamation while accidentally urinating on a corpse in the dark:

> I switched on my flashlight . . . and saw lying on the ground the body of a Pole, drenched in my urine. A notebook and scraps of Piłsudski's proclamation lay next to the corpse. In the . . . notebook, his expenses, a list of performances at the Krakow Dramatic Theater, and the birthday of a woman by the name of Maria-Louisa. I used the proclamation of Piłsudski, marshal and commander-in-chief, to wipe the stinking liquid from my unknown brother's skull, and then I walked on, bent under the weight of my saddle.

To think this was the very document I was holding in my hands! I wondered whether it was really such an unlikely coincidence. Probably thousands of copies had been printed, so why shouldn't one of them have ended up in the archive—it's not as if the Hoover had received the exact copy with Babel's urine on it, although Freidin did start making jokes to the effect that we should exhibit the proclamation "side by side with a bottle of urine." The joke was directed at the Hoover staff, who kept hinting that the exhibit would be more accessible to the general community if all those books and papers were offset by "more three-dimensional objects." Somebody suggested we construct a diorama based on the ending of "The Rabbi's Son," with pictures of Maimonides and Lenin, and a phylactery. Freidin maintained that if we included the phylactery, we would have to have "the withered genitalia of an aging Semite," which also appear at the end of the story. The diorama idea was abandoned.

Finding the Piłsudski proclamation made me realize that, even if the withered genitalia were lost to posterity, textual objects related to Babel's writings might still be uncovered. I decided to look for materials related to my favorite character in the 1920 diary, Frank Mosher, the captured American pilot whom Babel interrogates on July 14:

A shot-down American pilot, barefoot but elegant, neck like a column, dazzlingly white teeth, his uniform covered with oil and dirt. He asks me worriedly: Did I maybe commit a crime by fighting against Soviet Russia? Our position is strong. O the scent of Europe, coffee, civilization, strength, ancient culture, many thoughts. I watch him, can't let him go. A letter from Major Fauntleroy: things in Poland are bad, there's no constitution, the Bolsheviks are strong . . . An endless conversation with Mosher, I sink into the past, they'll shake you up, Mosher, ekh, Conan Doyle, letters to New York. Is Mosher fooling—he keeps asking frantically what Bolshevism is. A sad, heartwarming impression.

I loved this passage because of the mention of Conan Doyle, coffee, someone called Major Fauntleroy, and the "sad, heartwarming impression." Furthermore, "Frank Mosher" was the alias of Captain Merian Caldwell Cooper, future creator and producer of the motion picture *King Kong*. This really happened: in Galicia in July 1920, the future creator of *King Kong* was interrogated by the future creator of *Red Cavalry*. And when I looked up Merian Cooper in the library catalog, it was like magic: Hoover turned out to hold the bulk of his papers.

Merian Cooper, I learned, was born in 1894, the same year as Babel. He served as a pilot in the First World War, commanded a squadron in the Battle of St.-Mihiel, was shot down in flames in the Argonne, and spent the last months of the war in a German prison, where he "was thrown with Russians a good deal" and developed a lifelong aversion to Bolshevism. In 1918 he was awarded a Purple Heart. In 1919 he joined nine other American pilots in the Kosciuszko air squadron, an official unit of the Polish air force, to combat the Red menace under the command of Major Cedric Fauntleroy. Cooper took his pseudonym, Corporal Frank R. Mosher, from the waistband of the secondhand underwear he had received from the Red Cross.

On July 13, 1920, the Associated Press reported that Cooper had been "brought down by Cossacks" behind enemy lines in Galicia. According to local peasants, Cooper had been "rushed by horsemen of Budyonny's cavalry," and would have been killed on the spot, had not an *unnamed English-speaking Bolshevik* interfered on his behalf. The next day, July 14, the Frank Mosher entry appears in Babel's diary.

Although Cooper left a "sad, heartwarming impression" on Babel, Babel seems to have left no particular impression on Cooper, who recorded nothing of their "endless conversation." Of his time in the Red Cavalry, he has written only of his interrogation by Budyonny, who invited him "to join the Bolshevist army as an aviation instructor." (Babel was right, by the way; Mosher *was* fooling when he pretended to wonder whether he had committed "a crime by fighting against Soviet Russia.") Refusing to become a flight instructor, Cooper found himself "the 'guest' of a Bolshevist flying squadron for five days. I escaped, but was recaptured after two days, and taken under heavy guard to Moscow." He spent the winter shoveling snow from the Moscow railway line. In the spring, he escaped Vladykino Prison in the company of two Polish lieutenants, and hopped freight trains up to the Latvian frontier ("We adapted the American hobo methods to our circumstances"). At the border, they were obliged to bribe the guards. Cooper handed over his boots, and made another barefoot entrance in Riga.

One of Cooper's fellow pilots, Kenneth Shrewsbury, had kept a scrapbook—and, by a marvelous stroke of luck, it had also ended up at Stanford. Using a dry-plate camera, Shrewsbury had documented the entire Polish campaign, as well as an initial stopover in Paris. (There was a group portrait of the entire Kosciuszko squadron standing outside the Ritz; a long shot of the Champs-Élysées, eerily deserted except for a single horse-drawn carriage and two automobiles; and a close-up of a swan in what looked like the Tuileries.) For weeks I had been looking at 1920s photographs of Galicia and Volhynia, but these were the first that looked like the same place Babel was describing. Everything was there: a village clumped at the foot of a medieval castle, a church "destroyed by the Bolsheviks," airplanes, the handsome Major Fauntleroy, "Jews leveling a field," "Polish mechanics," mounted troops riding past a pharmacy in Podolia—and Cooper himself, looking just as Babel described him, big, American, with a neck like a column. In one photograph he was smiling slightly and holding a pipe, like Arthur Conan Doyle.

•

Cooper turned to filmmaking in 1923, in collaboration with fellow Russo-Polish veteran Captain Ernest B. Schoedsack. Looking for "danger, adventure, and natural beauty," they went to Turkey and filmed the annual migration of the Bakhtiari tribe to Persia (*Grass: A Nation's Battle for Life*); next, in Thailand, they filmed *Chang: A Drama of the Wilderness* (1927), about a resourceful Lao family who dig a pit outside their house to catch wild animals. All kinds of animals turn up in the pit: leopards, tigers, a white gibbon, and finally a mysterious creature called a *chang*, eventually revealed to be a baby elephant. Cooper claimed that, while filming *Chang*, he was able to predict the cast's behavior based on phases of the moon. A passionate aeronaut, Cooper often looked to the sky for answers: among his papers I found a letter from the 1950s outlining his plan to colonize the solar system, in order to both stymie the Soviets and solve California's impending crises of human and automobile overpopulation.

In 1931, the year Babel published "The Awakening," Cooper devised the premise for *King Kong*: on a remote island, a documentary filmmaker and his team discover the "highest representative of prehistoric animal life." The documentary filmmaker would be a composite of Cooper and Schoedsack: "Put us in it," Cooper instructed the scriptwriters. "Give it the spirit of a real Cooper-Schoedsack expedition." The team would bring the prehistoric monster to New York City to "confront our materialistic, mechanistic civilization."

I borrowed *King Kong* from the library that week. Watching the gigantic ape hanging off the Empire State Building, swiping at the biplanes, I realized that Babel had painted an analogous scene in "Squadron Commander Trunov." At the end of the story, Trunov stands on a hill with a machine gun to take on four bombers from the Kosciuszko squadron—"machines from the air squadron of Major Fauntleroy, large, armored machines . . . The airplanes came flying over the station in tighter circles, rattled fussily high in the air, plunged, drew arcs . . ." Like King Kong, Trunov has no plane. Like King Kong, he goes down. From the DVD notes, I learned that the pilots in the close-up shots of the Empire State Building scene were none other than Schoedsack and Cooper themselves, acting on Cooper's suggestion that "We should kill the sonofabitch ourselves." In other words, King Kong and Commander Trunov were both shot down by members of the Kosciuszko squadron.

The other fascinating detail of *King Kong*'s production is that the set for Skull Island was used at night to represent Ship-Trap Island in Cooper and Schoedsack's *The Most Dangerous Game*, an adaptation of Richard Connell's 1924 short story. *The Most Dangerous Game* finds the two stars of *King Kong*, Robert Armstrong and Fay Wray, again marooned on a tropical island, where they must again contend with a primitive monster: a mad Cossack cavalry general who hunts shipwrecked sailors for sport, attended by his mute sidekick, Ivan. ("A gigantic creature, solidly made and black bearded to the waist," Ivan "once had the honor of serving as official knouter to the Great White Tsar.")

I reported these findings to Grisha Freidin. "Well, look, there he is! Squadron Commander Trunov!" he exclaimed, peering at the film still I had brought, showing King Kong and the navy planes. "The image must have been in the collective unconscious," he mused. "You know what we should do? We should go back to Hoover and look at all the anti-Bolshevik posters. I am certain that we will find one representing Bolshevism as a giant ape."

He telephoned the archive directly and asked them to run a search for "ape" and "propaganda" in the poster database. The eighteen-page printout was waiting for me when I got there. Unfortunately, it included not just the keyword ape but any word beginning with ape—in any language.

The actual apes, once isolated from items such as *"Apertura a sinistra"* and *"25 lat Apelu Sztokholmskiego"* proved to be few in number. First was a German poster of an ape in a Prussian hat grabbing a woman in one paw and holding in the other a club labeled "Kultur." I had no idea how to interpret this image, but decided it wasn't related to Bolshevism. Next was a Hungarian poster whose central figure, described in the catalog as an "ape man," looked more like an extremely ugly human, covered in blood, which he was attempting to wash off in the Danube at the foot of the parliament.

Just as I was starting to wonder how I would break the news to Freidin, I happened upon an Italian World War II poster: "La mostruosa minaccia torna a pesare sull'Europa." The monstrous menace of Bolshevism was represented as a bright red, embarrassed-looking ape, standing on a map of Europe and brandishing a sickle and hammer. The artist, possibly concerned that the ape hadn't come out menacing enough, had taken the precaution of representing a masked figure of Death standing behind its shoulder.

One ape on a map of Europe, the other on the Empire State Building. I took off the white gloves; my work here was done.

Or so I thought. First, my copy was sent back to me with a note: "Please call ASAP regarding portrayal of Cossacks as primitive monsters." I tried to explain that I myself wasn't calling the Cossacks primitive monsters—I was only suggesting that others had felt that way. The exhibit coordinator disagreed. Others, she said, *didn't* consider Cossacks to be primitive monsters: "In fact, Cossacks have a rather romantic image."

I debated citing the entry for Cossack in Flaubert's *Dictionary of Received Ideas*—"Eats tallow candles"—but instead I simply observed the likelihood of any Cossacks actually attending the exhibit was very slim.

"Well, that's really not the point. Anyway, you never know in California."

A few days later, I began to receive phone calls about the "three-dimensional objects." "Elif, glad I caught you! How would you feel if we put a fur hat in your Red Cavalry display case?"

I considered this. "What kind of fur hat?"

"Well, that's the thing, I'm afraid it's not quite authentic. Someone picked it up at a flea market in Moscow. But it looks, you know, like a Russian fur hat."

"Thanks so much for asking me," I said, "but I really think it should be up to Professor Freidin."

"Oh," she said. "Professor Freidin is not going to want that hat in the display case."

"No," I acknowledged.

The next day, the telephone rang again. "Okay, Elif, tell me what you think: we'll put, sort of lying along the bottom of your display case—a Cossack national costume."

"A Cossack national costume?" I repeated.

"Well—well—okay, *the problem is* that it's child's size. It's sort of a children's Cossack costume. But that's not entirely a bad thing. I mean, because it's in a child's size, it will definitely fit in the case, which might not happen with an adult-size costume."

Nearly every day they thought of something new: a samovar, a Talmud, a three-foot rubber King Kong. Finally they settled on a giant Cossack saber, also, I suspect, acquired at the Moscow flea market. They put the saber in a case that had no semantic link to sabers, so people at the exhibit kept asking me what it meant. "Why didn't it go in the display about 'My First Goose'?" one visitor asked. "At least that story has a saber in it."

By that time, the conference had begun. Scholars arrived from around the world: Russia, Hungary, Uzbekistan. One professor came from Ben-Gurion with a bibliography called "Babelobibliografiya" and a talk titled "Babel, Bialik, and Bereavement." But the star guests were Babel's children: Nathalie, the daughter from his wife, Evgeniya; and Lidiya, the daughter from Antonina Pirozhkova, with whom Babel lived his last years.

When it turned out that Antonina Pirozhkova would be in attendance, my classmate Josh was ecstatic. Josh's parents were *Star Wars* fans and his full name is Joshua Sky Walker; to differentiate him from other Joshes, he was often called Skywalker. Skywalker was also working on the exhibit and, based on photographs from the 1930s, had developed a crush on Pirozhkova.

"Man, do I hope I get to pick *her* up from the airport," he said.

"You do realize she must be more than ninety years old?"

"I don't care—she is so hot. You don't understand."

I did understand, actually. I had noticed some Cossacks in the Rodchenko book whom I would gladly have picked up from the airport, were it not that, in accordance with my prediction, none of them came to the conference.

Skywalker, however, got his wish: he and his friend Fishkin, a native Russian speaker, were appointed to pick up Pirozhkova and Lidiya, the Sunday before the conference. I was initially supposed to pick up Nathalie Babel, but Nathalie Babel had called the department to warn that she had a very heavy trunk: "You must send me a strong male graduate student. Otherwise, do not bother. I will take a bus." So a male graduate student had been sent, and I had the afternoon free. I was cramming for my university orals, trying to read all eighteen pounds of the *Human Comedy* in one month, and was desperately speed-reading *Louis Lambert* when the telephone rang. It was Skywalker, who had apparently broken his foot the previous night at the Euromed 13 dance party, and wanted me to go pick up Pirozhkova and Lidiya. "You can't miss them," he said. "It'll be, like, a ninety-year-old woman who is gorgeous and a fifty-year-old woman who looks exactly like Isaac Babel."

"But—but what happened to Fishkin?"

"Fishkin went to Tahoe."

"How do you mean, he went to Tahoe?"

"Well, it's kind of a funny story, but the thing is that their plane lands in half an hour . . ."

I hung up the phone and rushed outside to dump all the garbage that had accumulated in my car. Realizing that I didn't remember Antonina Pirozhkova's patronymic, I ran back inside and Googled her. I was halfway out the door again when I also realized I had forgotten how to say "He broke his foot" in Russian. I looked that up, too. I wrote BABEL in big letters on a sheet of paper, stuffed it in my bag, and ran out the door, repeating "Antonina Nikolayevna, *slomal nogu.*"

I got to SFO ten minutes after their plane had landed. For half an hour I wandered around the terminal holding my BABEL sign, looking for a gorgeous ninety-year-old woman and a fifty-year-old woman who looked like Isaac Babel. Of the many people at the airport that day, none came close to matching this description.

In despair, I called Freidin and explained the situation. There was a long silence. "They won't be looking for you," he said finally. "They're expecting a boy."

"That's the thing," I said. "What if they didn't see a boy and, you know, they took a bus."

"Well, my gut feeling is that they're still there, in the airport." He had been right about the Bolshevik ape, so I decided to keep looking. Sure enough, ten minutes later I spotted her sitting in a corner, wearing a white headband and surrounded by suitcases: a tiny elderly woman, nonetheless recognizable as the beauty from the archive photographs.

"Antonina Nikolayevna!" I exclaimed, beaming.

She glanced at me and turned slightly away, as if hoping I would disappear.

I tried again. "Excuse me, hello, are you here for the Babel conference?" She quickly turned toward me. "Babel," she said, sitting up. "Babel, yes."

"I'm so glad—I'm sorry you were waiting. A boy was going to get you, but he broke his foot."

She gave me a look. "You are glad," she observed, "you are smiling, but Lidiya is suffering and nervous. She went to look for a telephone."

"Oh, no!" I said, looking around. There were no telephones in sight. "I'll go, I'll look for her."

"Why should you go, too? Then you'll both be lost. Better you should sit here and wait."

I sat, trying to look appropriately somber, and dialed Freidin again.

"Thank goodness," he said. "I knew they would still be there. How is Pirozhkova? Is she very angry?"

I looked at Pirozhkova. She did look a bit angry. "I don't know," I said.

"They told me they would send a Russian boy," she said loudly. "A boy who knows Russian."

The atmosphere in the car was somehow tense. Lidiya, who did indeed look very much like her father, sat in the front seat, reading aloud from every billboard. "'Nokia Wireless,'" she said. "'Johnnie Walker.'"

Pirozhkova sat in the back and spoke only once the whole trip: "Ask her," she told Lidiya, "what is that thing on her mirror."

The thing on my mirror was a McDonald's Happy Meal toy, a tiny stuffed Eeyore wearing a tiger suit. "It's a toy," I said.

"A toy," Lidiya said loudly, half turning. "It's an animal."

"Yes, but what kind of animal?"

"It's a donkey," I said. "A donkey in a tiger suit."

"You see, Mama?" said Lidiya loudly. "It's a donkey in a tiger suit."

"I don't understand. Is there a story behind this?"

The story, to my knowledge, was that Tigger had developed a neurosis about being adopted and having no heritage, so Eeyore put on a tiger suit and pretended to be his relative. As I was thinking of how to explain this, another patch of orange caught my eye. I glanced at the dashboard: it was the low-fuel warning light.

"It's not my donkey," I said, switching off the fan. "It's my friend's donkey."

"What did she say?" Pirozhkova asked Lidiya.

"She said that it's her friend's donkey. So she doesn't know why he's wearing a tiger suit."

"What?" said Pirozhkova.

Lidiya rolled her eyes. "She said that the donkey put on the tiger suit in order to look stronger in front of the other donkeys."

There was a silence.

"I don't think she said that," said Pirozhkova.

We drove by another billboard: " 'Ted Lempert for State Senate.' "

"Ted Lempert," Lidiya mused, then turned to me. "Who is this Ted Lempert?"

"I don't know," I said. "I think he wants to be senator."

"Hmm," she said. "Lempert. I knew a Lempert once—an artist. His name was Vladimir. Vladimir Lempert."

"Oh," I said, trying to think of something to say. "I'm reading a novel by Balzac now about somebody called Louis Lambert." I tried to pronounce "Lambert" to sound like "Lempert."

We drove the rest of the way to the hotel in silence.

Babel's first daughter, Nathalie, looked younger than her age (seventy-four), but her voice was fathomless, sepulchral, with heavy French *r*'s.

"YOUR HAND IS VERY COLD," she told me when we were introduced. It was later that same evening, and all the conference participants were heading to the Hoover Pavilion for an opening reception.

"We have black squirrels here at Stanford," another graduate student told Nathalie Babel, pointing at a squirrel. "Have you ever seen a black squirrel?"

Nathalie glanced vaguely in the direction of the squirrel. "I CANNOT SEE ANYTHING ANYMORE," she said. "I cannot hear, I cannot see, I cannot walk. For this reason," she continued, eyeing the steep cement stairway to the pavilion, "everyone thinks I am always drunk."

At the top of the stairs, two Chinese men were taking turns photographing each other with Viktor Zhivov, a Berkeley professor with a kind expression and a tobacco-stained Old Believer beard.

"Lots of Chinese," I overheard someone say in Russian.

"True. It's not clear why."

"They're taking pictures with Zhivov."

"They want to prove that they've been to California. Ha! Ha!"

The two Chinese were, in fact, filmmakers, whose adaptation of the *Red Cavalry* cycle, *Qi Bing Jun*, was supposed to premiere in Shanghai the following year. (I believe the project was eventually canceled.) The screenwriter was tall, round-faced, smiled a lot, and spoke very good English; the director was short, slight, serious, and didn't seem to speak at all. Both wore large cameras around their necks.

In the Chinese *Red Cavalry*, the screenwriter told us, Cossacks would be transformed into "barbarians from the north of China"; the Jewish narrator would be represented by a Chinese intellectual. "There are not so many differences between Jews and Chinese," he explained. "They give their children violin lessons, and they worry about money. Lyutov will be a Chinese, but he will still have 'spectacles on his nose and autumn in his heart.'" At "nose," he touched his nose, and at "heart," he struck his chest. The director nodded.

Looking at the Chinese filmmakers, I remembered Viktor Shklovsky's account of how Babel spent the whole year 1919 writing and rewriting "a story about two Chinese." "They grew young, they aged, broke windows, beat up a woman, organized this or that"; Babel hadn't finished with them when he joined the Red Cavalry. In the 1920 diary, "the story about the Chinese" becomes part of the propaganda that Babel relays in the pillaged shtetls: "I tell fairy tales about Bolshevism, its blossoming, the express trains, the Moscow textile mills, the universities, the free food, the Revel Delegation, and, to crown it off, my tale about the Chinese, and I enthrall all these poor tortured people." At Stanford, we had it all: a university, free food, and, to crown it off, the Chinese.

Not all of the Russians were as delighted by the Chinese as I was. "We don't mess with your *I Ching* . . . ," I overheard one audience member saying.

Some Russian people are skeptical or even offended when foreigners claim an interest in Russian literature. I still remember the passport control officer who stamped my first student visa. He suggested to me that there might be some American writers, "Jack London, for example," whom I could study in America: "The language would be easier and you wouldn't need a visa." The resistance can be especially high when it comes to Babel, who wrote in an idiosyncratic Russian-Jewish Odessa vernacular—a language and humor that Russian-Jewish Odessans earned the hard way. While it's true that, as Tolstoy observed, every unhappy family is unhappy in its own way, and everyone on planet Earth, vale of tears that it is, is certainly entitled to the specificity of his or her suffering, one nonetheless likes to think that literature has the power to render comprehensible different kinds of unhappiness. If it can't do that, what's it good for? On these grounds I once became impatient with a colleague at a conference who was trying to convince me that the *Red Cavalry* cycle would never be totally accessible to me because of Lyutov's "specifically Jewish alienation."

"Right," I finally said. "As a six-foot-tall first-generation Turkish woman growing up in New Jersey, I cannot possibly know as much about alienation as you, a short American Jew."

He nodded: "So you see the problem."

The reception was followed by a dinner, which began with toasts. A professor from Moscow was proposing a toast to Pirozhkova. "In Russian we have an expression, a little-known but good expression, that we say when someone dies: 'He ordered us to live a long time.' Now I look at Antonina Nikolayevna and I think of Babel who died before his time, and I think, 'Babel ordered her to live a long time.' We are so lucky for this, because she can tell us all the things that only she knows. A long life to Antonina Nikolayevna!"

This toast struck me as both bizarre and depressing. I downed nearly a whole glass of wine and became light-headed to the extent that I almost told a dirty joke to Freidin's eighteen-year-old daughter, Anna. Anna, who was applying to colleges, had asked about undergraduate advising at Harvard. I told her about my freshman adviser, a middle-aged British woman who held advisee meetings in a pub—once I missed our meeting because they were checking IDs at the door—and who worked in the telecommunications office.

"The telecommunications office?"

"Uh-huh. I would see her there when I went to pay my phone bill."

"Did she have any other connection to Harvard, other than working in the telecommunications office? Was she an alumna?"

"Yeah, she got an MA in the seventies, in Old Norse literature."

Anna stared at me. "Old Norse literature? What good is an MA in Old Norse literature?"

"I think it's useful in telecommunications work," I said.

"Old Norse literature," Anna repeated. "Hmm. Well, it must be a *fecund* area of study. Aren't the Norse the ones who invented Thor, god of thunder?"

"Oh—I know a joke about Thor!" The joke involves the comic exchange between Thor and a farmer's daughter: "I AM THOR!" says Thor, to which the farmer's daughter replies: "I'm thor, too, but I had tho much fun!"

"So Thor comes down to earth for a day," I began, when I suddenly became conscious that Joseph Frank—the Stanford emeritus famous for his magisterial five-volume biography of Dostoevsky—had abandoned the lively discussion he had been having with a Berkeley professor about Louis XIII. Both were regarding me from across the table with unblinking interest.

"You know," I said to Anna, "I just remembered it's kind of an inappropriate joke. Maybe I'll tell you another time."

By now, every single person at the table was staring at me. Frank leaned over the arm of his wheelchair toward Freidin's wife, a professor at Berkeley, who was also in a wheelchair. "Who is that?" he asked loudly.

"That is Elif, a graduate student who has been very helpful to Grisha," she replied.

"Ah." Joseph Frank nodded and turned his attention to his pasta.

These events took a toll on me, and I overslept the next morning, missing the 9:00 a.m. panel on biography. I got to the conference center as everyone was leaving for lunch, and immediately spotted Luba, who is my height, with huge, sad gray eyes and an enormous quantity of extremely curly hair.

"Elishka!" she exclaimed. "Did you just wake up? Don't worry, I wrote everything down for you, in case you want to use it in a novel." We went to the student union for lunch, and Luba told me about the panel.

Three different people were writing biographies about Babel. The first, Freidin, presented on the Other Babel. The second, an American journalist, talked about her experiences researching Babel's life in 1962 Moscow. She had interviewed Babel's old acquaintance, the French chargé d'affaires, Jacques de Beaumarchais (descendant of the author of *Figaro*), and was followed by the KGB, whom Beaumarchais gallantly instructed *"Fichez le camp!"* but the KGB took her in for questioning anyway. The third, Werner Platt, a German who taught Russian history in Tashkent, read a paper called "Writing a Biography of Isaac Babel: A Detective's Task," largely about getting kicked out of various Russian archives and not managing to find out anything about Babel. On the premise that "good detective work means returning to the scene of the crime," the historian had made pilgrimages to Babel's old house in Odessa, the Moscow apartment, the dacha in Peredelkino—only to find that all had been torn down. Undiscouraged, Platt got on a bus to Lemberg. In his diary Babel had mentioned Budyonny's decision not to attack Lemberg in 1920: "Why not? Craziness, or the impossibility of taking a city by cavalry?" Looking around Lemberg, Platt concluded that, as Babel had implied by calling Budyonny's withdrawal "crazy," Lemberg was indeed a beautiful city.

His talk was poorly received. Someone had muttered: "For an incompetent scholar, everything is 'a detective's task.'" It seemed that some of the documents that Platt had been unable to access in the archives had been published years ago. "You can buy this in the Barnes and Noble," someone said.

Platt had also made some provocative claims about the lost manuscripts, which led to a free-for-all about the location and contents of the missing folders.

"Empty!" an unknown Russian had shouted. "The folders were empty!"

Nathalie Babel had stood up and taken the microphone— "The best part," Luba said, sitting up straighter and reading from her notebook in a deep, sepulchral voice.

"WHEN I WAS A LITTLE GIRL, I WAS TOLD THAT MY PUPPY WAS A WRITER." Pause. "LATER I HEARD PEOPLE TALKING ABOUT ISAAC BABEL, SAYING THAT HE WAS A GREAT WRITER." Pause. "TO ME, HE WAS MY PUPPY."

Long pause.

"I AM CONFUSED."

Another pause.

"I AM *CONFUSED*."

One minute, two minutes passed, in total silence. Finally, somebody asked Nathalie whether it was true that she was "still sitting on some unpublished letters."

Nathalie Babel sighed. "LET ME TELL YOU A STORY

ABOUT LETTERS." The story was that Nathalie Babel had come into possession of a trunk of her father's letters. ("Her puppy's letters," Luba explained.) "I KNEW THE BIOGRAPHER WOULD COME," she said, "BUT HE ANNOYED ME. SO I GAVE THE LETTERS TO MY AUNT. WHEN THE BIOGRAPHER CAME, I SAID, 'I HAVE NOTHING.'" And where were the letters now? Nathalie Babel didn't know. "MAYBE THEY ARE UNDER MY BED, I DON'T REMEMBER." The panel ended in pandemonium.

Later that afternoon, after the panel on Babel and World Literature, I rode my bike back to the graduate-student housing complex and nearly ran over Fishkin, who was standing outside wearing pajamas and smoking a cigarette. I welcomed him back from Tahoe, and asked how he was enjoying the conference. Fishkin, I learned, was not enjoying the conference. Not only was he in trouble about Tahoe, but Boris Zalevsky, a well-known twentieth-centuryist, had given him the finger in the parking lot.

"Is that a joke?" I asked.

"N-n-no!" said Fishkin, who stuttered at emotional moments. "He really did it, I swear!"

I had been baffled by Zalevsky's character ever since the question-and-answer session after that afternoon's panel. A famous professor of comparative literature had just read what struck me as an incredibly lame paper comparing a passage in *Madame Bovary*, in which flies are dying in the bottom of a glass of cider, to Babel's description of the death of Squadron Commander Trunov. (The similarity was supposedly that both Babel and Flaubert were aestheticizing the banal.) The moderator—my adviser, Monika Greenleaf—returning to the subject of those flies in the cider, had compared them to the inkwell full of dead flies at the miser's estate in *Dead Souls*, and also to Captain Lebyadkin's lyric about cannibalistic flies in a jar in Dostoevsky's *Demons*. I thought this was a much more promising line of comparison—in fact, Babel, too, had a passage about "flies dying in a jar filled with milky liquid" in a Tiflis hotel. A beautiful passage: "Each fly was dying in its own way." But before my adviser could get to her point about dead flies, Zalevsky had interrupted: "The Flaubert example was pertinent, but your example is not pertinent."

This had confused me, because I had actually liked Zalevsky's paper. It had been far more interesting than the one about "aestheticizing the banal" and the "rapture of perception." But if he was such a smart guy, why was he (a) praising a mediocre paper and (b) being rude to Monika, who had at her fingertips every fly that had ever drowned in the whole Russian canon?

"He must be bipolar," I told Fishkin. "So how did it happen?"

Fishkin had had his turn signal on and was about to pull into a parking spot when suddenly a car came around the corner from the opposite direction and slipped in before him. The driver of this car proceeded to give Fishkin the finger—and, as if that weren't enough, he had gone and turned out to be Zalevsky!

"What did you do?" I asked.

"I-I-I turned my head, like this"—Fishkin turned his head to the left—"so that he wouldn't see my face. Then I drove away."

Back in my apartment, I made some tea and settled down to get through some more Balzac. But there was no escaping from Babel.

In one of the critical forewords I found the following anecdote, which Balzac used to tell about his father's early career as a clerk to the public prosecutor in Paris, and which might justly be titled "My First Partridge":

> According to the custom of the time [Balzac's father] took his meals with the other clerks at his employer's table . . . The Prosecutor's wife, who was eyeing up the new clerk, asked him, "Monsieur Balzac, do you know how to carve?" "Yes, Madame," the young man replied, blushing to the roots of his hair. He plucked up his courage and grabbed the knife and fork. Being entirely ignorant of culinary anatomy, he divided the partridge into four, but with such vigor that he smashed the plate, ripped the tablecloth and carved right through to the wood of the table. The Prosecutor's wife smiled, and from that day on the young clerk was treated with great respect in the house.

As in "My First Goose," a young man starts a new job, goes to live among people from a potentially unwelcoming culture, and attains respect and acceptance through the mutilation of poultry.

The anecdote appears in Théophile Gautier's 1859 biography of Balzac. I wondered if it could be shown that Babel had read Gautier. Then I wondered whether there was anything to eat at home. There wasn't. I got in my car and was driving down El Camino Real when my cell phone started ringing. The phone played a cheerful melody, but the letters on the screen spelled "FREIDIN."

"Professor Freidin! What a pleasant surprise!"

"Elif, hello. I don't know if it is pleasant or a surprise, but, yes, this is Grisha."

Freidin was at a dinner for the conference participants. He was experiencing confusion due to the lack at this dinner of any graduate-student presence. "You are not here. Fishkin isn't here. Josh isn't here. Nobody is here. It looks—well, it looks strange. It's a bit embarrassing."

"But we weren't invited to the dinner," I pointed out.

Silence.

"I see. You were waiting to be *invited*."

I made the next U-turn and headed to the faculty club.

Of the four tables in the private room, three were completely full, and one completely empty. As I was considering whether to sit at the empty table by myself, Freidin noticed me and made a space between himself and Janet Lind, a professor who had edited the first English translation of the 1920 diary. The others at the table were Nathalie Babel; the American journalist; Werner Platt; a literature professor from Budapest; and a translator who had recently published the first English edition of Babel's collected works.

Freidin introduced me to Janet Lind and suggested that we might like to talk about *King Kong*. It rapidly emerged that she and I had very little to say to one another about *King Kong*. What little spark there had been in this conversation was soon extinguished by Nathalie Babel, who was staring at Lind with a fixed, unbenevolent expression. A chilly silence descended upon the table.

"JANET," Nathalie said finally, in her fathomless voice. "IS IT TRUE THAT YOU DESPISE ME?"

Janet Lind turned to her calmly. "I beg your pardon?"

"IS IT TRUE THAT YOU DESPISE ME?"

"I can't imagine what makes you say that."

"I say it because I would like to know if it is TRUE THAT YOU DESPISE ME."

"That is an extremely odd question. What gives you an idea like that?"

"I just think you were told that I'm a NASTY OLD WITCH."

"This is really extremely odd. Did someone say something to you?" Lind frowned slightly. "You and I have barely had any interactions."

"Even so, I had the impression—that you DESPISE ME."

This conversation continued for longer than one would have thought possible, given how clear it was that Janet Lind, for whatever reason, was just not going to tell Nathalie Babel that she did not despise her. Looking from Lind to Babel, I was struck by the nontrivial truth behind the Smiths song: "Some girls are bigger than others." It wasn't just that Nathalie Babel's face was physically larger—it was somehow visibly clear that she came from a different place and time, where the human scale was different, and bigger.

"Come, Nathalie," Freidin interceded.

She fixed him with her deep, watery eyes. "SOME PEOPLE DO DESPISE ME, YOU KNOW . . ." She sighed, and pointed at two wineglasses: "Which of these is my glass?"

"They're both yours."

"Oh? I can't see anything. Which is water?"

"It looks to me like they're both white wine."

Nathalie stared at him. "AND WHY DO I HAVE TWO GLASSES OF WINE?"

"Why do you say it like it's a bad thing? If it were me, I would think, 'This must mean that I've done something very good.' *Here*, however, is your water glass."

"Ah." Nathalie Babel took a drink of water.

There was a long silence.

"So," Platt said to Freidin, as the waiters were bringing out the entrées. "I hear that Slavic department enrollments are declining in the United States."

"Oh, do you? Well, you're probably right."

"Do you notice a decline here at Stanford?"

"I'd say we've had a pretty fair enrollment the past few years."

"What about graduate students—do you have many graduate students? I have somehow not seen your students."

"Here is Elif," said Freidin. "She is one of our graduate students."

Platt peered at me over the rims of his glasses for several seconds, then turned back to Freidin. "Yes—so. I see you have one specimen. Are there many others?"

By this point we had all been served some cutlets swimming in a sea of butter. These cutlets appeared to depress everyone. The Hungarian scholar even sent hers back, with detailed instructions. It reappeared a few minutes later, with no modification visible to the naked eye.

Toward the end of the meal, Lidiya Babel came over from her table, stood behind Nathalie's chair, put her arms around her shoulders, and patted her head. "My darling," she said, "how I love you! How *good* it is that we are all together!"

Nathalie glanced over her shoulder, with the expression of a cat who does not want to be picked up.

Freidin looked from Nathalie to Lidiya. "Thank you!" he exclaimed. "Thank you, Lidiya!"

Lidiya stared at him. "What for?"

"For coming! In your place maybe I would have hesitated."

"What do you mean to say—that you would find it difficult to travel with my mother?"

"No, of course not—but it's a long distance, an unknown place . . ."

"Speaking of your mother," Nathalie told Lidiya, "how old is she anyway? Some people say ninety-two, some people say ninety-six. Or is it a secret?"

"My mother is ninety-five."

"She doesn't look a day over ninety-three," said Freidin gallantly.

"It's true, she's in good health and looks well," Lidiya said. "However, not as well as she looked two years ago. But that isn't the main thing. The main thing is that everything is still all right *here*." She tapped her temple. "Her memory and her understanding."

When Lidiya went back to her table, Nathalie followed her with her eyes.

"THAT OLD WITCH WILL BURY US ALL," she remarked.

"Nathalie!" said Freidin.

She turned to stare at him. "YOU THINK I SHOULD KEEP MY MOUTH SHUT," she observed. "But—WHY? WHAT DO I HAVE TO LOSE? I HAVE NOTHING LEFT TO LOSE."

Freidin looked nonplussed. "Well, then, I guess you should risk everything," he said. And, making a visible effort to change the subject: "Nathalie, now that you're here, there is something I've been dying to ask you. What was your aunt's name? One sees it written so many ways. Meriam, Miriam, Mary, Maria—which was it?"

"Oh! Do tell us the correct spelling!" exclaimed Platt, his eyes lighting up.

Nathalie looked at him. "I don't understand what you mean by the correct spelling. Some called her Meriam, others Mary, others Maria. All three were used."

"How interesting," said Janet Lind, turning to Freidin. "I'm surprised you haven't already gone to Odessa and looked it up in the municipal register."

"I'm afraid there are many other surprises where that came from. I've always wanted to go to Odessa and look all these things up, but it somehow never happened."

"Why don't you go now?"

"For the same reason that the Babel conference is here, at Stanford: I don't really travel."

"Why not?" asked the American journalist.

Freidin explained that his wife's health kept him in the area, which I thought would end the discussion, but it didn't.

"Well, your daughter still lives with you, doesn't she?" someone asked. "Can't your daughter stay with her?"

"Anna is an enormous source of support and happiness, but she is eighteen years old, and she has a busy life of her own."

The journalist looked thoughtful. "You know what I think?" she said. "I think you should get her a dog."

Freidin stared at her. "Excuse me?"

"You should get your wife a dog," the journalist explained. "It will change her life."

"I really don't see what a dog has to do with any of this."

"The dog will change her life!"

"What makes you think that her life needs to be changed?" There was another silence. "There are various things that cannot be accomplished by a dog."

The journalist looked downcast. "I just thought that if she's sick, the dog can cuddle with her."

"Cuddling is not the problem," said Freidin firmly.

The journalist nodded. "I can see I've said something wrong," she said. "But I'm just crazy about dogs." She looked truly sorry.

"We did have a dog once, years ago," Freidin said, in a conciliatory tone, "called Kutya."

The Hungarian professor, a mournful-looking woman in gray, looked up with interest. "*Kutya* means 'dog' in Hungarian!" she said. She spoke in a head voice, a bit like a puppet.

"We think Kutya might have had some Hungarian blood. He had a complicated heritage—part German shepherd, part Labrador retriever, and part bass baritone."

"Your dog could *sing*? Did he also *speak*? We had a *cat* once who could speak."

Silence.

"What—" I ventured, and cleared my throat. "What did your cat say?"

The Hungarian professor stared at me. "'*I'm hungry*,'" she sang out.

The one person at the table who had remained completely silent during these exchanges was the English translator: a lithe, handsome man—a former dancer, I later learned—with high cheekbones, narrow eyes, and a faintly contemptuous expression. He spoke British English, with a hint of a foreign accent.

His translation was itself an enigma: there were passages of such brilliance that you would stare from the original to the English and wonder how anyone had arrived at anything so unlikely and yet dead-on, but there were also strange discrepancies. For example, at the end of "My First Fee," Babel writes, "I will not die before I wrest from the hands of love one more—*and this will be the last*—gold coin"; the translation reads: "I will not die until I snatch one more gold ruble (*and definitely not the last one!*) from love's hands." In "Guy de Maupassant," Babel writes: "Night *bolstered* my hungry youth with a bottle of '83 Muscatel." The translation says, "Night *obstructed* my youth with a bottle of Muscatel '83." The book was full of such odd changes. Babel says "at nine o'clock"; the translation says "shortly after eight." Babel says "at midnight"; the translation says "after eleven." Freidin didn't like the way "giving the fig" was rendered as "thumbing one's nose," or the passage in which the homeless poet during the Petrograd famine has "Siberian salmon caviar and a pound of bread in [his] pocket": on the grounds that "homeless people do not carry caviar in their pockets," Freidin considered the correct translation to be "salmon roe."

Because of these and other disagreements, we all ended up writing our own translations, with a note that "many translations were used in the preparation of this exhibit, including . . ."

Everything had seemed fine until the end of the dinner, when the handsome translator suddenly turned to Freidin.

"You know," he said, "I went to your exhibit yesterday, and I noticed something strange. Perhaps you can explain it to me." He had noticed his own book in a glass case, open to Babel's story "Odessa"—next to a caption quoting "Odessa" in a different translation.

"Copyediting," Freidin said promptly. "Hoover ran all our text through copyediting. You would not believe the changes they made." He told the story of the copy editor who had translated all the italicized Yiddish in such a way that *Luftmensch* (an impractical visionary) came out as "pilot"; *shamas* (the beadle of a synagogue) turned, via "shamus," into "private detective."

The translator looked completely unamused. "So you're saying that the Hoover copy editors changed my translation?"

"Well, I'm saying that these texts went through many different hands."

"But what am I supposed to think, as a translator? My book is put on display next to something I didn't write. Is it possible to take some sort of legal action?"

Freidin paused. "Michael," he said, "we all like your translation, and we are grateful to you. I want us to be friends. Let's not talk about legal action. It doesn't even make sense. We didn't charge admission for the exhibit."

"That isn't the point. The point is that there in the display case I see *my book*, and next to it I see a typed quotation *with mistakes*. And you're telling me nobody can be held accountable because you didn't charge admission?"

"Michael. I want us to be friends. Now let's be honest. Were there mistakes in the exhibit? Yes! There are mistakes everywhere. There are mistakes in the *Complete Works*, if it comes to that."

The translator, who had excellent posture, sat up even straighter. "What mistake? Do you mean in the notes? That was corrected in the paperback."

"No, I'm not talking about the notes."

"Well, frankly, I don't know what you *are* talking about."

"Michael, I want us to be friends. The *Complete Works* is very, very good. We all like it very much. But in translating Babel—in translating anyone—mistakes are unavoidable. *I* have found mistakes. *Elif* has found mistakes." The translator briefly turned his hooded eyes in my direction. "But *I want us to be friends*."

"Do you see what I'm up against?" Freidin demanded. We were standing outside the conference hall after dinner. The Chinese were about to give their presentation. A junior professor of symbolism was standing nearby, smoking.

"What happened?" the symbolist asked.

"What didn't happen? It was a dinner from Dostoevsky, that's all."

"In what sense? 'The Two Families'?"

"Well, there was that."

"And what else?"

"Well—" Freidin broke off, glancing into the hall, where two professors and one Chinese filmmaker were crawling under a table, doing something with extension cords. "Excuse me." As Freidin hurried into the conference room, Lidiya Babel came up the stairs trailed by several International Babel Scholars, who were perhaps hoping to learn the things that *only she could tell us.* "Do you know," one of them said, "of those two Chinese, one is a Muslim?"

"Which one?"

"The short one."

"Are there many Chinese Muslims?" Lidiya asked.

"He is not Chinese!" shouted a depressed-looking historian. Everyone turned and looked at him.

"I don't think he's really Chinese," the historian repeated.

"He does look—different," said Lidiya.

"Maybe he is a Uighur," Zalevsky suggested.

"Wha-a-at?"

"A Uighur, a Uighur, a Uighur."

"When I asked the other Chinese what his religion was," continued the first scholar, "he said to me, 'My religion is Isaac Babel.'"

"Very strange," said the historian.

Everyone turned to Lidiya Babel, as if awaiting some response.

"It's an interesting thing," she said slowly. "I once knew a man who married a German woman, and they went to China and photographed Chinese children. Their pictures were put in a book, and published: a book of photographs of Chinese children. But the really interesting thing is that when they asked the man what kind of women he preferred, he would always say: 'Oh, ethereal—like a butterfly.' But when you saw the German woman—she was completely round."

There was a long pause.

"Ah, yes," said the symbolist finally. "'The eternal disjuncture between reality and the dream.'"

"Completely round," repeated Lidiya Babel. "Whereas later, she ate nothing but cucumbers and black caviar, and now she's altogether thin. Of course, this was when black caviar in Russia sold for next to nothing."

I felt a strange feeling, close to panic. What if that was it, the thing that only she could tell us?

Inside the conference hall, the Chinese filmmakers sat at a long table in front of a flickering screen. The screenwriter smiled and made eye contact with everyone who came in. The director stared impassively into the back corner of the room. I wondered what he was thinking about, and whether he was really a Uighur.

"I used to be a student here at Stanford," the screenwriter began. "Right here. I used to study computer programming. I used to work all night in the computer cluster next door. Then I took a creative writing class to learn how to write stories. There, my teacher assigned Isaac Babel's story 'My First Goose.' This story changed my life."

I was amazed anew at the varieties of human experience: to

think we had both read the same story under such similar circumstances, and it had had such different effects on us.

"Babel was like the father to me," continued the screenwriter. "I consider myself Babel's son. Therefore, Nathalie and Lidiya are my sisters." Something in the air suggested that not everyone in the audience had followed him in these logical steps. "Today I was able to shake hands with Nathalie, Lidiya, and Pirozhkova. I feel that I touched Babel's hand. I hope Babel is up there watching us right now!"

Next, the director gave a short address in Chinese, and the screenwriter translated. "I had the foundations of my existence rocked by Isaac Babel's *Red Cavalry*. His prose is so concise." The director gave a little nod when he heard the English word "concise." He went on to express his admiration of Babel's deep understanding of the relationship between men and horses. He himself was a horseman, and had filmed the movie known as the first Chinese Western. He had made films in all genres, including action, war, and family.

"I am so grateful because here I met Babel scholars from all over the world and the universe," the address concluded. "I saw so much passion! I can't show you my film of Isaac Babel's *Red Cavalry*, because I haven't made it yet. Instead I will show you some of my film, the first Chinese Western, *Swordsmen in Double Flag Town*. Then you will see how I feel about horses, and maybe you will understand how I feel about Isaac Babel."

The DVD was inserted into somebody's laptop and projected onto a big screen. The sound didn't work. Yellow dunes flashed silently by, a desert, the galloping legs of a horse, a row of Chinese characters. "*Swordsmen in Double Flag Town!*" cried the director, flinging out one arm. These were the first words he had spoken in English.

•

Later that night, Matej and I met at the picnic tables outside the housing complex. The world had changed two years' worth since the biography class. I had moved from the apartment across from the Safeway to a studio on campus. Matej now bought his Winston Lights from Australia, instead of from the American Indians. Matej had brought four bottles of beer—three for him and one for me—and I told him my story about the two Chinese, about their gratitude for having met scholars from all over the world, and the universe. "I think I saw one of them this afternoon," Matej said. "I saw one scholar, who was from the world, talking to another scholar, who was from elsewhere in the universe."

The subject of interplanetary visitors reminded me to tell Matej about Cooper's plan to simultaneously resolve the West Coast population boom and the Sputnik crisis by exporting Californians to the moon.

"What—like Nikolai Fyodorov?" Matej riposted.

I had forgotten all about Nikolai Fyodorov, the influential Russian philosopher who declared the future tasks of mankind to be the abolishment of death, the universal resurrection of all dead people, and the colonization of outer space (so the resurrected people would have somewhere to live).

Fyodorov published almost nothing in his lifetime. He worked as a librarian in Moscow, where his visitors included both the aging Lev Tolstoy and the teenage Konstantin Tsiolkovsky who, in 1903—the year of Fyodorov's death—mathematically proved the possibility of spaceflight. Tsiolkovsky went on to become the "grandfather of Soviet cosmonautics," and Soviet cosmonautics was Cooper's bête noire: "So there really is a path from Fyodorov to Cooper!" I concluded.

"If there wasn't, you would find one anyway," Matej replied. "You remind me of a Croatian proverb: the snow falls, not in order to cover the hill, but in order that the beast can leave its tracks."

"What's that supposed to mean?"

"Well, it's kind of an enigmatic proverb."

We talked then about Matej's current object of study: something called "the problem of the person." The problem, Matej explained, was that personhood is revealed and constituted by action, such that the whole person is always present in every action—and yet the person isn't "exhausted" by any single action, or even by the sum of all her actions. The action of writing "My First Goose," for example, expresses Babel's whole person (it isn't the case that only part of Babel wrote "My First Goose," while part of him remained uninvolved); nonetheless, neither "My First Goose," nor even the sum total of Babel's writings, expresses everything about him as a person.

"One way of putting it is like this," Matej said. "When you're in love with someone, what exactly is it you love?"

"I don't know," I said.

"That's just it, you see—you love . . . *the person.*"

The person is never exhausted by his actions: there is always something left over. But what is that precious remainder—where do you find it?

Reflecting upon the problem of the person, I was brought to mind of a novel I had always liked, but never quite understood: Ivan Goncharov's *Oblomov* (1859), the story of a man so incapable of action or decision making that he doesn't get off his sofa for the whole of part 1. In the first chapter, Oblomov receives various visitors who are active in different spheres of human activity. In all these forms of activity, Oblomov deplores the absence of "the person." A socialite rushes in, talks of balls, dinner parties, and tableaux vivants, and then rushes away, exclaiming that he has ten calls to make. "Ten visits in one day," Oblomov marvels. "Is this a life? Where is the person in all this?" And he rolls over, glad that he can stay put on his sofa, "safeguarding his peace and his human dignity."

The second visitor, a former colleague from the civil service, tells Oblomov about his recent promotion to department head, his new privileges and responsibilities. "In time he'll be a big shot and reach a high rank," Oblomov muses. "That's what we call a career! But how little of the person it requires: his mind, his will, his feelings aren't needed." Stretching out his limbs, Oblomov feels proud that he doesn't have any reports to write, and that here on the sofa there is "ample scope both for his feelings and his imagination."

I saw now that the problem of the person was the key to Oblomov's laziness. So loath is Oblomov to be reduced to the mere sum of his actions that he decides to systematically *not act*— thereby to reveal more fully his true person, and bask in it unadulterated.

Oblomov's third visitor, a critic, arrives in rapture over the invention of literary realism. "All the hidden wires are exposed, all the rungs of the social ladder are carefully examined," he gushes. "Every category of fallen woman is analyzed—French, German, Finnish, and all the others . . . it's all so true to life!" Oblomov not only refuses to read any realist works, but becomes almost impassioned. "Where is the person in all this? . . . They describe a thief or a prostitute, but forget the person, or are incapable of depicting him . . . The person, I demand the person!" he shouts.

Thinking over the problem of the person in the context of literary realism, I remembered a sentence from Babel's diary that I had initially taken as a joke: "What is this gluttonous, pitiful, tall youth, with his soft voice, droopy soul, and sharp mind?" It wasn't a joke—the question was where, in these characteristics, was the person? *What* was the person? In a speech in 1936, Babel described a change in his view of literary production: formerly, he had believed that the events of their time were so unusual and so surprising that all he had to do was write them down and "they would speak for themselves," but this literature of "objectivism" had turned out "uninteresting." "In my work there had been no person," Babel concluded. "The person had escaped himself." Three years later, the NKVD took him in, and didn't let him finish. The person had escaped for good.

The conversation with Matej turned to the way people are formed by their influences, by the fatal roles of others in their lives. I remember saying that I didn't believe Babel when he described Maupassant as the most significant of his literary influences.

"I suppose you have some other influence in mind?"

"Well . . . Cervantes." My latest theory was based on Babel's incorporation into one of his stories of various elements from the biography of Cervantes, who had worked for seven years as a bookkeeper for the Spanish Armada.

"My fear when I listen to you," Matej said finally, "is you remind me of this German philosopher." This German, Leo Strauss, had written a commentary to Western philosophy, arguing that all the greatest philosophers had felt it necessary to encrypt their real ideas. In the commentary, Strauss took it as his mission to reveal the Other Plato, the Other Hobbes, the Other Spinoza, all saying things that Plato and Hobbes and Spinoza had left unspoken.

"A lot of the ideas he attributes to Spinoza are interesting," Matej said, "but if Spinoza really thought those things, why didn't he say so?"

As he spoke these words, two figures approached through the darkness: Fishkin and Skywalker.

"Elif!" said Skywalker. "Just the person we wanted to see. Isn't that right?"

"Yes," said Fishkin unhappily.

"Fishkin has something to tell you. Doesn't he?"

"Yes." Fishkin took a deep breath. "Remember how I said yesterday that Zalevsky gave me the finger? Well, actually it happened d-differently . . ." He trailed off.

"Ye-e-s?" Skywalker prompted.

"Actually," Fishkin said, "I gave *him* the finger. I had finally found a parking spot and was about to pull in—when all of a sudden this car came speeding from the opposite direction and stole my spot. Naturally, I gave the guy the finger. Then he gave me the finger, and I saw it was Zalevsky. Then I drove away. I meant to tell you the truth yesterday. But when I said Zalevsky gave me the finger, you were like, 'Oh my god, what a monster!'— I just couldn't tell you I did it first."

A straightforward relationship to factual truth never was one of Babel's top priorities. "I was a boy who told lies," begins one of the Childhood stories: "This came from reading." A later story about reading, "Guy de Maupassant," ends with a largely incorrect retelling of Édouard de Maynial's biography of Maupassant: "Having achieved fame, he cut his throat at the age of forty, bled profusely, but lived. They locked him in a madhouse. He crawled about on all fours and ate his own excrement . . ." Contemporary Babel scholarship has shown that "neither Maynial nor any other biographer has Maupassant walking on all fours or eating his excrement"; the image appears to be borrowed from either *Nana* (Count Muffat crawls at Nana's feet, thinking of saints who "eat their own excrement") or *Madame Bovary* (a reference to Voltaire on his deathbed, "devouring his own excrement"). In "Guy de Maupassant," Babel mentions neither Voltaire nor Zola nor Flaubert—except to claim that Maupassant's mother is Flaubert's cousin: a false rumor explicitly controverted by Maynial.

Was Babel trying to establish the independence of the person from his deeds—the independence of Maupassant, the person, from his factually accurate biography? Was it about the "premonition of truth" being more true than historical fact?

Walking back to my apartment, I passed the laundry room. Warm, detergent-scented air gusted from vents near the floor and a stereo in the open window was playing Leonard Cohen's "First We Take Manhattan": *I love your body and your spirit and your clothes.*

What is it you love, when you're in love? His clothes, his books, his toothbrush. All of the manufactured, formerly alienated commodities are magically rehabilitated as aspects of the person—as organic expressions of actions, of choice and use. After Eugene Onegin disappears in book 7, Tatyana starts visiting his abandoned estate. She looks at his pool cues, his library, his riding crop, "and everything seems priceless to her." "What is he?" she asks, poring over his books, examining the marks left by his thumbnail in the margins.

So, too, do scholars now pore over the articles that once

belonged to Babel. One historian has annotated the inventory of belongings confiscated from Babel's Moscow apartment, his apartment in the Great Nikolo-Vorobinsky Lane. (In her memoirs, Pirozhkova writes about how impressed she was to learn about the existence of the Great Nikolo-Vorobinsky Lane, whose name literally means "Great Lane of Nikolai and the Sparrows"; Babel told her the street was named after the nearby Church of St. Nikolai-on-the-Sparrows, which had been built "with the help of sparrows, that is to say, in order to raise money for its construction, sparrows were caught, cooked and sold." This was totally untrue, as *Vorobinsky* actually came from an archaic word for "spindle," only coincidentally sharing the same adjectival form as "sparrow," but Babel could spin a story out of anything.) Can one glimpse the person, in the list of objects?

Binoculars—2 pr.
Manuscripts—15 folders
Drafts—43 it.
Schematic map of the motor transport network—1 it.
Foreign newspapers—4
Foreign magazines—9
Notebooks with notes—7 it.
Various letters—400 it.
Foreign letters and postcards—87 it.
Various telegrams—35 it.
Toothpaste—1 it.
Shaving cream
Suspenders—1 pr.
Old sandals
Duck for the bath
Soapdish—1

The fifteen folders of manuscripts vanished, along with the nine others seized from Babel's dacha. As for the personal items, they were held for three months before being surrendered to the state as "revenue." According to receipts, the binoculars eventually brought in 153 rubles and 39 kopeks, but there is no record of what happened to Babel's rubber duck.

(2010)

AN INTERRUPTION

Chad Harbach

Over the course of the past century, mean global temperatures increased by 0.6 degrees C. This change seems slight but isn't: in the winter of 1905 my great-grandfather, a coppersmith, installed the roof on a new reef-point lighthouse two miles from Lake Michigan's shore. Each morning he drove out across the open ice in a horse and buggy laden with his copperworking tools; today the water that far from shore never freezes, much less to a depth that could support a horse's weight.

Well into the 1990s, such changes had happened gradually enough to seem salubrious, at least in the upper Midwest—a karmic or godly reward, perhaps, for hard work and good behavior. No snow in October! Another fifty-degree day in February! It was as if the weather, too, partook of the national feeling of post–World War II progress: the economy would expand, technology would advance, the fusty mores of a black-and-white era would relax, and the climate, like some index or celebration of all this, would slowly become more mild. This was America. Our children would not only have bigger cars, smaller stereos, a few extra years to find themselves—they'd have better weather, too.

Now we know what we've done. Or we should. The fuel-burning binge (and the beef-eating binge, and the forest-clearing binge) we've been on for the past hundred and fifty years, and especially the last sixty, and increasingly and accelerantly, has brought into view the most dangerous threat in the brief history of our civilization. It's become possible to glimpse the disappearance of so many things, not just glaciers and species but ideas and institutions, too. Things may never be so easy or orderly again. Our way of life that used to seem so durable takes on a sad, valedictory aspect, the way life does for any nineteenth-century protagonist on his way to a duel that began as a petty misunderstanding. The sunrise looks like fire, the flowers bloom, the morning air dances against his cheeks. It's so incongruous, so unfair! He's healthy, he's young, he's alive—but he's passing from the world. And so are we, healthy and alive—but our world is passing from us.

For a long time, we feared that we would destroy ourselves by a sudden spasm of bomb-dropping. We still fear this, and should: the bombs are everywhere, attached to missiles that are meant for us, for our cities and our skins, though they point toward the empty sky. Despite our fear, we've learned to rest almost easily in the idea that for nuclear catastrophe to happen buttons must be pushed; that though it's easy to push buttons the imaginative connection between the buttons and their consequences will not be lost; that no human being would willingly push those buttons and accept those consequences again. We may well be wrong about this, but it is possible we are right; each day that passes without nuclear disaster implies the hope of decades, centuries, eons of the same.

Global warming—and the other environmental disasters

that will exacerbate and be exacerbated by global warming—doesn't permit this hope. It takes forty years or more for the climate to react to the carbon dioxide and methane we emit. This means that the disasters that have already happened during the warmest decade in civilized history (severe droughts in the Sahel region of Africa, western Australia, and Iberia; deadly flooding in Mumbai; hurricane seasons of unprecedented length, strength, and damage; extinction of many species; runaway glacial melt; deadly heat waves; hundreds of thousands of deaths all told) are not due to our current rates of consumption, but rather the delayed consequences of fuels burned and forests clear-cut decades ago, long before the invention of the Hummer. If we ceased all emissions immediately, global temperatures would continue to rise until around 2050.

This long lag is the feature that makes global warming so dangerous. Yes, this is how we would destroy ourselves—not by punching red buttons in an apocalyptic fit but by appropriating to ourselves just a little too much comfort, a little too much warmth, a little too much time. Like Oedipus, we've been warned. Like Oedipus, we flout the warning, and we'll act surprised, even outraged, when we find out what we've done.

Warming of 3 degrees C—five times as much as has occurred since 1900—is a standard projection for the century just begun. Though such a change would cause unimaginable destruction, it doesn't constitute a worst-case scenario by any means; in fact, it's the amount of warming assumed by the U.S. Climate Action Report of 2002, a carefully combed and vetted State Department document that begins with a heartening quote from President Bush ("My Administration is committed to a leadership role on the issue of climate change"). Three degrees Celsius is a conservative composite of the numbers produced by our best supercomputer climate models, and it doesn't presuppose any of the dramatic events—the shutdown of the Gulf Stream, the disintegration of a major ice shelf, the collapse of the Amazon rain forest—that have climate scientists increasingly worried.

These computer models grow continually more sophisticated and detailed—but to truly understand how it's going to be, to know what life will be like with a warming of 3 degrees C, we would need a Borgesian computer model that stretched from the height of the thermosphere to the ocean floor; a computer model to account for the possible extinction, migration, or adaptation of every living species; a computer model to assess the reactions of cowed, calamity-shaken governments to widespread flooding, food and freshwater shortages, storm-wrecked shorelines, aggressively rising seas. In a few short decades, nothing will be as it is now, everything will have to be recalculated, and the task of laying out even one of the many possible scenarios is akin to imagining in full a science-fiction planet sort of like our own: no matter how many dozens upon dozens of novels you wrote, there would always be details and consequences that escaped your consideration, and, once recognized, forced you to reconsider the whole.

Certain consequences, however, are obvious and inarguable, because they're already under way. Increased rainfall and evaporation will intensify cycles of drought and flooding worldwide. The Climate Action Report describes an America where, within our lifetimes, "Drought is an important concern virtually everywhere. Floods and water quality are concerns in many regions." Equatorial countries—which depend on the decreasingly reliable summer monsoons for life-sustaining rains, and which tend to be hardest hit by El Niño's storms and droughts—will suffer even more.

Sea levels will continue to rise, partly due to glacial melt, but mainly because water expands as it warms. Higher seas, combined with increasingly powerful overwater storms, will devastate, destroy, or simply consume low-lying areas. The Dutch have begun making plans to abandon large tracts of their hard-won, dike-drained nation to the advancing sea. Tuvalu and other low-lying islands are reluctantly plotting the relocation of their entire citizenries. Some studies estimate that there will be 150 million environmental refugees by midcentury, largely as a result of flooding in poor countries like Bangladesh, where 13 million people live within three feet of sea level. The billions of dollars needed to rebuild New Orleans will be needed again and again and again, mostly by countries that don't have them.

Extirpation of other species has long been a human specialty, but global warming, combined with continued habitat destruction, will accelerate the process by orders of magnitude. Our coral reefs and alpine meadows will be destroyed. Tropical diseases like malaria and dengue fever will spread to ever higher altitudes and latitudes. Food production will be hampered or crippled in many regions, and some people, perhaps many people, will starve.

And so on. Only one feature of our otherwise forgotten twentieth-century world seems likely to remain and be reinforced— the supreme importance of wealth. Rich countries will do better than poor countries, rich households will do better than poor households, rich species (Homo sapiens and their pets) will do better than poor species (all the rest). Global warming will deepen the divide between haves and have-nots—Hurricane Katrina offers a one-off example of how this can occur even in the

United States, but the sharper distinction will be international. As poor countries are hammered by sudden disasters and longer-term droughts, shortages, and epidemics, wealthier countries will paradoxically and perversely provide less aid, as they struggle with their own resource problems and future uncertainties.

In a world of relative stability, governments can make decisions with relative leisure and even magnanimity. They think twice about bombing one another; they sometimes indulge ideals of generosity, equity, humanitarianism. This cannot remain true of a world where the most fundamental stability of all—the sameness of climate on which agrarian civilization was founded—has been casually discarded. Exiled from a more or less predictable world, we will become desperate and confused, and no computer program can model that desperation. Our president has declared a perpetual borderless war as a consequence of a single unforeseen attack; even a much saner administration may become unhinged when nothing, least of all the weather from one year to the next, can be relied on. Skirmishes or worse will flare as resources dwindle. Our isolation will grow as millions of fellow species become extinct. The suppressed nightmare of nuclear war will recur during daylight hours.

These are not worst-case scenarios. The worst-case scenarios are much worse.

Of all the crimes committed by our current administration—institutionalized torture, pursuit of war under false pretenses, et cetera—its ecological crimes are the most damaging and regret-table. George W. Bush has dismantled decades' worth of environmental legislation, but his worst offense has been to take the oil companies' despicable campaign of disinformation about global warming and make it national policy. Even in the not-so-likely event that our next administration fully understands the scope of the danger, the costs of these eight years of paralysis will prove incalculable.

In 1988, NASA's top climate scientist, James Hansen, testified before Congress that he was "99 percent sure" that human-induced global warming was under way. His words made the front page of the *Times* and marked the entrance of global warming into mainstream public discussion. The following year, Al Gore called Hansen to testify again; this time, the first Bush administration forced him to alter his prepared statement. A furious Gore called the incident "science fraud" perpetrated by the "Science Politburo of the Bush Administration."

But Bush Senior, who oversaw the Montreal Protocol that reversed the destruction of the ozone layer, was a staunch ecologist compared to his son. (In between, Clinton and Gore were crucial to the forging of the Kyoto Protocol, and generally much sounder on environmental matters, but also presided over a 14 percent increase in U.S. greenhouse emissions.) The second Bush has shown a Bolshevik flair for asserting ideological control over scientific inquiry. Hansen, who still heads NASA's climate program, was recently warned of "dire consequences" if he persisted in speaking out about the need for immediate reductions in carbon emissions. Scientists at the National Oceanic and Atmospheric Administration have been muzzled, too. The White House has altered or excised passages on climate change in several EPA reports; the former head exciser, Philip A. Cooney, took a job at ExxonMobil after resigning.

After his first congressional appearance, Hansen was criticized by many scientists for drawing premature conclusions. He alone understood the difference between science, which demands constant skepticism in a search for total certainty, and politics, which demands reasonable assessments of probabilities and costs. The rigors of science look like weakness and temporizing when viewed through the lens of politics. This is the same blurred distinction on which the second Bush has based his devious insistence on "sound science"—i.e., perfect foreknowledge of future events as a prerequisite for action.

Meanwhile the Pentagon has begun scenario-planning for abrupt climate change. A Department of Defense–commissioned report from 2003 begins by noting that "there is substantial evidence to indicate that significant global warming will occur during the twenty-first century" and goes on to envision the consequences of one abrupt-change scenario that has increasingly captured the attention of scientists—the shutdown of the Gulf Stream, which could plunge most of Europe into a deep chill while the rest of the world continues warming. The report isn't terribly imaginative or grammatical, but it is based on sound fundamentals: "With at least eight abrupt climate change events documented in the geological record, it seems that the questions to ask are: When will this happen? What will the impacts be? And, how can we best prepare for it? Rather than: Will this really happen?"

The authors go on to conclude that, while superior wealth and resources would allow the United States to adapt moderately well to such a scenario, we would find ourselves in a world "where Europe will be struggling internally, large numbers of refugees are washing up on [U.S.] shores, and Asia is in serious crisis over food and water. Disruption and conflict will be endemic features of life." Such conclusions force us to consider the most cynical of all possible interpretations of our indifference to global warming: on some level, we believe not only that we'll be fine, but that our relative advantage over other countries will actually increase. Instead of yielding aspects of our dominance to bigger nations like China and India, we'll maintain our hold over a troubled world—an idea as unethical as it is dubious.

The United States, with 5 percent of the world's population, produces 25 percent of the world's greenhouse gases, and thus is disproportionately responsible for the warming that has occurred so far and will occur in coming decades. The Climate Action Report maintains—and the White House continues to insist—that U.S. "strategies are expected to achieve emission reductions comparable to the average reductions prescribed by the Kyoto agreement, but without the threats to economic growth." Two paragraphs later, it's made clear that our emissions are scheduled to increase by 43 percent between 2000 and 2020—a "comparable" amount, somehow, to the 7 percent reduction prescribed by Kyoto.

It's often said that Kyoto doesn't matter, because the cuts prescribed are so small as to be wholly inadequate—but our refusal to go even this far has brought the international political effort to address global warming to a dead halt. Kyoto expires in 2012, and governments should now be creating far more ambitious post-Kyoto plans, but such plans are unthinkable in the absence of U.S. economic leadership. EU countries can act as responsibly as they like, but China and India, the slowly waking behemoths of U.S.-style fossil-fuel use, will do nothing until the United States demonstrates that a grand-scale transition to renewable energy can be achieved by big industrial countries.

This is the responsibility incumbent on us, and its fulfillment could easily be couched in the familiar, voter-friendly language of American leadership, talent, and heroism. But it has not been. Instead we are welcoming the prospect of running shipping routes over the thawed North Pole, and scheming to drill for fresh oil beneath what used to be tundra. Instead of enacting a Manhattan Project for renewable fuels, we continue building technologically fossilized infrastructure at massive cost. After a profit-minded turn away from coal-fired power in the eighties and nineties, scores of new coal plants are scheduled to be built in this country by 2025. China and India are following suit, adding coal-fired capacity as fast as they can. A slow, self-congratulatory creep toward sustainability—a small investment in solar power, a fleet of "green" SUVs that get thirty miles a gallon—is no match for billions of dollars of deathly infrastructure. Once built, these plants will remain online for decades, pouring gigatons of carbon into the air, unless some humanitarian-minded nation sends its fighter planes to bomb them.

Hard, but not impossible, for a free democratic people to circumvent their government. In the past year, there's been a definite uptick in public attentiveness to global warming, spurred by Elizabeth Kolbert's quietly harrowing three-part piece in *The New Yorker* and then by the horrors of Katrina. New books abound and are selling well. A full-length documentary debuted at Sundance. ABC News and *60 Minutes* have run prime-time specials. *Rolling Stone* publishes pieces by Al Gore and Bill McKibben. And yet the impression on our consciousness remains a dangerously shallow one. An accumulation of editorials has not amounted to a political movement, much less a transformation in our thinking. There remains an eerie discrepancy between the scope of the problem and our attention to it.

This is true not just of the pollsters' America, that amorphous

TV-watching body that extracts convenient messages—Drive that SUV! Build a five-bedroom house when the kids leave home!—from their administration's silence. It's true of the mainstream press and the left, as well. The *Times* continues to give column inches to global-warming skeptics, as if such skeptics existed outside the protected biosphere of petroleum-company funding. *The Nation* devotes as much space to the dangers of warming as anyone, but it also publishes "A 'Top Ten' List of Bold Ideas," which aims at "positive, aggressive post-Bush (and post–New Democrat) near- and long-term change." So what do progressives boldly wish for? A thirty-hour workweek and universal day care— but the words "global warming" are nowhere to be found, and the weakly worded "investing in conservation and renewable energy" rates only an honorable mention. This is as perverse as it is typical. Imagine a historian in the year 2080, reading such lists as she researches the vexing question of how even educated, "progressive" people could have refused to face what was happening.

If such a thing as a literary/political/intellectual left exists, it is defined by its capacity for imaginative and sympathetic reach—by its willingness to surmount barriers of difference (class, distance, nationality) and agitate for a more equitable distribution of the goods and goodnesses that make up our idea of human (and nonhuman) well-being. To be able to imagine what it might be like to be tortured, or to live in abject poverty, or under the watchful eyes of U.S. Predator drones—this capacity is crucial to the project of any political left in a wealthy country. But in the case of global warming, our collective imagination has failed us utterly.

There seems to be a persistent if unstated resistance on the part of the left to the precepts of ecology. Environmental causes haven't captured the attention of our subtlest thinkers and writers, but remain cordoned off to be pursued by nature lovers and nonprofiteers. In fact, global warming represents the third great crisis of technological civilization. The first two have not been resolved—they stay with us, in the form of third world sweat-shops and slums (the brutal conditions and wealth discrepancy that first spurred Marx and Engels) and stockpiled hydrogen bombs (the application of each new technology to the art of kill-ing humans). The third promises to overwhelm them both, even while it exacerbates them.

The most powerful and cogent critique that can currently be leveled against our mode of capitalism is that markets fail to account for ecological costs. In a crowded world of finite size, our political economy values only acceleration and expansion. Scarce natural resources like clean air and water, not to mention more complex systems like rain forests or coral reefs, are either held at nothing or seriously undervalued. Corporations could clear-cut all our forests, reduce croplands to swirling dust, turn rivers to con-veyors of toxic sludge, deplete supplies of minerals and metals, double and redouble carbon emissions—and all our economic indicators would show nothing but robust growth until the very moment the pyramid scheme collapsed. Indeed, most of these things are happening, with only scattered opposition. When our math improves, when the costs of our products fully reflect the resources used and the wastes produced—especially CO_2: then and only then can capitalism begin to become a viable and hu-mane economic system.

Meanwhile, it feels strange to be alive and well, strange to keep riding the wave of our wild prosperity, strange to feel the warmth of the February sun on our necks. Do we know what's happen-ing or don't we? It seems like we know, it seems like everyone knows—the news is out, the science corroborates our senses, until it seems impossible not to know—but we refuse to believe it. We've been taught to imagine ever longer and happier and healthier lives for ourselves—we can't help half-consciously numbering the walks we'll take, the books we'll read and write, the grandchildren we'll hoist in the year 2060. And maybe these dreams will come true. Maybe, as the Pentagon report suggests, the same privileged caste of people who engineered the coming disasters will live in fifty years much as they do now, buffered from harm by money and medicine and force of arms. The weather will be an erratic and dangerous spectacle, economies and ecosystems will collapse, millions will die elsewhere in the world, but we'll seal our borders, abandon our ideas of nature, buy Canada ("the Saudi Arabia of freshwater"), and adapt.

Fifty years after that? We won't be around. Those who will be can fend for themselves, and call us what they like.

(2006)

WHAT DO YOU DESIRE?

Emily Witt

On a Monday last April, in line at JFK Airport to board a plane to San Francisco. Before me stood a silver-headed West Coast businessman. His skin had the exfoliated, burnished sheen of the extremely healthy; his glasses were of an advanced polymer; he had dark jeans. He wore the recycled ethylene-vinyl acetate shoes that are said never to smell. His fleece coat was of an extraordinary thickness and quality, with a lissome external layer that would not pill. He seemed like the sort of man who would pronounce himself a minimalist and say that everything he bought was selected for its extraordinary craftsmanship and beautiful design. But the silver fox's computer bag was a cheap thing with netting and buckles that said *GOOGLE* on it. The person in front of him in line wore a Google doodle T-shirt with Bert and Ernie where the *O*s would be. In front of him was a Google backpack.

Until I left San Francisco it never went away. It was embroidered on breast pockets, illustrated with themes of America's cities, emblazoned on stainless-steel water bottles, on fleece jackets, on baseball caps, but not on the private coach buses that transported workers to their campus in Mountain View, where they ate raw goji-berry discs from their snack room and walked about swathed, priestlike, in Google mantles, with Google wimples and Google mitres, seeking orientation on Google Maps, Googling strangers, and Google chatting with friends, as I did with mine, dozens of times a day, which made the recurrence of the logo feel like a supremacist taunt.

My first day in the city I sat in a sunlit café in the Mission District, drank a cappuccino, and read a paper copy of the *San Francisco Chronicle* that lay anachronistically on the counter. I overheard someone talking about his lunch at the Googleplex. "Quinoa cranberry pilaf," I wrote down. And then, "coregasm." Because that was the subsequent topic of discussion: women who have spontaneous orgasms during yoga. The barista was saying how wonderful it was that the issue was receiving attention, coregasms being something a lot of women experienced and were frightened to talk about. Those days were over.

The people of San Francisco were once famous for their refusal of deodorant and unnecessary shearing. Sometimes, walking down the street, past gay construction workers and vibrator stores, I was reminded that this was the place where Harvey Milk was elected (and assassinated), where the bathhouses had flourished (and closed). But most of the time I noticed only that the people of San Francisco appeared to have been suffused with unguents and botanical salves, polished with salts, and scented with the aromatherapeutics sold in the shops that lined Valencia Street. The air smelled of beeswax, lavender, and verbena, and the sidewalks in the Mission glittered on sunny days. The food was exquisite. There was a place in Hayes Valley that made liquid-nitrogen ice cream to order. I watched my ice cream magically pressured into existence with a burst of vapor and a pneumatic hiss. This miracle, as the world around me continued apace, just moms with Google travel coffee mugs talking about lactation consultants. Online, people had diverted the fear of sin away from coregasms and toward their battles against sugar and flour. "Raw, organic honey, local ghee, and millet chia bread taming my gluten lust" was a typical dispatch. "Thank goodness for ancient grains."

At night I was alone, and I would walk down the street listening to sermons in Spanish from the storefront churches and the electronic hum of the BART train below. The city was a dream world of glowing screens and analog fetishism, of Google, orgasms, stone fruits, and sparkles. A Greek chorus of the homeless and mentally ill connected these fragments into deeper conspiracies, until I began to see conspiracies myself. I would walk down the sidewalks of the Mission and note their glittery resemblance to my powdered blush in its makeup compact. "This sidewalk looks like Super Orgasm," I would think, Super Orgasm being the name of the particular shade of blush I own. My makeup reveled in contemporary sexual politics: FOR HIM & HER read the sticker on the back of my paraben-free foundation. I contemplated a possible economic index comparing the cost of a pint of honey-lavender ice cream to the federal minimum hourly wage. I ran to Golden Gate Park, where giant birds of prey gazed hungrily upon glossy dachshunds. The cyclists passed in shoals, dressed in Google bicycle jerseys.

I had never had a coregasm and my sexual expectations conformed to widely held, government-sanctioned ideals. I was single, and now in my thirties, but I still envisioned my sexual experience eventually reaching a terminus, like a monorail gliding to a stop at Epcot Center. I would disembark, find myself face-to-face with another human being, and there we would remain in our permanent station in life: the future.

In San Francisco, people thought differently. They sought to unlink the family from a sexual foundation of two people. They believed in intentional communities that could successfully disrupt the monogamous heterosexual norm. They gave their choices names and they conceived of their actions as social movements. I had come to San Francisco to observe this sexual vanguard, but I did not think their lessons applied to me. "But what is your personal journey?" they would ask, and I would joke about this later with my friends.

Public Disgrace is an online pornography series that advertises itself as "women bound, stripped, and punished in public." It is the creation of a thirty-year-old San Francisco–based porn director and dominatrix named Princess Donna Dolore. Princess Donna conceived of the project in 2008, during her fourth year of working for the pornography company Kink.com. In addition to directing, Donna performs in the shoots, though she is not usually the lead.

When Princess Donna is scouting locations for *Public Disgrace* she looks for small windows (they need to be blacked out) and spaces (they need to look crowded). For outdoor shoots she usually works in Europe, where public obscenity laws are more forgiving. Before each shoot, Princess Donna coordinates with the female lead to establish what she likes or doesn't like and produces a checklist of what the performer will take from her civilian audience. Some models are happy only with groping, some have rules against slapping, and some are willing to go so far as to be fingered or spit on by the audience.

For female performers, the draw of *Public Disgrace* lies in Donna's directorial prowess. Princess Donna is an experienced orchestrator of complicated fantasies of group sex, public sex, and violent sex. Such situations tend to be, as Princess Donna puts it, "kind of tricky to live out in real life." She is also a deft manipulator of the human body. Female performers trust her to extend the boundaries of their physical capacities.

The job description for *Public Disgrace*, posted at Kink.com, reads: "Sex between male dominant and female submissive; domination by female and male dom; secure bondage, gags, hoods, fondling, flogging, and forced orgasms with vibrators." For four to five hours of work, performers earn between $1,100 and $1,300, plus bonuses for extra sex acts with cameo performers who can show a clean bill of health.

A week after I arrived in San Francisco, I attended a *Public Disgrace* shoot. The shoots are open to the public, a public that's encouraged to actively participate. Novelty is important to the world of porn, so audience members are recruited through the internet but restricted to attending one shoot a year.

The venue of the shoot I attended, a bar called Showdown, was on a side street haunted by drug addicts and the mentally ill just south of the Tenderloin, next to a Vietnamese sandwich shop and a flophouse called the Winsor Hotel (reasonable rates daily-weekly). When I arrived, several people were standing under the red arrow outlined in yellow lightbulbs above the entrance, waiting to get in, including a group of young men and a heterosexual couple in their thirties. We signed releases and showed our photo IDs, and a production assistant took a mug shot of each of us holding our driver's license next to our face. Then she gave us each two drink tickets that could be redeemed at the bar. "Depending on how wasted everyone seems to be I will give you more," she promised.

•

That evening's performer, a diminutive blonde who goes by the stage name Penny Pax, flew up to San Francisco from her home in Los Angeles especially for the *Public Disgrace* shoot. She had told Donna that one of the first pornos she ever watched was *Public Disgrace*, and since she got into the business herself she had been anxious to make one. Her personal request for the evening was that Princess Donna attempt to anally fist her.

The bar was a narrow room with a sense of history attached to it, of an older San Francisco that was a working-class mix of Irish and Italian immigrants. Old-fashioned smoked-glass lamps hung over the wooden bar. A color-copied picture of Laura Palmer from David Lynch's television show *Twin Peaks* hung on the wall, next to a stopped clock with a fake bird's nest in the cavity where a pendulum should have been. Behind the front area with the bar was a dark square room with black wallpaper patterned with alternating illustrations of two parrots on perches and a vase of flowers. The crew from Kink had rigged lighting overhead.

Princess Donna arrived with a small entourage, wearing a vacuum-tight black minidress that flattered her exceptionally perfect breasts. Donna is an extraordinary physical presence in any group of people, and her stature plays integrally into her authority. She is five foot seven with long, almost alarmingly thin limbs that make her seem taller. She has large, brown, Bambi-ish eyes that, the night of the shoot, were complexly shadowed and wreathed in fake eyelashes, which Kink purchases in quantities of several hundred at a time. Her long brown hair was tied up in a high ponytail. She has a tattoo of a biologically correct heart on her left shoulder and a cursive inscription that says *Daddy* on her inner right forearm. She strode into the room carrying a black vinyl purse from which a riding crop protruded. With her minidress she wore tan cowboy boots, which made the length of her legs appear heronlike. A neck bruise the size of a silver dollar that I had noticed during my first meeting with her a week before had faded.

Donna stood before the bar with the palindromically stage-named male performer, Ramon Nomar, surveying the room. He pointed up to several hooks on the ceiling and to a metal Juliet balcony over the bar. Donna nodded without a word. They retreated to the back. I asked a production assistant where the female performer was. Penny Pax, she said, was having "quiet time."

Soon, the music was silenced (Kink had its own music, cleared of rights, to play). The bartender removed his gingham shirt and his tie and suddenly was wearing nothing but his waistcoat. Donna came out to make some announcements to the assembled crowd, which was well on its way to getting soused.

"You might think we are doing things to the model that are mean or humiliating, but don't," said Donna. "She's signed an agreement." According to the agreement, the crowd had permission to poke the model, fondle her, and finger her, but only if they washed their hands and had neatly trimmed fingernails. A fingernail trimmer was available if necessary. "I'm going to be watching you like a hawk to make sure you're not doing degrading things to her pussy," Donna said. She continued: "You're allowed to spit on her chest but not her face. You can give her a hard spanking, but you are not allowed to give her a hard smack." She pulled her production assistant over to her physically. "If Kat is the model"—here Kat bent over obligingly—"this would be a reasonable distance from which to spank her." Donna mimed responsible spanking practice.

The model, Donna went on to explain, could not leave the set bruised because she had another shoot coming up this week. Donna said that therefore at some point she might have to forbid certain practices to ensure Penny's body remained unmarked.

Donna concluded her speech with a more theoretical exposition. The whole point of *Public Disgrace*, she explained, is that it's supposed to seem spontaneous, and that "you guys are not supposed to know that we're coming here." Taking video was forbidden, photographs with phones were fine, but the most important thing: "Don't ignore us. I'm going to walk her in with a sign that says I'M A WORTHLESS CUNT. So react to that." She repeated that nail clippers and files were available for anyone who wanted them and reminded the audience to wash their hands in the bathroom before touching the model. Then she returned to the back room.

A few minutes later Donna emerged with Penny Pax and Ramon in tow. Penny was small, just over five feet tall, with full natural breasts, milky white skin, and a chin-length bob of corn-silk blond. Her eyes were the rich azure of a blue raspberry Blow Pop. She was very pretty, and decidedly not plastic or spray-tanned. She looked like a model in a JCPenney catalog. She wore a denim miniskirt, white high heels, and a white tank top. Donna looked her over, then deftly pulled the straps of Penny's tank top off her arms and folded them down. She spun Penny around, unhooked her white padded bra, and tossed it to one side. From a black duffel bag under a table Donna picked up and put back various coils of rope, judging the weight and length of each one. Meanwhile Ramon stared—the only word for it is lovingly—at Penny's breasts, which hung pendulously down, stretch marks visible. Grabbing them, Donna executed a complicated-looking tie, uplifting the breasts to bra elevation by winding the rope around each one. She pulled the straps of Penny's tank top back over her shoulders, then tied Penny's arms behind her back.

"Look at that," said Donna, surveying her work and turning Penny around. "You look gorgeous." Meanwhile Ramon stepped in and looked over Penny with the tender carnivorousness of a dime-store bodice ripper. He ran his hand over Penny's body from behind, turned her around and examined her, kissed and inhaled her hair, then put his hand up her skirt and began feeling her while staring intently at her body. This was his way of preparing for the shoot. Ramon was from Spain and had a sharp accent. He rarely smiled. He wore a tight black T-shirt that showed off his impressive pectorals, black pants, and black combat boots. He was just over six feet tall, tan, and sculpted like an Iberian Bruce Willis. This was an attractive couple. Donna hung a sign, which indeed read I'M A WORTHLESS CUNT, around Penny's neck, then grabbed Penny roughly by the hair and took her out the door.

Now the cameras were recording. Now we could redeem our drink tickets. The bar was full, mostly with men. These men I would divide into two groups: the openly slavering, confident about the righteousness of their lust, and the self-conscious, worried about breaking the taboos of touching and insulting a woman. They were joined by a smattering of females, some of whom were there with their boyfriends, others who had come together in pairs. Donna had exchanged her cowboy boots for patent leather high heels and now strode through the door purposefully, she and Ramon on either side of Penny, who looked up at her tall handlers with baleful blue eyes.

"Tell everybody why you're here," ordered Donna, as the people drinking at the bar feigned surprise. "I'm a worthless cunt!" said Penny. Using some kind of professional wrestling trick, Ramon lifted her up by her neck and sat her on the bar. Working together, Donna and Ramon stuffed a cocktail napkin in her mouth and taped it into a gag, taking turns slapping her on her face and her breasts. They ripped off her spotless white tank top. The rope had cut off circulation to Penny's breasts and they looked painfully swollen.

"Who wants to touch it?" asked Donna. "Who wants to play with this worthless little cunt?" The bar patrons obligingly hit, fingered, and spanked her. From her handbag, from which the riding crop still menacingly protruded, Donna now withdrew a device crepitating with electric sparks and started shocking Penny with it. Ramon removed what remained of Penny's clothes, then his belt, and began gently swiping it at Penny, who was soon pinioned on the floor.

"I thought it was your dream," goaded Donna. "I thought it was your dream to shoot for this site. You didn't come ready?" She looked around the room. "What's her name?" she demanded. "Everyone knows what her name is."

"Worthless cunt!" yelled the crowd.

"What pretty girl wants to grab her titties?" A woman in attendance obliged. Ramon took off his pants, balancing on each foot as he pulled them over his combat boots. He was not wearing any underwear; his penis looked like the trunk of a palm tree. The bar patrons burst into applause.

He picked Penny up and had sex with her against the bar as the extras continued to smack at her breasts. Penny, still gagged, was wide-eyed. Her mascara had begun to run in rivers down her face. She had the option of halting everything with verbal and nonverbal cues, but she did not exercise it. Suddenly Donna stopped the show. "Everyone, I have an announcement," Donna said, as she removed the ropes still tied around Penny's breasts. "No more smacking this boob," she said, pointing to the right one, which had red marks on it. They resumed shooting.

Ramon, who had biceps like cannons, hoisted Penny around the room and the crowd followed, vying with one another for a good sight line. He was able to walk around holding Penny in one arm, wielding the zapper in the other. "Zap me!" requested a male audience member. Ramon rolled his eyes and did so without breaking rhythm. "Ouch," said the guy, looking sore. Ramon removed Penny's gag and guided her into a blow job, during which Penny theatrically gagged. Donna stood by, slapping and shocking, and then tag-teamed in. Using her hands, she made Penny ejaculate, to the delight of the crowd. After fifteen or twenty minutes, Donna called for a break.

Paused in the middle of his exertions, Ramon looked up at the ceiling with superintense concentration. Penny was on the floor. He picked her up and sat her on the bar. He and Donna tenderly tucked her hair back from her face and wiped off her sweat and the grime from the floor with Cottonelles. Donna, like a trainer during a boxing match, removed Penny's false eyelashes, gave her water, and kissed her on the cheek. During this reprieve from shooting, the crowd, which had been as verbally abusive as directed, seemed sheepish.

"You are beautiful and I'd take you to meet my mother!" yelled one man who had been particularly enthusiastic about yelling "worthless cunt." Ramon asked for a drink. "What do you want?" said the bartender. "A soda," said Ramon. "Porno guy wants a soda!" echoed the loud man.

When shooting resumed, a female audience member, heavily tattooed and wearing a miniskirt and a ragged T-shirt that had two skeletal hands printed across her breasts, had a go at Penny's body. Things continued in this way for more than an hour. Chairs were knocked over. Drinks were spilled. The bartender had by now removed his vest and was shirtless. The crowd was drunk and excited, although not entirely unembarrassed. "Make that bitch choke," shouted the shouty man. Then: "Sorry!"

Donna began to wind things down. "Okay, guys," she said, to prepare the audience, "the potshot's not the end, though." The crowd cheered. With the cameras off, Ramon and Penny had vanilla missionary sex on a table to get to the point where he could ejaculate. He nodded when he was ready, then put Penny on the floor, and masturbated until he came on her face. Again the room burst into applause.

The performers took a break. Ramon's job was now done. With the room's attention focused on Penny he yanked off his sweaty T-shirt, flung it into a corner, and wandered off into a dark part of the bar, naked but for his combat boots. Like a long-distance runner who has just crossed the finish line, he walked it off, moving his arms in circles, wiping the sweat from his face with his arm, and taking deep breaths. Nobody noticed him. Eventually he recovered his composure, toweled off, and put his black jeans back on. Penny, meanwhile, rested primly on a chair and sipped water. Her expression was, in a word, elated.

I joined Donna at the bar. What was going to happen next?

"I want to get my hand all the way in her ass," she said. "She's never done that before and she wants to try it."

Princess Donna sat Penny Pax down on a bar table. She had a Hitachi Magic Wand and a bottle of lubricant. "I need all the room that's in her holes for my hand," she announced, and the audience deferentially took a step back. After Donna accomplished her task, the crowd chanted, "Squirt, squirt, squirt, squirt," and then Penny did. I watched all this from a corner, standing next to Ramon, who had a towel around his bronzed shoulders and was drinking a bottle of pilsner.

Shooting was coming to a close. Donna and Ramon moved

Penny back to the bar and strung her up by her wrists to the metal balcony. I saw Donna in a corner, carefully wiping down a beer bottle with a sanitizing wipe. And that was the final shot of the evening: Penny tied up and suspended from the railings of the balcony by her wrists, while a member of the audience penetrated her with a beer bottle. Ramon, now shirtless and in jeans, casually sparked the zapper across his pectoral muscles a couple of times, then reached out and zapped Penny on the tongue she offered to him with a scream. Then it was done. With a debonair flourish, Ramon effortlessly picked up the tiny starlet and carried her out of the room in his arms.

Kink interviews its female performers before and after every shoot. It's a de-escalation strategy that reminds the viewer—if he watches it (Kink does not release the demographics of its audience, but studies have found that 98 percent of paid porn is watched by men)—of the controlled conditions of what he just watched, and confirms that the activity was consensual and that the model has recovered. Penny wandered out for her postgame interview wearing pink glasses, a gray bathrobe, and a pair of Uggs. But for her smeary mascara, she looked like a college student on her way to a dormitory bathroom. Donna arranged Penny's bathrobe to reveal her breasts. Other than that, like most postgame interviews with athletes, this one was a little bland.

Donna: So, Penny, how did you enjoy the shoot this evening?
Penny: I had a great time, it was amazing. There was so much going on.

Heckling audience member #1: I actually want to take you out for lunch later!

Heckling audience member #2: You have really pretty eyes!

Donna: All right, everybody, hold on. Tell me what your favorite parts were.

Penny: Probably, uh, just the getting handled by everyone and not really knowing how many hands were on me, or who was touching me . . . And then the—I don't know, did you get your fist in my butt?

Donna: I did.

Penny: Well, that was awesome. Yay! I can't wait to see it!

Donna: Yeah, that was rad. Round of applause for the anal fisting!

Audience applauds.

Donna: And you also said that you had never squirted like that before?

Penny: Yeah, that was ridiculous. How did you do that?

Donna: Magic fingers. Years of practice.

Penny: Yeah, it was amazing.

Donna: What were the most challenging parts?

Penny: Uh, probably putting your fist in my butt? That was pretty challenging. It felt really full.

Donna: On a scale of one to ten, how would you rate your happiness leaving the shoot?

Penny: Eleven!

Applause. Whistles.

Donna: So is it safe to say that you would come back and shoot for the site again?

Penny: Yes.

Donna: Do you want a shower?

Penny Pax nods.
Donna: Let's get you a shower!
Male audience member: A golden shower!
Female audience member: Can I come?

After this conclusion, Penny and I retreated to a stairwell behind the bar. Penny, I learned, is twenty-three years old. I asked if she had been working in the industry since she was eighteen. No, she said, she wishes. She had only been in the industry for six months. Before working in porn she was a lifeguard in Fort Lauderdale. Being a lifeguard in Fort Lauderdale had been pretty boring. I asked her about the shoot. I wanted to know how it had felt.

"It's a little uncomfortable in the beginning, for the anal," she said. (She was presumably referring to a moment early in the shoot when Ramon jumped up on the bar, stuffed a lemon in Penny's mouth, and had anal sex with her. "Nice boots, man!" someone in the audience yelled. Penny made a nonverbal cue to slow down and Donna jumped over and slathered her with lubricant.) "But my body warms up pretty quickly and then there's no discomfort." Slightly incredulous, I asked if there were moments then of genuine pleasure. She looked at me like I was crazy. "*Yeah*. Like the whole thing! The whole thing." She apologized for not being more articulate and explained she was in a state of delirium. "We call it 'dick drunk.'"

I rode back to the Mission in a van with Donna and Penny and Ramon. Penny and Ramon were both sleeping over at the landmarked Moorish castle that houses Kink. They usually work in mainstream porn in the San Fernando Valley, but enjoy coming to

San Francisco. In the shoot he was doing tomorrow for New Sensations in Los Angeles, Ramon lamented, they wouldn't even let him pull the girl's hair. I surmised that making more extreme pornography if you're a performer is like wanting to write like Beckett if you're a writer.

I left Penny and Ramon wandering the lobby in their gray bathrobes and stepped out into the cold San Francisco night. I walked west to Valencia Street, where I found a scene of unexpected destruction. Broken glass filled the sidewalks. The windows of every storefront—TACA Airlines, an adjacent property management company, the boutique after that, and on down the street—had been shattered. The windshields of the cars lining the street had been systematically bludgeoned. A new apartment complex under construction had *FUCK THIS SHIT* spray-painted on a column. I stared at the hanging fragments of glass and the garbage bins tipped over on the sidewalk. Then I crossed to the undamaged side of the street and bought myself an ice cream sandwich. I asked the cashier what had happened. He described a dozen protesters dressed in black. The following day was May 1. I knew strikes were planned in Oakland, but on this side of the bay nobody had seemed particularly interested in Occupy Wall Street.

I took some photos of the destruction and posted them to the websites of the great technology corporations with written exclamations of bafflement. Then I deleted the posts. I tried to think about the sex I had just watched. In the early years of broadband internet, *Frontline* had made a documentary called "American Porn." ("It's a multibillion-dollar industry—and growing. In a wired world, can anything stop it?") After interviewing various porn industry stalwarts, the male anchor had attended a shoot not unlike the one I just watched and had walked out in disgust.

While I certainly worried about what I had seen, I could not find it in myself to feel that level of indignation. I ate my ice cream sandwich and went to sleep.

Over the course of the next several weeks I watched Princess Donna direct and star in more films. I watched her perform in a Roller Derby–themed episode of a series called *Fucking Machines*, where she wielded a drill retrofitted with a giant dildo. I watched her train for her new role as director of a Kink property called *Ultimate Surrender*, a girl-on-girl wrestling tournament. For three eight-minute rounds, two women wrestled each other. The goal was for one woman to pin the other and molest her for as long as possible. For the fourth round, the winner has sex with the loser wearing a strap-on dildo. It's one of Kink's most popular properties and is sometimes shot before a live studio audience. Princess Donna also directs a series called *Bound Gangbangs*, and one day was inspired to do a shoot where all the men were dressed as panda bears. I watched this, too, and was surprised to find it beautiful.

I, personally, was not having sex while all this was going on. Not that the sex I would've had, if I'd been having sex, would've been anything like the sex that was going on at the Kink castle. The Kink actors were more like athletes, or stuntmen and stunt-women performing punishing feats, and part of what fascinated me was the ease with which they went in and out of it, the comfort with which they inhabited their bodies, their total self-assurance and sense of unity against those who condemned their practice. I possessed none of those qualities.

I had made no conscious decision to be single, but love is rare and it is frequently unreciprocated. Because of this, people around me continued to view love as a sort of messianic event, and my friends expressed a religious belief that it would arrive for me one day, as if love was something the universe owed to each of us, which no human could escape. I had known love, but having known love I knew how powerless I was to instigate it or ensure its duration. Whether love was going to arrive or not, I could not suspend my life in the expectation of its arrival. So, back in New York, I was single, but only very rarely would more than a few weeks pass without some kind of sexual encounter.

What even to call these relationships? Most of my friends had slept with one another and I had slept with many friends, too. Sometimes years separated sexual encounters. Things thought buried in the past would cycle around again, this time with less anxiety and greater clarity, in a fluid manner that occasionally imploded in horrible displays of pain or temporary insanity, but which for the most part functioned smoothly. We were souls flitting through limbo, piling up against one another like dried leaves, circling around, awaiting the messiah.

After a decade or so of living this way, with occasional suspensions for relationships that would first revive my belief in romantic love and its attendant structures of domesticity, and then once again fail and extinguish them, I started finding it difficult to revere the couple as the fundamental unit of society. I became a little ornery about it, to be honest: that couples paid lower taxes together, that they could afford better apartments, that there were so few structures of support to ease the raising of a child as a single person, that the divorced experience a sense of failure, that failed marriages are accompanied by so much logistical stress on top of the emotional difficulties. All this because we privilege a certain idea of love. The thought of the natural progression of couples, growing more and more insular, buying nicer and nicer furniture, shutting down the world, accruing things, relaxing into habit, scared me. As I grew older, I found it difficult to distinguish romantic love from other kinds of connections: the platonic love for the friends I did not want to have sex with, the euphoric chemical urges toward people I had sex with but did not love. Why was love between couples more exceptional? Because it attached itself to material objects, and to children? Because it ordered civilization? I probably would not have a baby without love, and buying a home seemed impossible for all kinds of reasons, but I could have sex. I had a body.

A few weeks before I decided I should go to California and watch people make porn, this revised outlook toward my prospects— that I did not need to see my life as an unanswered question, in permanent suspension for the answer of a relationship—resulted in deliberate immersion in New York's sexual fray. A relationship had ended, I kept running into old friends, I was internet dating; it was all happening. Then all of it imploded. First, I inadvertently caused someone emotional devastation. Second, I was told I might have been exposed to chlamydia. Third, I therefore might have given chlamydia to someone else. Fourth, and this really was the worst part, I received an email from an acquaintance that accused me of destroying her friend's relationship.

The next day, sitting in the packed waiting room of a public health clinic in Brooklyn for the un- and underinsured, I watched a clinician lecture her captive, half-asleep audience on how to put on a condom. We waited for our numbers to be called. In this cold, adult daylight, I examined what I had done. I thought about the suggestion, in the email from my acquaintance, that I "stop pantomiming thrills" and "starkly consider the real, human consequences of my real-life actions." A single person's need for human contact should not be underestimated. Surrounded on all sides by my imperfect fellow Americans, I thought many were also probably here for having broken some rules about prudent behavior. At the very least, I figured, most people in the room knew how to use condoms.

The clinician responded with equanimity to the occasional jeers from the crowd. She respectfully said no when a young woman asked if a female condom could be used "in the butt." After her lecture, while we continued to wait, public health videos played on loop on monitors mounted on the wall. They dated from the 1990s, and dramatized people with lives as disorderly as mine, made worse by the outdated blue jeans they wore. The brows of these imperfect people furrowed as they accepted diagnoses, admitted to affairs, and made confessional phone calls on giant cordless phones. Men picked each other up in stage-set bars with one or two extras in fake conversation over glass tumblers as generic music played in the background to signify a partylike atmosphere, like a porn that never gets to the sex. They later reflected on events in *Real World*–style confessional interviews. From our chairs, all facing forward in the same direction, awaiting our swabbing and bloodletting, we witnessed the narrative consequences. (One of the men has a girlfriend! And gonorrhea! Now he has to tell his girlfriend that he's bisexual and that he has gonorrhea!) The videos did not propose long-term committed relationships as a necessary condition of adulthood, just honesty. They did not recriminate. The New York City government had a technocratic view of sexuality.

The federal government had different expectations. Following the phone call I had looked up chlamydia on Google, which led me to the website for the Centers for Disease Control and Prevention. The government suggested that the best way to avoid chlamydia was "to abstain from vaginal, anal, and oral sex or to be in a long-term mutually monogamous relationship with a partner who has been tested and is known to be uninfected." Porn might be a fantasy, but at least it is not a fantasy that defies all interpretation. The suggestion of abstinence came with a more realistic reminder to use condoms. I usually used condoms, but this time I had not used a condom, so now I used antibiotics. When the lab results came back weeks after my visit to the Brooklyn clinic it turned out I did not have chlamydia. None of us had chlamydia.

Still, I didn't have sex again for nearly seven months.

The women at Kink came to porn for various reasons. Bobbi Starr, a twenty-nine-year-old who won *Adult Video News*'s Female Performer of the Year award in 2012, was raised in a Pentecostal Christian family in San Jose, California, and was homeschooled until middle school. She trained as a swimmer, competed in the Junior Olympics, and earned a scholarship to study music at San Jose State University. Although she had always considered herself sexually adventurous, she was twenty-two years old and working as a classical musician when she watched porn for the first time. Sitting down with a male friend, who was surprised at her lack of awareness, she watched several videos, including one called *Bong Water Butt Babes*. Very little needs to be said about this video except that the bedroom set is covered in sheets of plastic. Starr was mesmerized, applied for a job at Kink, enjoyed the bondage work, and within a year got an agent and moved to Los Angeles.

I asked her about pain. She recalled an "authentic BDSM experience" she had with a Kink dominatrix named Maitresse Madeline. "I had my head in the pit and she was flogging me and caning me and single-tailing me and doing all these really, really intense corporal activities with me and then she started tickling me and I just completely broke," she said. "At some point I came out and just cried on her chest and then she started crying." She described the experience as cathartic. "Through her dominating me and me subbing to her we had this really unique experience. I think that she and I are better partners, we have a better working relationship because of it, I think we have a better friendship because of it, I think it's easier for us to communicate."

One day, I watched Princess Donna have her makeup done for a shoot with the porn phenom James Deen. (James Deen is the first male porn star of the internet age to amass a vocally enthusiastic following among women. His popularity seems explicable not by his slight physique but by the way he gazes at his partners and whispers urgently in their ears—he manages to convey genuine, ardent desire. In real life he reminded me of the boy in the eighth grade who went around snapping girls' bra straps.) Another model wandered in, a lanky woman wearing hot pants and a bra that enclosed each breast in its own beribboned dirndl. A tattooed tendril of morning glories climbed the length of her very long leg. Donna introduced her to me as Rain DeGrey, and told me that she, Donna, had directed Rain's first shoot five years ago.

We went into a sort of lounge in the next room that had wall-to-wall carpeting and sofas. On one sofa a young woman with wet hair, wearing a gray bathrobe, barely out of adolescence if at all, sat painting her toenails a vivid sapphire. Her stage name was Katherine Cane. Rain DeGrey sat on a chair in front of me, applying sedimentary layers of Jergens bronzer as we talked.

Rain DeGrey described herself as a "24/7 lifestyle kinkster" and "pansexual." She told me that for years she had denied the fact that bondage and flogging turned her on. She knew that even in the Bay Area it was not something you could just tell people, that she would be judged for her preference.

"Finally you're like, 'Hey, it's okay if normies think I'm a freak,'" she told me. "And the day that I came out as kinky I felt fifty pounds lighter." One day, she was tied up in her local dungeon, the Citadel, getting flogged by a friend, when someone suggested she try to do some of this stuff professionally.

Her first shoot was for the Kink site Wired Pussy, which at the time was under Donna's direction. For the first scene they shot together, Donna stood over Rain DeGrey with a cattle prod. Donna told her if she moved the shoot would end.

"I don't know if you've ever tried to sit still on your hands and knees and not move while someone cattle prods you," said Rain.

Five years later, Rain DeGrey, who does not have a college degree, has bought herself a four-bedroom house with her earnings from Kink. She is very grateful to Donna for her counsel and support.

"I was actually on set for her *Bound Gangbangs* that she did, where she took on eight dicks." Rain stood up. She proceeded to demonstrate a play-by-play of everything that had happened, which ended with Donna on the floor, "this little, limp, sweaty, fucked rag doll. James Deen's just kicking her as hard as he can and she loves it."

Rain DeGrey returned to her chair and resumed her ceaseless application of self-tanning lotion. The chemical baby-powder scent of it wafted over us. I said nothing.

"I don't know if you've ever had cum in your eyes?" she asked.

"No," I said.

"That's like a super-duper hard limit for me," said Katherine Cane, shaking her head in dismay.

"It blinds you," said Rain.

"It stings horribly," said Katherine.

"Do you realize the dedication that takes?" asked Rain. "That's how committed she is."

Committed to what? To getting guys sitting in their studio apartments to jerk off to you for $30 a month? Not an insignificant accomplishment, but enacting a fantasy of violence for personal reasons was one thing; doing so for money was another. I held my tongue, and Rain continued.

"We're told our entire lives how fragile and delicate our bodies are," she said. She adopted a tone of mock concern. " 'Don't go out late at night, someone might mug you.' 'You've got to be careful, bad things will happen to you.' And there's a certain liberation in challenging your body, and getting beaten or distressed in some way and realizing you're actually tougher than you realized."

She looked over at Katherine, who had finished her pedicure and had her toes out in front of her. "Know what I mean?"

"Exactly," Katherine responded.

"It is a very empowering experience to realize you're not as fragile as you've been told your whole life," said Rain.

"But it's just as empowering to let yourself break down, in my opinion, because you go to a place that is so vulnerable and scary that a lot of people don't want to acknowledge it because it's your weakest point possible," said Katherine.

"The vulnerability," agreed Rain.

"Like you're safe to be your completely base, your most broken-down, crying, you can't even talk."

I didn't say anything, but here's what I thought: There was no great truth about the human condition that I would discover through celibacy.

•

Princess Donna makes a lot of porn: on average she does a couple of shoots a week, and she's been directing for eight years. Unsurprisingly, she sometimes gets bored and wants to try something different. When Princess Donna proposes a project, her boss, Kink CEO Peter Acworth, must approve it. Sometimes there are conflicts. Early in her career Donna proposed doing a series called *Dirty Girls*, which she described to me as "like girl–girl sex, but like rough sex, but not with, like, a dom/sub relationship but just like going at it, with like fisting and spitting and dunking people's heads in toilets, lots of anal, stuff like that." Acworth decided not to give the green light, but Kink thought the request was interesting enough that they posted an online debate between Donna and Acworth.

> Peter: So the fisting is really the most important thing to you.
> Donna: Clearly a lot of people like fisting and girls dominating each other and spitting on each other. It's still pretty extreme.
> Peter: I don't know how much for the male customers . . . you know for the male viewer I don't know how much fisting actually adds to it.
> Donna: I've had so many male viewers ask me for fisting. Like on Insex [Donna's previous employer] when I worked there they were always like, yeah, "fisting fisting fisting fisting." I think there's a lot of guys who think fisting is hot. I think you don't think it's hot.

Donna then proposed a lesbian gangbang site, which also did not pass, and then started experimenting with the tactics that

would go on to become *Public Disgrace*. She started while still filming for Wired Pussy, doing a series of shoots in New York where
she would wire up the performer and shock her under her clothes
in public places. These were popular, so Donna did a Wired
Pussy shoot where she invited members of the public. Eventually
she got the go-ahead to make *Public Disgrace* a recurring series.

I had insisted to myself that I wanted a long-term, committed
relationship, of the kind celebrated by the CDC and most happy
endings (of the narrative sort). I had decided that any other kind
of sexual relationship was a "waste of time." Having committed
myself to a limited worldview I saw not as limited but rather as
dignified and adult, I was able to distance myself from the very
question I had gone west to investigate—one that was turning
into a major question of my adult life: If love could not be relied
upon to provide an idyllic terminus to one's sexual history,
and naïve performative attempts at a noncommittal sex life resulted only in health scares and hurt feelings, how best to still
carry out a sexual existence?

In San Francisco, the right to be a lawfully wedded couple
was not taken for granted, but this question was still pursued
with a cheerful, pragmatic determination. It came accompanied
by Google spreadsheets, jargon, discussion groups, community
centers, dietary changes, and hallucinogens. San Francisco's
sexual vanguard might overuse words like "consciousness" and
"mindfulness," but the success of their politicization of sex had
repercussions that reached across the country. The mind-set
could sometimes seem grim, or at least all that talking kind
of dampened the feeling of spontaneity. But they meant it:
"Polyamory is a decolonizing force," one person explained to

me. "If you want to transform society, it includes our intimate relations."

I met with everyone I could. I met a group of Google employees in their early twenties, beneficiaries of the country's most elite educational institutions, now applying their sharp minds to the investigation of multiple concurrent relationships. They all did yoga, were extremely attractive, and accompanied their sexual experimentation with controlled consumption of psilocybin mushrooms and MDMA. They spoke of primary and secondary relationships, and described a world in which jealousy and possessiveness were the sins to overcome. I attended the cultlike meetings of a group of people who have devoted themselves to the female orgasm. After a "game" at one meeting, where I stood directly in front of a male stranger who looked in my eyes and repeatedly demanded answers to the question "WHAT DO YOU DESIRE?" for several minutes, I went home, drank almost a full bottle of wine, and wept.

I took the train across the bay to Oakland for a quiet dinner with several anarchists, to talk about anarchist ideas of sexuality. They all wore black and spoke of their decisions with a seriousness that my friends in New York might have derided. The anarchists cooked kale and dressed their pasta with cashew pesto from a jar. Oakland's soft summer warmth came as a welcome relief from San Francisco's miserable microclimates. We dined with the windows open and the evening sun flooding into an apartment lined with books.

In another part of Oakland I met with a radical queer activist who had a platonic partner, a sexual partner, and a rotating cast of people with whom she "played." (The really tough part, she admitted, was the scheduling.) I asked if her platonic partner was not just her roommate, or a friend, but she explained that it involved a deeper commitment: going to holidays at each other's family homes, caring for each other when sick—everything expected of a husband or wife except for the sex. It wasn't any easier than marriage, either: they were in couples' therapy.

In the past twenty years, in San Francisco especially, the celebration of choice over systems has coincided with the advent of new technology and an influx of money and entrepreneurs. One result has been the healthy, humane workplaces presented by Google, Facebook, Twitter, and the other Bay Area companies and their acceptance of individual expression in the corporate workplace and of families in all their forms. These changes made for a better working experience, but they also made it easier to complacently watch the flourishing of unfamiliar digital monopolies, to partake in the consumer delights produced by unprecedented inequality with a mistaken sense of political agency, and to pay to watch a woman get gangbanged on the internet with a clean conscience, because the producers used the rhetoric of the fair and just. The ghosts of the formerly ostracized, including the untimely dead, haunted the city. The consensus was that we honored the dead and the formerly oppressed by enacting the present utopia.

The wealth and the corporate culture that produced it defied the old models of good and bad. Google's motto, "Don't be evil," had been adopted across a range of industries. Evil, unfortunately, remained loosely defined: we would know it when we saw it. But all we saw on our computers were our photographs, our friends, our broken hearts, our writing, our search terms, our sexual fetishes.

The friendly blandness of Google's interface bestowed blessing on the words that passed through its sieve. On Google, all words were created equal, as all ways of choosing to live one's life were equal. Google blurred the distinction between normal and abnormal. The answers its algorithms harvested assured each person of the presence of the like-minded: no one need be alone with her aberrant desires, and no desires were aberrant.

Googling "tiny blonde tied up and ass fucked in public" will lead you to a video I saw recorded in San Francisco one April evening. In life, the sex I saw there did not upset me, but when I arrive at the video via Google I want to turn it off. The whole motivation of our new sexual paradigm might be to ensure that nobody will be alienated, but porn is a medium where the expression of one person's happy sex life can easily shade into another person's estrangement.

I watched how my friends became anxious when the subject of porn came up. Some people enjoyed watching it as part of a daily routine. Some felt enslaved by their desire for it. Others saw their real-world sexual experiences reduced to a corny mimicry of porn, and wished they could somehow return to a time when porn was less ubiquitous, or was just soft-focus tan people having relatively unadventurous sex by a swimming pool. Since more men than women watch porn, the occasional imbalance of knowledge caused distress all around and was perceived at times as an imbalance of power. Porn made people jealous, it hurt feelings, it made them worry about whether their partners were attracted to them, or to the kind of people they watched in porn, who might have a different hair color, skin color, or bra size. Because porn loves the taboo, it was also sometimes racist and misogynist.

It's tempting to think that life before internet porn was less complicated. There are sexual acts in porn that it would not occur to many people to attempt. We have more expectations now about what kind of sex to have, and how many people should be involved, and what to say, and what our bodies should look like, than we might have had at a time when less imagery of sex was available to us. But if the panoply of opportunity depicted in porn seems exaggerated, the possibilities are no less vast outside the internet. The only sexual expectation left to conform to is that love will guide us toward the life we want to live.

What if love fails us? Sexual freedom has now extended to people who never wanted to shake off the old institutions, except to the extent of showing solidarity with friends who did. I have not sought so much choice for myself, and when I found myself with no possibilities except total sexual freedom, I was unhappy. I understood that the San Franciscans' focus on intention—the pornographers were there by choice—marked the difference between my nihilism and their utopianism. When your life does not conform to an idea, and this failure makes you feel bad, throwing away the idea can make you feel better.

The panda gangbang took place deep in the basement of the Kink armory, where rivulets of the long-suffocated Mission Creek still trace a path between moisture-eaten columns, and the air hangs heavy with a stony dampness. On the day of the shoot, a glow of warm light punctured the center of a cavernously empty space. Bathed in this warm glow, a young woman named Ashli lay sleeping, impervious to the stygian immensity of her surroundings. Her sleek black hair was draped over her shoulder; a small silken bow of the palest pink pinned it away from her face into a girlish side part. The hem of her pink dotted-swiss dress had been carefully arranged to reveal a glimpse of her upper thigh through the gauze. On her feet she wore six-inch patent leather high heels embellished with lace. She slumbered on a bed of green leaves in a simulated bamboo forest beneath wraiths of mist produced by a Rosco Hazemaker puffing gently away beyond the circle of light, the sound of which seemed not to disturb her.

The panda bears approached her from behind. They waved their horrible paws and sniffed inquisitively. One stood over her nibbling at a frond of bamboo. Another gently stroked her hair.

"Now poke her or kick her," ordered Donna from the darkness. The pandas fell upon her. The sound of ripping gauze and a snapped bra strap broke the quiet. They fondled and slapped at her now-exposed breasts. She awoke and screamed in fear. "But I love pandas, I love pandas!" she cried out.

The panda shoot was a taxing one. Donna hovered around the bears, using metal clamps to keep the furry folds of their costumes from hiding the action. They took turns with Ashli without conferring much. Finally the pandas retired to their bamboo bowers and the shoot was over.

(2013)

THE INTELLECTUAL SITUATION
(THE HYPE CYCLE)

The Editors

By now everyone is familiar with *the hype cycle*. You know the drill: the ginned-up enthusiasm of publicists combines with word of mouth (and blog) to create so-called buzz. Articles appear, posing one of three questions. For the new artist: Is this the next big thing? For the established artist (or restaurateur): Will stratospheric expectations be met? For the figure whose stock is down: Can a comeback be staged? Then the release date arrives, or the premiere, or opening; at last the thing itself can contend with its reception. But, wait, now backlash surges alongside the ongoing hype. And understandably, too: it's not nice being force-fed even the tastiest food. But hold on a second, here comes the backlash-to-the-backlash . . .

One way of defending yourself against hype, with its incessant promise of the new, is to adopt a blasé attitude: whatever it is, you've seen it five times before. And it could be said that hype, too, is old hat. After all, the rapid boom and bust of stylistic trends and individual reputations has been going on for as long as there's been a bourgeoisie. Proust is clear on the purely formal character of bourgeois taste. Mme Vinteuil doesn't know when she promotes her favorite pianist whether she really likes how he plays; she just needs a name to bid up, to burnish her own. It's part of running a salon. Staying ahead of other people's taste is how you show that your taste reflects independent judgment, and not just your inevitable location on a chart where everybody's "favorite" music and books correspond exactly to his income level and education. Poor bourgeoisie! They try to show it's not all about the money, and next thing you know their relationship to culture is seized by the same buy low/sell high imperative. "I was listening to Franz Liszt before Pitchfork ever even *mentioned* him," they must have said to one another in what early adopters were already calling the belle epoque.

In the 1950s, America's first era of mass affluence, this bourgeois problem became a problem of mass taste. The art critic Harold Rosenberg referred to "the herd of independent minds." And yet the hype cycle has become faster and more domineering within living memory. Something started to happen in the late eighties, when those sumptuously oversized Vintage trade paperbacks (matte for International, glossy for Contemporary) began to appear, and Miramax had its first big hit with *sex, lies, and videotape* (1989). Both Vintage and Miramax succeeded in appealing to mass taste by flattering it as discriminating, classy, refined—and throwing in some sex: Vintage International's first reprint in the series was *Lolita*. Meanwhile, in 1990, Sonic Youth signed with Geffen Records. This last development was probably the most important, since hype-and-backlash today afflicts popular music most of all. Thus what was called "college rock" during the eighties became known as "indie rock" just when its independence from corporate sponsorship and mainstream taste was most in doubt.

Nirvana claimed to have signed with Geffen because Sonic

Youth led the way. And Nirvana were the first great victim-beneficiaries of the hype cycle (according to which all victims are beneficiaries, and all beneficiaries victims). By 1994 the phenomenon was sufficiently familiar that a documentary on the so-called Seattle scene could be called *HYPE!*

Do a LexisNexis search and you see the usage of "hype" growing pretty steadily from 1987 (when the database begins), and then suddenly jumping by 50 percent between 1996 and 1997. It's curious: just as a historic stock market bubble gets under way, the culture pages begin to bristle with a term that invariably suggests the overvaluation of would-be works of art. This suggests an unconscious understanding of the truth: the hype cycle replaces aesthetic judgment with something closer to speculative investment in securities.

Of course, there was never any such thing as truly independent aesthetic judgment. No cultural artifact ever appears out of nowhere, to be taken purely on its own terms; there is always what reception theory calls "a horizon of expectation." And who would want to possess independent aesthetic judgment anyway? It would mean you were impervious to the enthusiasms of your friends and the arguments of critics; it would mean that you were a total blockhead, ineducable, stupid. So the problem with hype is not that it prevents you from disappearing into a solipsistic reverie over the Monet coffee table book that—if you had to figure out aesthetics all by yourself—would be your favorite object in the universe. Nor is the problem of hype that things get overhyped. Inaccuracy is built into the notion: we say "overhyped" and "underhyped," we don't say "correctly hyped." Besides, as Harold Bloom has shown, it's possible to overhype even Shakespeare.

No, the problem with hype is that it transforms the *use value* of a would-be work of art into its *exchange value*. For in the middle (there's no end) of the hype cycle, the important thing is no longer what a song, movie, or book *does* to you. The big question is its relationship to its reputation. So instead of abandoning yourself to the artifact, you try to exploit inefficiencies in the reputation market. You can get in on the IPO of a new artist, and trumpet the virtues of the Arctic Monkeys before anyone else has heard of them: this is hype. Or you issue a "sell" recommendation on the overhyped Arctic Monkeys: this is backlash. But there are often steals to be found among recently unloaded assets: "Why's everybody hatin' on the Arctic Monkeys?" says the backlash-to-the-backlash. The sophisticated trader is buying, selling, and holding different reputations all at once; the trick in each case is to stay ahead of the market. And the rewards from this trade in reputations redound to your own reputation: even though the market (i.e., other people) dictates your every move, you seem to be a real individual thinking for yourself.

No one will admit to being the 100 percent tool whose taste is 100 percent social positioning. Probably no one *is* that person. But anyone sensitive to art is also sensitive enough to feel his true aesthetic judgments under continuous assault from publicists, bloggers, journalists, advertisers, reviewers, and assorted subcultural specimens. Hype-and-backlash overwhelm the artifacts that supposedly occasion them. At this point a basic inversion takes place. Never mind the moon; look at the finger pointing at the moon. Is it pointing too high, or too low? It makes you want to turn away from that overhyped satellite altogether. But there are perversities involved with ignoring hype, too. There's the person who demonstrates his individuality by patently false proclamations: "*The Sopranos* has nothing on *Friends*." Or the person who by promoting a revival of some "underrecognized" artist wastes his time and others': "J. F. Powers is the greatest American novelist of the twentieth century." Or you shut yourself off from the world and read only Dante. Some people even proclaim discrimination itself hopelessly snobbish, and just watch whatever's on.

Hype-and-backlash might seem simply to speed up and democratize the process of criticism; everybody's a cultural critic now. But this is mistaken. Real criticism of art sometimes attempts the correction of reputations (as when T. S. Eliot encouraged everyone to drop Shelley and pick up Donne), but that's not its main task. Real criticism can take the form of a monograph or a long review, or just a few words mumbled to a friend. In any case, it judges art with reference to the work's internal logic and generic and historical situation. And criticism, which relies on impressions and arguments, is always susceptible to opposite impressions and counterarguments.

Now look at the bullying charticles assembled by lifestyle journalists: the approval matrices and hype-and-backlash sine curves that now disfigure even such a once-proud publication as *Les Inrockuptibles*. Where the critic tells you what you *should* think—a proposition you're free to reject—the charticler tells you what you *do* think, already. The charticler takes his prejudices and dresses them up as sociology. You are told to get in line by someone pretending the line has already formed; the only comfort is when still others fall in behind you.

The strange thing is that we are not glad when other people like what we like, or vice versa. You'd think these would be happy occasions—as if the candidate you loved won the election. Hurrah! And indeed the excitement of buzz is a protopolitical phenomenon; the collective apprehension of the next big thing is a bit like being on a march. You learn, for example, from the recent Nirvana biography that the pleasure of hearing the band play a small club in 1990 owed a lot to the audience's feeling that they were going to be huge: "Everyone was going around saying, 'This is the band that's going to make it.'"

The really potent work of art implies a promise to change everything—surely the world can't bear the awareness induced by true art!—that's always renewed and always broken. What reveals the promise as broken is that everyone's now a fan of the art in question, and still the world goes on as before. Hence the backlash. And if ever the artifact recovers its uncontested popularity, it will be as the work of a "classic" director, writer, or band, which status implies it's no longer a threat to anyone. People can still feel, in the face of all evidence, that a new album might change everything; not so a box set. That's how it goes: hype, then backlash, then oblivion or the collector's edition. The hype cycle has become the emotional life of capitalism, an internalized stock market of aesthetic calls and puts. It testifies first to the power and then, almost as soon, to the impotence of mere culture. It's how the public expresses faith in itself, and a still more unshakable belief in its irredeemability: if we all like something, it can't be good. The extent of the hype cycle's corruption of our minds can be measured by the frequency with which you hear people complaining that environmentalism has grown so fashionable, so chic, so trendy. Try to imagine a similar complaint from another political era: "I was totally into democracy—before they extended the franchise. I was all about socialism—but it became so working class."

(2008)

THE FACE OF SEUNG-HUI CHO

Wesley Yang

The first school shooter of the 1990s was an Asian boy who played the violin. I laughed when I heard an account of the rampage from my friend Ethan Gooding, who had survived it. Ethan forgave me my reaction. I think he knew by then that most people, facing up to a real atrocity, as opposed to the hundreds they'd seen on TV, didn't know how to act.

Ethan had left New Providence High School in central New Jersey for the progressive utopia of Bard College at Simon's Rock in Great Barrington, Massachusetts. Simon's Rock was a school for high school juniors and seniors ready for college-level work, a refuge for brilliant misfits, wounded prodigies, and budding homosexuals. Ethan was a pretty bright kid, brighter than me, but mostly he was a budding homosexual. One day in gym class at New Providence, Ethan made a two-handed set shot from half-court using a kickball while dressed in buttercup-yellow short-shorts and earned the nickname "Maurice." This was not a reference to E. M. Forster's frank novel of gay love, but to Maurice Cheeks, the great Philadelphia 76ers point guard. The unintended resonance was savored by those few of us who could discern it. Ethan had a striking pre-Raphaelite pallor set off against flaming red cheeks and lips with the puckered epicene aspect that speaking the French language too young will impart to a decent American mouth. None of this in itself meant, necessarily, that he was going to become gay, but then—well, he was.

Gay-bashing was less of a hate crime back then and more of a patriotic duty, particularly in a race-segregated, heavily Catholic suburb like New Providence. At Youth and Government, the YMCA-sponsored mock legislature attended by suck-ups with Napoleon complexes, the "governor" from our school introduced a bill to "build an island of garbage off of the Jersey Shore" where we could "put all the homosexuals." We all chortled along, none more loudly than the closet cases in our midst. It was the kind of place you wanted to flee so badly that you trained yourself to forget the impulse.

But then there was a place called New York, only a half hour's drive away. We made our first anxious forays into New York City nightlife, Ethan and I and Jasper Chung, the other Korean kid from my high school (himself a governor of the mock legislature, and also a closet homosexual). We tried to get into the back room of the Limelight, where the real party was happening. "Try to look cute," Ethan told me, brushing my hair with a concerned, appraising look. Then he sucked in his cheeks, which I guess was his way of looking cute, or at least making his face less round. It would be more than a decade and a half before I learned what a smile could do for you (it is one way to hold at bay the world's cruelty), so I made a fish-eyed grimace in emulation of David Gahan of Depeche Mode. They never let us into the back room.

Those were the wild Peter Gatien days, when the place was still bristling with drugs and prostitution, most of which managed to pass us by. But we were assailed by a phalanx of sweaty, shirtless Long Island beefcake. Ethan would, to my frightened astonishment, meet other guys, and go off into a dark corner with them, and leave me to fend for myself, which I was not equipped to do. I'd get dehydrated and wear an anxious scowl. I would attempt some rudimentary sociological and semiotic reading of the scene that swirled all around me. I couldn't relax.

Not that I was myself homosexual. True, my heterosexuality was notional. I wasn't much to look at (skinny, acne-prone, brace-faced, bespectacled, and Asian), and inasmuch as I was ugly, I also had a bad personality. While Ethan was easing himself into same-sex experimentation, I was learning about the torments and transports of misanthropy. "That kid," I remember overhearing one of the baseball players say, "is a misfit." No one ever shoved my head in a locker, the way they did the one amber-tinted Afghani kid, or PJ, the big dumb sweet slow kid, and nobody ever pelted me with rocks, as they did Doug Urbano, who was fat and working class (his father was a truck driver, and sometimes, when he lectured us about the vital role that truck drivers play in the American economy—they really do, you know—he was jeered). But these judgments stayed with me.

Jasper once told me that I was "essentially unlovable." I've always held that observation close to my heart, turning to it often. It's true of some people—that there's no reason anyone should love or care about them, because they aren't appealing on the outside, and that once you dig into the real person beneath the shell (if, for some obscure if not actively perverse reason, you bother), you find the real inner ugliness. I knew lots of people like that— unloved because unlovable. Toward them I was always cold. Maybe I held them at arm's length to disguise from myself our shared predicament. And so, by trying to disguise something from yourself, you declare it to everyone else—because part of what makes a person unlovable is his inability to love.

One day we were hanging out with Ethan in Jasper's room over winter break. Ethan was telling us all about Simon's Rock, and—this might be an invented memory; it feels real, yet I can't rely on it; the very feeling of reality makes me distrust it—Ethan told me that I reminded him of this weird Asian guy at his school, whom he then proceeded to describe. Ethan, cherubic complexion notwithstanding, could actually be pretty mean. He was proud of his ability to wound with a well-chosen phrase coined in an instant, which is not to say that I didn't aspire to the same facility. It's just that he really had it. In any case, Wayne, my double, was an Asian boy ill at ease in the world, and he had a chip on his shoulder. His father had been an officer in the Taiwanese air force, and his mother had been a Suzuki-method violin teacher. For a time, Wayne had been among the best violinists in the world in his age group. He was headed along the familiar track of Asian American assimilation. By the time he arrived at Simon's Rock, he had other things to prove.

The gay guys liked to tease Wayne and intimate that he might be one of them. It was good-natured ribbing, gentle to the extent that it was not tinged with gay malice; and who could begrudge them their share of malice—a little or a lot—given the world they were entering? On top of everything else, an incurable illness spread by the kind of sex you were already having or else aching to have was killing off a whole generation of your predecessors. You could get a rise out of Wayne, and he deserved it: here he was at this place where people were finally free to be who they really were, and who he really was turned out to be someone who didn't want other people to be free to be who they were. He had fled Montana only to discover his continuing allegiance to its mores. And who knows, conceivably he was even a bit bi-curious. "How tough are you?" Wayne's friends used to ask him, egging him on. "I'm tough!" he would shout.

By now the story of Wayne Lo has been well told, though he has not become a figure of American legend. (His certified authentic "murderabilia" drawings were fetching just $7.50 on his website at the time his jailers shut it down.) On Monday, December 14, 1992, a package arrived for him in the mail from a North Carolina company called Classic Arms. It contained two hundred rounds of ammunition that Wayne had ordered using his mother's credit card. The school's dean held the package, and, after questioning Wayne about what was inside it (Wayne assured him that it was a Christmas gift), gave it back to him. Liberals! They'll hand over the ammunition that their enemies will use to kill them.

Ethan told his version of the story to Jasper and me over hamburgers at the A&W Restaurant at the Short Hills mall. Wayne had started hanging out with some other students who wanted to rebel against the orthodoxy of difference at Simon's Rock. They listened to Rush Limbaugh and joked about killing people. They were suspicious of Jews and blacks and homosexuals and . . . did they make an official exception for Asians? Wayne wrote a paper proposing a solution to the AIDS crisis: kill them all. He lacked the imagination to come up with the island of garbage disposal. Then, according to psychiatrists hired by his defense, Wayne was overtaken by a "somatic hallucination"—not heard, but directly experienced in his body—of God urging him to punish the sinners of Simon's Rock.

It was a more innocent time, in a way. The Berlin Wall had come down. Crime rates were beginning the historic fall they were to make during the 1990s. American soldiers were ensconced in the Persian Gulf, having recently kept the armies of Saddam Hussein from entering the land of the two holy places. People didn't know about school shooters back then. They still thought that Asian men were happy to be (as Ethan liked to call us) the Other White People. Or even, as many people were suggesting, the New Jews. And for the most part, Asian people were happy—and are. I mean, maybe they were nerds, maybe they were faceless drones, but did anybody know they were angry? What could they be angry about? They were getting rich with the rest of America—and reassuring everyone of our openness and our tolerance for everyone prepared to embrace the American dream.

Lo went around the campus with the Chinese-made SKS Carbine rifle that he bought in a neighboring town. He shot and killed two people and wounded four others. Had his rampage not ended prematurely when his rifle repeatedly jammed (cheap Chinese junk), he might have set a record that no one was going to best. Instead, he called the police and negotiated his surrender.

The perpetrator of the largest mass murder in American history was an Asian boy who wrote poems, short stories, a novel, and plays. I gazed at the sad blank mug of Seung-Hui Cho staring out at the world on CNN.com—the face-forward shot that was all the press had before they received Cho's multimedia manifesto, mailed on the day of the shootings, with its ghastly autoerotic glamour shots (Cho pointing gun at camera; Cho with a hammer; Cho pointing gun at his head). I felt, looking at the photo, a very personal revulsion. Millions of others reviled this person, but my own loathing was more intimate. Those lugubrious eyes, that elongated face behind wire-frame glasses: *He looks like me*, I thought.

This was another inappropriate reaction. But the photo leapt out at me at a funny time in my life. I had gone to New York five years earlier, to create a life for myself there. I had not created a life for myself there. I had wanted to find the emerging writers and thinkers of my generation. I had found the sycophants, careerists, and media parasites who were redefining mediocrity for the twenty-first century. I had wanted to remain true to myself as a writer, and also to succeed; I wanted to be courageous and merciless in defense of the downtrodden, and I wanted to be celebrated for it. This was a naïve and puerile desire, and one that could not be realized—at least not by me, not in this world. It could not be done without a facility (and a taste) for ingratiation that I lacked. It could not be done without first occupying a position of strength and privilege that I did not command—because, as Jesus said, to him who hath, more will be given; nor without being enterprising and calculating in a way that I wasn't—because, as Jesus went on to say, to him who hath not, even that which he hath will be taken from him. It seemed to me that every kind of life, and even the extinction of life, was preferable to the one that I was living, which is not to say I had the strength either to change my life, or to end it.

And then to be confronted by that face. Because physiognomy is a powerful thing. It establishes identification and aversion, and all the more so in an age that is officially color-blind. Such impulses operate beneath the gaze of the supervisory intelligence, at a visceral level that may be the most honest part of us. You see a face that looks like yours. You know that there's an existential knowledge you have in common with that face. Both of you know what it's like to have a cultural code superimposed atop your face, and if it's a code that abashes, nullifies, and unmans you, then you confront every visible reflection of that code with a feeling of mingled curiosity and wariness. When I'm out by myself in the city—at the movies or at a restaurant—I'll often see other Asian men out by themselves in the city. We can't even look at each other for the strange vertigo we induce in one another.

Let's talk about legible faces. You know those short, brown-toned South American immigrants that pick your fruit, slaughter your meat, and bus your tables? Would you—a respectable person with a middle-class upbringing—ever consider going on a date with one of them? It's a rude question, because it affects to inquire into what everyone gets to know at the cost of forever leaving it unspoken. But if you were to put your unspoken thoughts into words, they might sound something like this: Not only are these people busing the tables, slaughtering the meat, and picking the fruit, they are the descendants of the people who bused the tables, slaughtered the meat, and picked the fruit of the Aztecs and Incas. The Spanish colonizers slaughtered or mixed their own blood with the princes, priests, scholars, artisans, warriors, and beautiful women of the indigenous Americas, leaving untouched a class of Morlocks bred for good-natured servility and thus now tailor-made to the demands of an increasingly feudal postindustrial America. That's, by the way, part of the emotional undertow of the immigration debate, the thing that makes an honest appraisal of the issue impossible, because you can never put anything right without first admitting you're in the wrong.

So: Seung-Hui Cho's face. A perfectly unremarkable Korean face—beady-eyed, brown-toned, a small plump-lipped mouth, eyebrows high off his eyelids, with crooked glasses perched on his nose. It's not an ugly face, exactly; it's not a badly made face.

It's just a face that has nothing to do with the desires of women in this country. It's a face belonging to a person whom, if he were emailing you or sending you instant messages and you were a normal, happy, healthy American girl at an upper-second-tier American university—and that's what Cho was doing in the fall of 2005, emailing and writing instant messages to girls—you would consider reporting to campus security. Which is what they did, the girls who were contacted by Cho.

First, you imagine, they tried to dissuade him in the usual way. You try to be polite, but also to suggest that you'd actually prefer that your correspondent, if he could, you know, maybe, oh, I don't know, *disappear from your life forever? How about that?*—and you had to do this subtly enough not to implicate yourself in anything damaging to your own self-image as a nice person, but then not so subtly that your correspondent would miss the point. When Cho missed the point, the girls had to call the campus police. They did not want him arrested, and they did not press charges. They just had to make clear that while Cho thought he was having one kind of encounter (a potentially romantic one), he was in fact having another kind of encounter (a potentially criminal one), and to show him that the state would intervene on their behalf if he couldn't come to terms with this reality. And so, the police didn't press any charges, but they did have a man-to-man talk with Cho, and conveyed to him the message that it would be better if he cut it out.

Seung-Hui Cho's is the kind of face for which the appropriate response to an expression of longing or need involves armed guards. I am not questioning the choices that these girls made; I am affirming those choices. But I'm talking about the Cho that existed before anyone was killed by him—the one who showed proficiency in beer pong at the one fraternity party his room-mates took him to, and who told his roommates he had a girl-friend named Jelly who was a supermodel from outer space; who called one of his roommates to tell him that he had been on va-cation with Vladimir Putin; and who emailed Lucinda Roy, di-rector of the creative writing program, seeking guidance about how to submit his novel to publishers. "My novel is relatively short," he wrote. "It's sort of like *Tom Sawyer*, except that it's really silly or pathetic, depending on how you look at it."

Of course, there are a lot of things that Cho might have done to change his social fortunes that he declined to do. Either out of incompetence, stubbornness, or plain old bat-shit craziness, Cho missed many boats that might have ferried him away from his dark fate. For one, he could have dressed a little bit better. He might have tried to do something with his hair. Being a little less bat-shit crazy couldn't have hurt. Above all, he could have cultivated his taste in music. He was "obsessed with download-ing music from the Internet," the press reported, putting a sinis-ter cast on something that everyone of a certain age does. But the song he continually played on his laptop, driving his roommates to distraction, wasn't some nihilistic rhapsody of wasted youth. It wasn't Trent Reznor of Nine Inch Nails saying he wanted to fuck you like an animal, and it wasn't the thick lugubrious whine of James Hetfield of Metallica declaring that what he'd felt, and what he'd known, never shone through in what he'd shown.

No, it was the cruddiest, most generic grunge-rock anthem of the nineties, Collective Soul's "Shine." "Shine" came out in 1994, and you only had to hear the first minute to know that whatever was truly unyielding about the music Nirvana spawned by breaking punk into the mainstream was already finished. The song cynically mouths "life-affirming" clichés noxious to the spirit of punk rock, but then, these are not, given the situation, without their own pathos. You could picture the Cho who stalked around campus not saying a word to anyone, even when a classmate offered him money to speak, coming home in silence to listen to these lyrics repeat in an infinite loop on his laptop, and even, one day, to write them on his wall:

> Teach me how to speak
> Teach me how to share
> Teach me where to go
> Tell me will love be there (love be there)

> Whoa-oh-oh-oh, heaven let your light shine down.

"You were the single biggest dork school shooter of all time," opined one internet chat board participant, and it was hard to disagree. Cho was so disaffected that he couldn't even get the symbols of disaffection right. In the fall of 2005, when he made the mistake of instant-messaging girls, Cho was also attending Nikki Giovanni's large creative writing class. He would wear reflector glasses with a baseball cap obscuring his face. Giovanni, who believed that openness was vital to the goals of the class, stood by his desk at the beginning of each session to make him take off the disguise. He later began showing up with a scarf wrapped around his head, "Bedouin-style," as Giovanni put it. When the attendance sheet was passed around, he signed his name as a question mark.

The class set Cho off, somehow—maybe because he had enrolled in the hope that his genius would be recognized, and it was not recognized. He began snapping pictures of female classmates with his cell phone camera from underneath his desk. Eventually, many of the seventy students enrolled in the class stopped coming. That's when Giovanni went to Lucinda Roy and insisted that Cho be barred from her workshop. She refused, in the words of one article about it, to be "bullied" by Cho.

"He was writing, just weird things," Giovanni told *The New York Times*. "I don't know if I'm allowed to say what he was writing about . . . He was writing poetry, it was terrible, it was not like poetry, it was intimidating."

Giovanni's personal website has a list of all her honors and awards and another page for all the honorary degrees she has earned—nineteen since 1972—and a brief biography that identifies her as "a world-renowned poet, writer, commentator, activist, and educator," whose "outspokenness, in her writing and in lectures, has brought the eyes of the world upon her." Oprah Winfrey has named her one of her twenty-five living legends. "We are sad today, and we will be sad for quite a while," the sixty-three-year-old eminence told the convocation to mourn Seung-Hui Cho's victims. "We are not moving on, we are embracing our mourning."

It's a perfectly consistent picture: Giovanni the winner of awards, and Giovanni the wise and grandmotherly presence on *Oprah*. But if you knew more about the writing of Nikki Giovanni, you couldn't help but wonder two things. What would the Nikki Giovanni of 2007 have made of a poem published by the Nikki Giovanni of 1968, and what would the Nikki Giovanni of 1968 have made of the Nikki Giovanni of the present? The Nikki Giovanni of 1968 wrote this:

Nigger
Can you kill
Can you kill

Can a nigger kill
Can a nigger kill a honkie
Can a nigger kill the Man
Can you kill nigger
Huh? nigger can you
kill
Do you know how to draw blood
Can you poison
Can you stab-a-Jew
Can you kill huh? nigger
Can you kill

Back then Giovanni was writing about a race war that seemed like it really might break out at home, even as the country was fighting what she saw as an imperialist war in Vietnam. Black militancy was something that many people admired, and many more felt sympathy toward, given the brutal history of enslavement, rape, terrorism, disenfranchisement, lynching, and segregation that blacks had endured in this country. And so you wonder what would have happened if, for instance, Cho's poems (and thoughts) had found a way to connect his pain to his ethnic identity. Would Giovanni have been less intimidated if she could have understood Cho as an aggrieved Asian man, instead of an aggrieved man who happened to be Asian? Or if he were black and wrote the way he did? Or if he were Palestinian and managed to tie his violent grievances to a real political conflict existing in the world? (Can you bomb-a-Jew?) Giovanni knows black rage, and she knows the source of women's bitterness. We all do. We know gay pride. We know, in short, identity politics, which, when it isn't acting as a violent outlet for the narcissism of the age, can serve as its antidote, binding people into imagined collectivities capable of taking action to secure their interests and assert their personhood.

Cho did not think of himself as Asian; he did not think of himself ethnically at all. He was a pimply friendless suburban teenager whom no woman would want to have sex with: that's what he was. And it turned out that in his imagination he was a warrior on behalf of every lonely invisible human being in America. This was his ghastly, insane mistake. This is what we learned from the speech Cho gave in the video he mailed to NBC News. For Cho, the cause to fight for is "the dorky kid that [you] publicly humiliated and spat on," whom you treated like "a filthy street dog" and an "ugly, little, retarded, low-life kid"—not just Cho, not just his solitary narcissistic frenzy, but also that of his "children," his "brothers and sisters"—an imagined community of losers who would leave behind their status as outcasts from the American consensus and attain the dignity of warriors—by killing innocent civilians.

Cho enclosed his speech, too, in the NBC packet, as "writings."

You had everything you wanted.
Your Mercedes wasn't enough,
you brats,
your golden necklaces weren't enough,
you snobs,
your trust fund wasn't enough . . .

You have vandalized my heart,
raped my soul
and torched my conscience.
You thought it was one pathetic, bored life you were
    extinguishing.

I die like Jesus Christ,
    to inspire generations of the weak and defenseless people.

Cho imagines the one thing that can never exist—the coming to consciousness and the joining in solidarity of the modern class of losers. Though his soft Asian face could only have been a hindrance to him, Cho did not perceive his pain as stemming from being Asian: he did not perceive himself in a world of identity politics, of groups and fragments of groups, of groups oppressing and fighting other groups. Cho's world is a world of individually determined fortunes, of winners and losers in the marketplace of status, cash, and expression. Cho sees a system of social competition that renders some people absolutely immiserated while others grow obscenely rich.

When I was at Rutgers I knew a guy named Samuel Goldfarb. Samuel was prematurely middle-aged, not just in his dimensions, which were bloated, and not just in his complexion, which was pale but flushed with the exertion of holding himself upright—sweat would dapple the groove between his upper lip and nose—but above all in something he exuded, which was a pheromone of loneliness and hostility. Samuel had gone off to Reed College, and, after a couple of years of feeling alienated in that liberal utopia, he had returned east. Samuel was one of the students at Rutgers who was clearly more intellectually sophisticated than I. He knew more, he had read more, and it showed. He was the kind of nominal left-winger who admired the works of Carl Schmitt before many others had gotten onto that trend, and he knew all about the Frankfurt School, and he was already jaded about the postmodernists when others were still enraptured by the discov-

ery of them. In addition to being the kind of leftist who read a
Nazi legal theorist to be contrarian, Samuel was also the kind of
aspiring academic so contemptuous of the postmodern academy
that he was likely to go into investment banking and make pots
of money while jeering at the rest of humanity, because that was
so much more punk rock than any other alternative to it. He identified his "lifestyle"—and, of course, he put that word into derisive
quote marks when he used it—as "indie rock," but Samuel's irony
had extra bite to it, real cruelty and rancor, that was tonally off-
kilter for the indie rock scene, which, as it manifested itself at
Rutgers, was taciturn to the point of autism, passive-aggressive,
and anti-intellectual, but far too cool and subdued for the exertions of overt cruelty.

You saw a look of sadness and yearning in Samuel's face when
he had subsided from one of his misanthropic tirades—there was
no limit to the scorn he heaped on the intellectual pretensions of
others—and it put you on guard against him. What you sensed
about him was that his abiding rage was closely linked to the
fact that he was fat and ugly in a uniquely unappealing way, and
that this, compounded with his unappealing rage, made him
the sort of person that no woman would ever want to touch. He
seemed arrayed in that wild rancor that sexual frustration can
bestow on a man, and everything about his persona—his corus-
cating irony, his unbelievable intellectual snobbery—seemed a
way to channel and thus defend himself against this consuming
bitterness. He was ugly on the outside, and once you got past
that you found the true ugliness on the inside.

And then below that ugliness you found a vulnerable person
who desperately needed to be seen and touched and known as a
human phenomenon. And above all, you wanted nothing to do
with that, because once you touched the source of his loneliness,

there would be no end to it, and even if you took it upon yourself to appease this unappeasable need, he would eventually decide to revenge himself against a world that had held him at bay, and there would be no better target for this revenge than you, precisely because you were the person who'd dared to draw the nearest. This is what you felt instantly, without having to put it into words (it's what I felt, anyway, though it might have been pure projection), the moment you met Samuel. For all that he could be amusing to talk to, and for all that he was visibly a nice guy despite all I've just said, you were careful to keep your distance.

Samuel used to complain about declining academic standards. He said that without much work he was acing all of his classes. This was a way of exalting himself slightly while mostly denigrating others, which made it an exemplary statement of his, but it was also a suspect statement, since no one had asked. One day, while I was in the history department's front office, I noticed a plastic crate full of hanging folders. In one of those folders, I found my own academic transcript in its entirety. Then I looked for Samuel's. Like mine, it was riddled with Ds and Fs. And while what Samuel had said about academic standards and his own aptitude was surely true, it was also true that he had lied—and I suppose I understand why. If your only claim to self-respect was your intellectual superiority, and you had more or less flunked out of Reed College because of the crushing loneliness and depression you encountered once you realized that liberal utopia wasn't going to embrace you as it did the willowy, stylish high school outcasts who surrounded you—and if your grades weren't much better at Rutgers (a pathetic public university, even though you hated Reed more), you might be forced to lie about those grades, because they were the public face of all you had left—your intellectual superiority—and even after all you'd endured, or maybe because of it, your public face still mattered. Unaware that the contrary evidence was there for anyone to check (it should not have been) or that a person inclined to check it existed (I should not have looked), you would assume that you could tell this lie without being caught.

I mentioned this incident to a mutual acquaintance, who proceeded to tell Samuel, who accused me of making up lies about him, and turned me into the great enemy of his life—he was clearly looking for one—which was too bad and a little disconcerting, because, as I explained to him, he and his grades had never meant anything to me. And yet I had only read two transcripts, his and mine, mostly because I suspected, correctly, that he was telling lies. Samuel had been wronged by me, and it would have been right for me to apologize, but I had some hostility of my own, so instead I told him that he was ugly on the outside, but even uglier on the inside, and that he meant nothing to me, and his enmity counted for nothing to me. And this was true. I had recognized him as a person with whom I had some mutual understanding—overlapping interests and, most of all, overlapping pretensions—but I never wanted him as a friend. The image this whole affair calls up is the scene in *Born on the Fourth of July* in which two paraplegics in wheelchairs start wrestling around in anger, and then tip each other into a ditch by the side of the road, and fall out of their wheelchairs, and roll around on the ground in the dirt, from which they are unable to lift themselves.

I saw Samuel Goldfarb at a coffee shop near Union Square about a year ago. He was chatting up the Eastern European counter girls. You could tell that he was a regular. He had put on a lot of weight and lost more of his hair, and his skin had lost none of its sebaceous excess. He had really become, at thirty-two or thirty-three, the ruined middle-aged man that he already seemed on the cusp of becoming in youth. He seemed like a nice, harmless guy, but then you could still discern loneliness and sexual desperation clinging to him, though it had lost some of its virulence. I was glad to see his resignation. And I knew that he was probably very rich, and I felt weirdly good on his behalf to know that if he had to be lonely, if he had to be one of the millions of sexually null men in America—and for all I knew, he could have studied *The Game* and become a world-class seducer in the intervening years, though it seemed unlikely ("Hey, guys—quick question for you—do you believe in magic spells?"—I couldn't see it)—at least he could be rich.

Lack of money had taught me the value of money. I had learned that when I didn't have it—and by this I mean, really having none of it, as in, like, nothing, which was most of the time—I would become extremely unhappy. And that when I did have it, even a little bit of it, which was rare, my despondency was assuaged, and I became like a dry and dwindling houseplant that would rally and surge up from out of its dolor when watered. I deduced from this pattern that what I needed to do was find an occupation that would pay me a salary—it was amazing to think how long I had gone without one—and then I would have money all the time, and then I would be, if not happy, at least okay. And to come to this realization seemed a little bit like the moment in *1984* when Winston Smith decides that he loves Big Brother, but then even more than that it just felt like growing up and it felt like life. And so I figured that Samuel was fine; and while I was very far from fine, I thought someday I'd catch on to something and I'd eventually be fine, too.

And maybe I still will, at that.

•

A friend of mine wrote a book about online dating. She talked to hundreds of people about their experiences. Online, you become the person you've always known yourself to be, deep down. Online, you're explicit about the fact that you are paying for a service, and you're explicit about the fact that what you're paying for is to get what you really want, and what you're paying for is the ability to remove that annoying bit of residual romantic non-sense that gets us into annoying situations in life where we have to face up to the fact that we are rational profit maximizers in nothing so much as those intimate areas where we pretend to be otherwise. And so, people on the dating sites disclose what they really want, and also what they really don't want.

This friend talked to one man from Maryland who put up his profile on Match.com one night a few years back. This man had good reason to think he would do well on the site. He made more than $150,000 a year; he was white; he was over six feet tall. The next morning, he woke up and checked his account. Over the course of the previous night, he had gotten many responses. How many responses had he gotten? How well could he expect to do, being a man able to check off, without lying, boxes that certified that he made more than $150,000 a year, that he was six feet four inches tall, and that he was white? How well do you think he was going to do on that site where people disclosed what they really wanted out of life and also what they really didn't want?

He had gotten six thousand responses in one night. The fact was that if there was something intriguing or beautiful about that man—and there's something beautiful about us all, if you look deeply enough—someone was going to take the trouble to find it out, and they'd love him for that thing, not because he was six feet four inches tall, and not because he made more than $150,000 a year. You'd find out about his love of truth and poetry, to the extent that it existed, or at least his ability to make you laugh, or his own ability to laugh at things that made you laugh, too—things on TV. You could watch TV together. Because the thing you wanted to do was to find true love and have that true love coincide with everything else that you wanted from life, so that you could have all the benefits of one kind of ease, and all the moral credit that others had to win by forgoing that kind of ease (but you could have it all, so why not?), and so you were going to put yourself in a position to do that. And you weren't going to answer the ads of anyone with beady, lugubrious eyes in a forlorn, brown-tinted face, and if that person wrote you a message, you weren't going to write him back, and you'd probably even, if it seemed like it was necessary, block all further emails from that person. And you'd be right to do that. You'd be behaving in the way that any rational person in your situation would behave. We all agree that the rational thing to do is to shut every trace of that person's existence out of your view. The question, though, is—what if it's not you shutting out the losers? What if you're the loser whom everyone is shutting out? Of course, every loser is shutting out an even more wretched loser. But what if, as far as you know, you're the lowest person at the low end of this hierarchy? What is your rational move then?

You wake to find yourself one of the disadvantaged of the fully liberated sexual marketplace. If you are a woman, maybe you notice that men have a habit of using and discarding you, pleading their own inconstancy and premature emotional debauchery as a sop to your wounded feelings. If you are a man, maybe you notice that the women who have been used and discarded by other, more highly valued men are happy to restore (for a while) their own broken self-esteem by stepping on you while you are prone, and reminding you that even a society of outcasts has its hierarchies. Indeed, these hierarchies are policed all the more ruthlessly the closer to the bottom you go.

For these people, we have nothing but options. Therapy, selective serotonin reuptake inhibitors, alcoholism, drug addiction, pornography, training in mixed martial arts, mail-order brides from former Soviet republics, sex tours in Southeast Asia, prostitution, video-game consoles, protein shakes and weight-lifting regimens, New Age medicine, obsession with pets or home furnishings, the recovery movement—all of which are modes of survival as opposed to forms of life. Each of these options compensates for a thing, love, that no person can flourish without, and each, in a different way, offers an endlessly deferred resolution to a conundrum that is effectively irresolvable. You could even say that our culture feeds off the plight of the poor in spirit in order to create new dependencies. You might even dare to say that an undernourished human soul—desperate and flailing, prone to seeking voluntary slavery in the midst of freedom and prosperity—is so conducive to the creation of new markets that it is itself the indispensable product of our culture and our time, at once its precondition and its goal.

There's a familiar narrative we all know about high school losers. It's the narrative of smart sitcoms and even edgy indie films. The high school loser grows up, fills out, goes to Brown or RISD, and becomes the ideal guy for every smart, sensitive, quirky-but-cute girl with glasses (who is, in turn, the female version of the loser made good). The traits that hindered him (or her) in one phase of life turn out to be a blessing in another, more enlightened phase, or else get cast aside. For many people, this is an accurate description of their experience—it is the experience of the writers and producers of these stories.

In the indie film version of Seung-Hui Cho's life, the escort Cho hired a few weeks before his massacre wouldn't have danced for him for fifteen minutes in a motel room and then shoved him away when he tried to touch her. Not every one of the girls he tried to talk to would have recoiled in horror from him. Something would have happened in that film to remind him, and us, of his incipient humanity—that horribly menaced and misshapen thing. He would have found a good-hearted person who had perhaps been touched in some way by the same hysteria—and don't we all know something about it?—that had consumed Cho's soul. And this good-hearted girl or boy would have known how to forgive Cho for what he couldn't forgive himself—the unbearable, all-consuming shame of being ugly, weak, sick, poor, clumsy, and ungifted.

We know that Cho had dreamt of this indie film ending. He had been dreaming of it for a long time. In the spring semester of 2006, he wrote a story about a boy estranged from his classmates: "Everyone is smiling and laughing as if they're in heaven-on-earth, something magical and enchanting about all the people's intrinsic nature that Bud will never experience." But eventually the boy meets a "Gothic Girl," to whom he breaks down and confesses, "I'm nothing. I'm a loser. I can't do anything. I was going to kill every god damn person in this damn school, swear to god I was, but I . . . couldn't. I just couldn't."

Cho's short story about the Gothic Girl should have ended, but did not, with this declaration. Instead, he and the girl steal a car and drive to her house, where she retrieves "a .8 caliber automatic rifle and a M16 machine gun," and the story concludes when she tells the narrator, "You and me. We can fight to claim our deserving throne."

In real life, there was no Gothic Girl, no *me* to Cho's *you*, no other willing actors—whether sympathetic, heroic, or equally violently deranged—to populate the self-made movie of his life.

Having failed to make it as a novelist—he really did send a book proposal to a New York publisher—Cho decided to make a film. This was a familiar trajectory, with a twist. He was going to collaborate with all the major television networks on it. In the days before his date with a self-appointed destiny, Cho was spotted working out in the college gym. He wanted his scrawny arms and chest to appear more credibly menacing than they were. How many of those men working their arms to the point of exhaustion were driven by the vain notion that they could improve their sexual prospects in the process? Cho had no such illusions. He was preparing a spectacle for the world to witness on TV, and he needed to look the part.

(2008)

RISE OF THE NEURONOVEL

Marco Roth

The last dozen years or so have seen the emergence of a new strain within the Anglo-American novel. What has been variously referred to as the novel of consciousness or the psychological or confessional novel—the novel, at any rate, about the workings of a mind—has transformed itself into *the neurological novel*, wherein the mind becomes the brain. Since 1997, readers have encountered, in rough chronological order, Ian McEwan's *Enduring Love* (de Clérambault's syndrome, complete with an appended case history by a fictional "presiding psychiatrist" and a useful bibliography); Jonathan Lethem's *Motherless Brooklyn* (Tourette's syndrome); Mark Haddon's *The Curious Incident of the Dog in the Night-Time* (autism); Richard Powers's *The Echo Maker* (facial agnosia, Capgras syndrome); McEwan again with *Saturday* (Huntington's disease, as diagnosed by the neurosurgeon protagonist); *Atmospheric Disturbances* (Capgras syndrome again) by a medical school graduate, Rivka Galchen; and John Wray's *Lowboy* (paranoid schizophrenia). And these are just a selection of recently published titles in "literary fiction." There are also many recent genre novels, mostly thrillers, of amnesia, bipolar disorder, and multiple personality disorder. As young writers in Balzac walk around Paris pitching historical novels with titles like *The Archer of Charles IX*, in imitation of Walter Scott, today an aspiring novelist might seek his subject matter in a neglected corner or along some new frontier of neurology.

What makes so many writers try their hands and brains at the neuronovel? At the most obvious level, the trend follows a cultural (and, in psychology proper, a disciplinary) shift away from environmental and relational theories of personality back to the study of brains themselves, as the source of who we are. This cultural sea change probably began with the exhaustion of "the linguistic turn" in the humanities, in the 1980s, and with the discredit psychoanalysis suffered, around the same time, from revelations that Freud had discounted some credible claims of sexual abuse among his patients. Those philosophers of mind who had always been opposed to trendy French poststructuralism or old-fashioned Freudianism, and the mutability of personality these implied, put forth strong claims for the persistence of innate ideas and unalterable structures. And in neuroscience such changes as the mind did endure were analyzed in terms of chemistry. By the early nineties, psychoanalysis—whether of a Lacanian and therefore linguistic variety, or a Freudian and drive-oriented kind—was generally considered bankrupt, not to mention far less effective and more expensive than the psychiatric drugs (like Prozac) that began to flow through the general population's bloodstream. The new reductionism of mind to brain, eagerly taken up by the press—especially *The New York Times* in its Science pages—had two main properties: it explained proximate causes of mental function in terms of neurochemistry, and ultimate causes in terms of evolution and heredity.

Many scientists and philosophers acknowledge that they understand more about how damaged brains work—or, rather, don't work—than about the neurochemistry of the normal brain. And yet, in its popular journalistic form, the new reductionism can or will soon describe all human behavior, from warfare to soul making. The British physician, philosopher, and neuro-skeptic Raymond Tallis has summarized the doctrine: "A convergence of evolutionary theory, neuroscience, and other biological disciplines has led countless thinkers to claim that we are best understood as organisms whose entire panoply of behavior is directly or indirectly related to organic survival."

New scientific discoveries may be less important for the change in the novel than the triumphal march of scientific advancement recounted in books like Daniel Dennett's *Consciousness Explained* (1991) and Steven Pinker's *How the Mind Works* (1997). Culture-shaping institutions like the *Times* can't easily respond to Dennett's and Pinker's arguments and analyses, which the average journalist remains unprepared to evaluate, but it has been impossible to ignore their superbly confident rhetoric. Here is the philosopher Dennett:

> Fiery gods driving golden chariots across the skies are simpleminded comic-book fare compared to the ravishing strangeness of contemporary cosmology, and the recursive intricacies of the reproductive machinery of DNA make [Bergson's] élan vital about as interesting as Superman's dread kryptonite. When we understand consciousness— when there is no more mystery—consciousness will be different, but there will still be beauty, and more room than ever for awe.

The program was to develop a full redescription of consciousness in scientific terms. A corollary program in philosophy of mind was the "eliminativism" of Paul and Patricia Churchland, who dismiss "folk psychological" terms (such as happiness, sadness, excitement, anxiety, et cetera) as constituting a hopelessly and indeed meaninglessly imprecise vocabulary without bearing on the actual activities of the brain.

In 1949, Lionel Trilling could write, "A specter haunts our culture—it is that people will eventually be unable to say, 'They fell in love and married,' let alone understand the language of *Romeo and Juliet*, but will as a matter of course say, 'Their libidinal impulses being reciprocal, they activated their individual erotic drives and integrated them within the same frame of reference.'" The joke is now quaint; the possibility of an orthodox everyday Freudianism turned out to be no more ultimately threatening than the other specter Trilling was alluding to. Today people, or a certain class of university-educated ones, are likelier to read books like *The Female Brain* than to consult any psychoanalytic writer on female sexuality, and to send emails like this almost serious one I received from a friend:

> In advance of your date in Brooklyn, there are one or two things to know and one or two things to get ready to do! First we should hope that N is postmenstrual and therefore on an estrogen up. Day twelve of the menstrual cycle would be best. Testosterone will be kicking in with a bit of androgen on top of the estrogen, making N somewhat aggressively sexual. Of course she will also be speeding toward ovulation and will be at her verbal and intuitive best. So, use a condom and do a lot of looking in her eyes (girls are prewired at birth for mutual gazing, unlike boys). Give her a lot of face. Her capacity to read emotions and her need to evaluate the facial expressions of those around her

will be at a peak (setting in motion circuits established during estrogen flushes in utero and the massive estrogen marination which took place during infantile puberty and hyped-up during adolescence).

So: smile!

In this language, one now needs more words than ever to say "They fell in love," and we haven't even got past the first minute of the first date.

This is a problem: What to do after psychoanalysis, and before Dennett's mystery-banishing total explanation of consciousness has arrived? Of course, it's not as if midcentury novels were case studies written in Freudian jargon. But an era in which analysis, rather than neurology, was taken to offer the most authoritative account of personality was an era more friendly to the informal psychological explorations of novelists. After all, introspection of the self and observation of others were Freud's main tools—as they remain the novelist's.

The change we are discussing here was arrestingly summarized in one of the rare recent novels of psychoanalysis, Daniel Menaker's *The Treatment* (set in the early 1980s but published in 1998). In our new age—or so complains Dr. Morales, the oracular shrink in Menaker's novel—"Treatment will no longer consist of explorations of significance and spirit and mystery, but quick fixes, twelve steps, behavioral adjustment, and pills." Morales's elegy for the old ways, delivered in a comic Cuban accent, begins with a claim to be the last Freudian,

the last of a line that estretches from Moses to Aristotle through Cicero to our good Lord Jesus Christ and Aquinas and Maimonides and Shakespeare and Montaigne and finally to Freud and then to me. A line of fascination with and respect for the dignity, the very concept of the human soul . . . Freud will die, as Marx will die. And all that will be left of those nineteenth-century giants of intellect will be the unpityingly neutral doctrines of Sharles Darwin. Darwin is the man who must bear the responsibility for the end of meaning.

Ian McEwan's *Enduring Love* (1997) effectively inaugurates the genre of the neuronovel, and remains one of its more nuanced treatments. The narrator, Joe Rose, is a science journalist, a self-styled man of the enlightenment. Elitist but meritocratic, Joe is given to saying things to his girlfriend like "Don't you think I'm some kind of evolutionary throw forward?" Despite this weakness for self-congratulation, he is a decent guy who has the bad luck to become the object of a love with no cause but the deluded lover's neurochemistry. The demon lover, one Jed Parry, meets Joe for the first time as part of a group of men trying to save a boy from being blown away in a hot air balloon. The accident, or accidents, happen while Joe is on a picnic with his girlfriend Clarissa, a Keats scholar.

Because he is a science writer by profession, McEwan's Joe is a narrator of realist fiction capable of reflecting on his realism, or rather Zolaesque naturalism. An addict of facts, Joe provides an alibi for McEwan's moments of lyricism—"The silence appeared so rich as to have a visual quality, a sparkle or hard gloss, and a thickness too, like fresh paint"—and can also comment, in the next sentence, "This synesthesia must have been due to my disorientation." Joe correctly diagnoses the madman relatively early in the novel; it's convincing everyone else he's right that takes time. His girlfriend won't believe him and neither will the police until the final scene, when Parry holds a knife to Clarissa's throat. Suffering from de Clérambault's, Parry is beyond reason or persuasion—as Joe (a Darwinian) had always alleged.

In 1997, McEwan was still the sort of writer to challenge somewhat the correctness of Joe's neurological reductionism. Joe's rejection of any talking cure in favor of a thoroughgoing evolutionary psychology and medicalization had costs that the novelist tried to acknowledge: "From day one," Clarissa the humanist writes to Joe, "you saw [Parry] as an opponent and you set about defeating him, and you—we—paid a high price . . . Do you remember me suggesting to you early on—the night you walked out on me in fury—that we ask him in and talk to him? You just stared at me in disbelief, but I'm absolutely certain that at that time Parry didn't know that one day he would want you dead. Together we might have deflected him from the course he took."

This balanced weighing-up of the case no longer attracts McEwan as a writer. He has now firmly taken sides in a debate he was earlier content to stage with some subtlety. As he confided in a recent *New Yorker* profile, "Poor Greg [McEwan's son] had to study *Enduring Love* in school. He had a female teacher. And he had to write an essay: Who was the moral center of the book? And I said to Greg, 'Well, I think Clarissa's got everything wrong.' He got a D. The teacher didn't care what I thought. She thought that Joe was too 'male' in his thinking. Well. I mean, I only wrote the damn thing."

Perhaps so that no one would miss the point again, McEwan largely abandoned his earlier ambiguity when he wrote *Saturday* (2005), in favor of stark biological determinism. That novel evokes recent history—September 11, the street protests against the Iraq war—but only as background music incidental to a central conflict. This is the struggle between mental normals—who are really exceptional normals like the neurosurgeon Perowne, his barrister wife, and their musician son and poet daughter— and the subnormal Baxter, a violent thug suffering from the incurable, genetic brain-wasting disease Huntington's chorea. Here McEwan changes the narrative voice from the first person of *Enduring Love* to a more authoritative limited omniscient third person. We're always in Perowne's scientific mind, a mind capable of reflecting on itself in up-to-date terms of neuroscience, though we also catch glimpses of his creator guiding us, as in the surgeon's reflections on the superiority of neuroscience to ordinary language. When Perowne drives by an antiwar demonstration, a host of half thoughts arise, on war, death, terrorism, the justness of the cause. A voice tells us that all this occurs in "the preverbal language that linguists call mentalese. Hardly a language, more a matrix of shifting patterns, consolidating and compressing meaning in fractions of a second . . . Even with a poet's gift of compression, it could take hundreds of words and many minutes to describe." Of course McEwan has almost done just that, even down to the color of Perowne's thoughts—"a sickly yellow"—but only while conceding the insufficiency of his chosen medium, like a painter ruing the fact that he is not a photographer.

Despite how often we're told that Huntington's disease is the main cause of Baxter's uncontrolled aggression and wild mood swings, it's still tempting to declare him, rather than the neurosurgeon, the most human character in *Saturday*. Blindsided by a car that shouldn't be there, then lied to, and humiliated in front of his friends, he is a wronged man seeking revenge. When he's about to rape Perowne's daughter, he's momentarily bedazzled and soothed by her impromptu poetry recitation and gets knocked into a coma. Ah, the evolutionary advantages of memorizing Matthew Arnold!

By the novel's lights, however, Baxter is simply an incurable. *Saturday* turns into a defense of post-Thatcherite Britain's class system as well as the global imbalance of power by substituting the medical for the social. Some people are simply thugs, for reasons with nothing to do with social organization; in this respect they resemble terrorists. As Perowne reflects, "There are people around the planet, well-connected and organised, who would like to kill him and his family and friends to make a point." Perowne knows there is no talking to such people, and this time the novel contains no Clarissa to propose to him that conversation might have spared bloodshed.

In McEwan's work, the neurologically abnormal are foils more than actual characters; their main purpose is to be defeated by normals of the better sort.

But there is another set of neurological novels in which the author inhabits a cognitively anomalous or abnormal person and makes this character's inner life the focus of the novel, soliciting our sympathies. McEwan's neuronovels are of the hard variety; these other books are soft neuronovels.

Books like Lethem's *Motherless Brooklyn* (1999), with its Tourettic narrator, load almost the entire burden of meaning and distinctiveness onto their protagonists' neurologically estranged perceptions of our world. In doing so, they move what has traditionally been a minor character to the front of the novel. Idiots or the insane can dispense ironic wisdom—think of Shakespeare's pretension-puncturing fools—or serve as objects to show off the protagonist's sympathy and understanding in novels like Balzac's *Médecin de campagne* or Dickens's *Nicholas Nickleby*. Septimus Smith, the schizophrenic or shell-shocked First World War vet in *Mrs. Dalloway*, offers a contrast to the bright world of postwar aristocratic London, as well as a useful sympathetic object for Woolf's title character. There are also the more existentially troublesome Pip in *Moby-Dick* and, of course, American literature's signature idiot, Benjy in Faulkner's *The Sound and the Fury*. And yet it would be strange, if not impossible, to retell *The Sound and the Fury* exclusively from Benjy's point of view, which is in effect what many of the neuronovels set out to do.

In *Motherless Brooklyn*, the orphaned narrator afflicted (or blessed) with Tourette's syndrome determines to solve the mystery of his beloved boss's most foul and unnatural murder. This boss was the man who gave him a chance in life, and he has been knocked off by his brother. The plot is *Hamlet* by way of Philip Marlowe. The novel shows an agreeable openness about its derivative character, and perhaps the real purpose of such a conceit, poised between high and low, between realism and genre fiction, is to provide cover for the author to engage in the kind of stylistic experimentation habitual to modernist novelists doing interior monologues. Faulkner's Benjy spoke in a strange and addled voice—but then so did Faulkner's other characters, along with those of Joyce, without their needing to be mentally damaged. When Lethem's Tourettic narrator describes himself as "a human freak show," "a carnival barker, an auctioneer, a downtown performance artist, a speaker in tongues, a senator drunk on filibuster," this justifies or excuses the freewheeling language of his creator. While posing as a sort of observing doctor, like Oliver Sacks, the author indulges an experimental impulse that would today otherwise be seen as pretentious. The modernist desire to gather and combine the heterogeneous voices of entire regions and nations—"to forge in the smithy of my soul the uncreated conscience of my race"—led to novels open to the whole range of human language, from curses to visionary lyricism. When Lethem puts his words into the mouth of a Tourettic character, the very act of medicalization marginalizes the experimental impulse, marking any remnant modernism as a case for abnormal psychology.

The entire effect of Lethem's neurologically prompted "carnival barker" is similar to the one contained in the sentences from McEwan quoted above: "The silence appeared so rich as to have a visual quality, a sparkle or hard gloss, and a thickness too, like fresh paint. This synesthesia must have been due to my disorientation." The reader is presented simultaneously with an effect and a diagnosis of its cause; the writer indulges in some fancy language or rare perceptions, and then hastens to explain why, on medical grounds, this is allowed.

The *Motherless Brooklyn* model—which is also followed by Haddon's *Curious Incident of the Dog in the Night-Time*, Galchen's *Atmospheric Disturbances*, and Wray's *Lowboy*—in fact attempts a synthesis between what had seemed to be two distinct and increasingly divergent modes: on the one hand, American realism, ending with the "research novel"—novels stuffed with facts, names, things, impressing the reader with the author's store of "nonfiction" knowledge—and, on the other hand, the novel of consciousness, of interiority, of linguistic play and estranging description associated with high modernism.

But to ground special perceptions and heightened language in neurological anomaly ends up severely circumscribing the modernist project. The stylistic novelty and profound interiority of *Ulysses* or *To the Lighthouse* were called forth by normal protagonists—an ad salesman, a housewife—and were proposed as new ways of describing everyone and anyone from the inside out. Modernism seemed revolutionary as long as it threatened to become general; the neuronovel refashions modernism as a special case, odd language for describing odd people, different in neurological kind, not just degree, from other human beings. In this way, the "experimental" writing of neuronovelists actually props up rigid social conventions of language use. If modernism is just the language of crazy, then real men must speak like Lee Child.

Galchen's *Atmospheric Disturbances* exhibits the perils of this mixture of objective (medical) realism with an attempt to write a novel of subjectivity. The novel is narrated entirely from the point of view of Leo Liebenstein, a man who, suffering from Capgras syndrome, believes his wife has been replaced by an exact replica. The delusion sets in when Liebenstein wakes up, Gregor Samsa–like, from uneasy dreams—and from a migraine. "I was then a fifty-one-year-old male psychiatrist with no previous hospitalizations," he tells the reader, as though giving a medical report on himself. What happens next, however, and for the subsequent two hundred or so pages, is not a medical report but the flight of a damaged mind. Liebenstein, who still believes he can tell sane from insane—he's a psychiatrist, after all—decides to go in search of his "real" wife.

In a gentlemanly review, James Wood placed *Atmospheric Disturbances* in the European modernist tradition of the unreliable narrator, like Hamsun's *Hunger* or Svevo's *Zeno's Conscience*, as well as the novel of love, like Proust's *Un Amour de Swann*. Galchen's novel, he claims, "is a relentless exploration of how a man could fail to see clearly the woman he loves. We are all afflicted at times with the cataracts of the quotidian, where routine clouds our ability to notice what we once loved about the person we live with—this is the novel's universal appeal." "Cataracts of the quotidian" is a lovely phrase, but in order to write it, Wood must blur his own vision. For it is not the case, as Wood suggests, that "Leo has, perhaps, a version of Capgras syndrome, whose victims come to think that an impostor has replaced a family member or friend." There is no "perhaps" about it. Leo does have Capgras syndrome, and the novel depends on its medical precision to be something other than the ravings of a lunatic, and an unsympathetic lunatic at that. Liebenstein is vain and annoying, his narration both leaden and showy: "She, the woman, the possible dog lover, leaned down to de-shoe." Here is a man who can't say that his wife takes off her shoes. There must be something wrong with his brain. He's also a man who mistakes the verbose for the descriptive: " 'Oh,' I said, my palms beginning to sweat as random sensuality carbonated up to my cortex."

After Leo has followed his allegedly missing wife's trail to Argentina, her native country, he comments on the practice of memorializing the missing of the 1970s Dirty War: "People naturally perseverate on their personal tragedies, even though such perseveration doesn't really serve anyone, neither the living nor the dead. I mean, there's research on these things. It's simply not a practical use of time to think constantly of the dead." Such a reflection, at once unfeeling and pretentious (why does he have to say "perseveration"?), is of a piece with Liebenstein's jerkish personality, which his disorder neither explains nor excuses. Meanwhile, Liebenstein's tics and riffs effectively bury the actual plot of the novel: Rema, Liebenstein's wife, who is there the whole time as her husband raves and treats her like an alien, must keep her cool in order to save her marriage. She even runs after him to Argentina. That she thinks the marriage is worth saving at extraordinary cost is assumed but never addressed. The novel, it turns out, makes most sense not from a neurological standpoint, but under the lens of an old-fashioned Freudian interpretation. For we learn that Rema's father may have been "disappeared" during the Dirty War, although it's possible he just walked out, and we also know that Rema has married a man who would be roughly her father's age, were he still alive, or around. So Rema seems predestined to love an absent older man, an Oedipal rather than neurological mystery—but not one the novel attempts to illuminate.

Of course, you can make Liebenstein's delusion into an allegory of a universal condition, as Wood does, but only at the expense of novelistic and medical specificity both. In some way, perhaps we all suspect our loved ones of being impostors—but if this is so, how can it be that some people have Capgras syndrome and most do not? The difference in degree is a difference in kind. But a neuronovel like Galchen's wants to have it both ways—to combine the pathological and the universal. Even as it relies on something like a readerly meaning impulse—we want to be able to generalize or approximate or metaphorize the rare neurological condition into some kind of experience compatible with our own—it also baffles and frustrates the same impulse. Any possibility of the necessary interpretive leap is disavowed by the pathological premise of the novel itself. By turning so aggressively inward, to an almost cellular level, this kind of novel bypasses the self, let alone society, or history, to arrive at neurology: privacy without individuality. And the deep logic of the story is likewise not one of irony or fate or comeuppance, but simple contingency; the etiology of a neurological condition is biological, not moral. And mere biological contingency has a way of repelling meaning.

The aesthetic sensation a reader gets from the neuronovel is not the pleasure of finding the general in the particular, but a frustration born of the defeat of the metaphoric impulse. We want to make the metaphor work, to say, "Yes, we are all a bit like a paranoid schizophrenic sometimes" or, "Yes, as Mark Haddon's autistic narrator needs to separate the foods on his plate and not let them touch, to sort colors into good and bad, so am I in my impulse to classify a new genre." But this would be to indulge the worst tendency of literary criticism, whether of a jargony and sectarian or burbling and humanistic type: to insist on meaning or relevance when there isn't any, or when the works themselves actually foreclose it. Instead the reader has to admit to himself that his brain doesn't work like an autistic person's, a Capgras sufferer's, and that when he loves or works or fears or talks, his ordinary neurons fire or misfire for ordinary rather than extraordinary reasons, whatever these may be.

In other words, the neuronovel in its present form presents the experience of a cognitive defeat. We imagine that science might get there, but it hasn't yet. What's strange is that science, as it moves in the direction of a total redescription of the mind in terms of the brain, may merely be replicating and systematizing the earlier insights of the psychological novel. A recent nonfiction book is called *Proust Was a Neuroscientist*. But insofar as the title's claim is true, Proust was a neuroscientist not by cribbing from contemporary case studies, but by observing himself and others outside of any consulting room. Surely the way for a novelist to be a neuroscientist today is still to *anticipate* rather than follow the discoveries of brain science. It would be no surprise if a novelist could still describe and mimic traits of cognition that neurology can't yet experimentally confirm.

The question, then, is why novelists have ceded their ground to science. And from the writer's perspective, if not from the reader's, an allegorical interpretation of the neuronovel does seem possible. Is the interest in neurological anomaly not symptomatic of an anxiety about the role of novelists in this new medical-materialist world, which happens also to be a world of giant publishing conglomerates and falling reading rates? Are novelists now, in their own eyes and others', only special cases, without specialized and credentialed knowledge, who may at best dispense accurate if secondhand medical (or historical or sociological) information in the form of an entertaining fictional narrative? And is the impulse to write not an inexplicable compulsion, a category of disorder outside the range of normal? Do writers need special institutions that recognize and treat their mental peculiarities, without granting these any special visionary status? (Such institutions are known as MFA programs.) Perhaps the writer also needs an understanding spouse who will not leave him when he creates her double, or a family that tries to accommodate his strange habits. Most novelists also have grounds for fearing that Ian McEwan, tribune of the healthy brain, will defeat them in the combat over readers and their money. To put all this more simply, the neuronovel tends to become a variety of meta-novel, allegorizing the novelist's fear of his isolation and meaninglessness, and the alleged capacity of science to explain him better than he can explain himself.

By comparison with most nineteenth-century novels, and even with most twentieth-century modernist novels of the "stream of consciousness" school, the neuronovels have in them very little of society, of different classes, of individuals interacting, of development either alongside or against historical forces and expectations. Iris Murdoch (whose fate it was to become better known, through her husband's memoirs, as an Alzheimer's patient than as a novelist) observed that the twentieth-century novel had lost both religion and society. A midcentury novelist who wanted to write about society had first to take pains to reconstruct it, to research something that to George Eliot or Dickens had been more or less spontaneously available. And the twentieth-century decline of religion meant a common moral frame of reference couldn't be taken for granted, either. So postwar writers as different as Nabokov and Sarraute and Bellow were thrown back on themselves. But at least they retained that subject matter: the personal, the self. It now seems we've gone beyond the loss of society and religion to the loss of the self, an object whose intricacies can only be described by future science. It's not, of course, that morality, society, and selfhood no longer exist, but they are now the property of specialists writing in the idioms of their disciplines. So the new genre of the neuronovel, which looks on the face of it to expand the writ of literature, appears as another sign of the novel's diminishing purview.

(2009)

FISH ROT

Rebecca Curtis

It was at the Cerebus Center, which had become like home to me, that I met him, and I knew after five minutes of hearing him talk that he could be the one to make me happy again, even though he was talking to another girl, not me, and even though everyone at the Cerebus Center, me, too, had Fish Rot. Needless to say, I hadn't had sex in a long time. Definitely the last time it happened George Hubs Junior was president, or maybe George Hubs Senior was president. I'd stopped hoping, and decided my sister's "prophetic dream" was wrong. I won't have a baby and carry it wrapped in a blue shawl through my sister's hallway, I thought.

"You were newly recovered from a long illness," my sister had told me excitedly when describing her prophetic dream. "You were very happy," she said. "You were walking down my hallway carrying a baby in your arms. It was wrapped in a blue shawl!"

Why was I at her house if I'd just had a baby? I asked. Where was my husband? She didn't know, my sister said sadly.

I didn't care about having a baby but liked the thought that

I'd recover. I was thirty-nine. I never considered meeting a man at a detox joint where nearly every denizen had Fish Rot.

When I was down during my illness, I thought: At least I have family. Every six months my whole family went to my older sister's house in Idaho and hung out in her mansion, hiked in the nearby woods, and soaked in her hot spring; my older sister and her husband, my nieces, ages four and six, my younger sister, her husband, and our parents. None of the rest of us liked our parents, because our mother criticized us a lot and our father was a kid rubber who'd often find my nieces playing Legos or video games in the living room and start massaging their legs and backs, and none of us liked seeing it, and my nieces were too small and scared to move away or something like that, but my sister and I carried spray bottles around with us that we'd filled with water, and whenever he started massaging my nieces one of us would say quietly, "No," and spray him until he backed off. For whatever reason, he hated water. So I got down sometimes, but I had family; those visits weren't perfect, but they meant something to me. They meant I had family. Friends, an inheritance, and a place to go if I ever lost everything, job, ability to think, stuff like that. And until I spent my savings, I had my savings, and when I got lonely, I lay in my bedroom in New York and drew the curtains and pretended my last horrible boyfriend, a screenwriter who told me I should move to Bulgaria because Bulgarian men might like me, was in the room. When I learned I got it, I called him, because my doctor said I should, and I said, "Goatboy, you might have Fish Rot." He said, "Leah, I don't have Fish Rot, but I'm sorry you do." A month later I saw his picture in *Tick-Tock*, he'd married a girl who was dark haired, very pretty, and slender.

Since I got it I'd changed, but mostly for the better, in my head. At first it was hard. Most doctors I saw, the ones my insurance liked, said I needed a psychiatrist. I didn't test positive for Fish Rot.

"But it's an immune-system-response test," I told them, "and Fish Rot *disables* the immune system."

"But people *do* test positive," they said. "And you don't."

I did research on the internet about Fish Rot. I told everyone I knew that Fish Rot was the fastest-spreading infectious disease in America. It was true. It was true even then, when George Hubs Senior was president.

"Then why don't *I* know about it?" they said.

"Cover-up," I said. "Look on the internet. It has to do with the Centers for Disease Control, the Infectious Disease Society of America, the FDA, Nazis, and the government."

Then they said, "Oh, really," but it was too complicated to explain about Pear Island, the bioterror research done under a government program in the fifties by doctors who were also scientists, witnesses, and war criminals, and who now headed the CDC and IDSA and said that Fish Rot didn't exist. "Fish Rot is for fish," these doctors said. And stuff like that. "Once I had a fish rot," they said. "So I flushed it." These doctors and organizations said that very few people in America actually had Fish Rot, but that a lot of hypochondriacs thought they did. If anyone still had symptoms of Fish Rot after a month of oral meds, these doctors said, it was "Post–Fish Rot Syndrome," and these people could be made happy with a vitamin B shot, or should get a cat.

Some doctors said it couldn't be cured.

Of course, the economy wasn't the best. Lots of people, even healthy ones, were getting cancer or having heart attacks, and 75 percent of Americans were overweight or obese, and extreme weather such as hurricanes was happening a lot on the coasts, and our American armies were struggling to subdue fanatical rebels in Iraq, so I knew that in the grand scheme I was lucky to have hands, arms, legs.

But I felt depressed because I'd spent all my money on Fish Rot. I was pretty down when I met Prince Horndrak, or Lord Kradnroh, or whatever, at the Cerebus Center, I was low as low, desperate.

My older sister got it first. When she got it, I thought: Hahaha, she *would* get Fish Rot.

I loved her, but she didn't take care of herself. Worked too hard, bought bottled water at LilPrincessCafé for her kids. Every time she passed a LilPrincessCafé, and one stood on every corner of every Boise block, she stopped the car, she could be ten minutes from home in her SUV and the girls would see one and go, "We're thirsty, LilPrincessCafé, LilPrincessCafé!" and she'd say, "Now, girls, we're ten minutes from home, we have water we can drink for free at home," and they'd go, "LilPrincessCafé!" and she'd stop and buy them Bottled Waters, Hot Chocolates, and Madeleines. I couldn't afford the cheapest item at LilPrincessCafé, which was "Use the Bathroom: 50 cents." My nieces were four and six but they had every hand-wiz, talk, and music device, they had I-Grab, SoundGenie, and Surround-Siren-V. I thought: She deserves Fish Rot. I had an eighties-style boom box.

My sister kept working with Fish Rot. Her left leg and arm would go numb one day and she'd make her husband drive them both to work. The fingers on her left hand got soft and itchy. They puffed up and the skin cracked and bled. Then her fingers grew white, spongy, porous bulbs on them. She bought gloves. The gloves smelled like fish. She and her husband were accountants. She told her insurance company, "You're going to pay for IV antibiotics for Fish Rot, for twelve months, for eighteen months, for as long as I want."

Their policy was, no IV antibiotics for Fish Rot.

"No, we're not," they said.

Mold grew between her toes.

She bathed in hydrogen peroxide every night after work, but it didn't help.

She found a doctor, one of a group of rogue doctors called Fish Rot Society of America who'd all had Fish Rot, and so believed it existed and had learned how to treat it so they didn't rot. Soon she was paying this doctor, known by his patients as "the Cowboy" because he rode Fish Rot into the ground and was bowlegged and had a square jaw and floppy brown hair and was sort of hot, $30,000 a month for IV antibiotics to treat her Fish Rot. This doctor believed that his patients should also get acupuncture and eat special green algae plants that pull lead from the body and all sorts of shit. My sister paid up the wazoo for this doctor's services and soon her savings were shot. She got to lie on the Cowboy's massage bed and have the Cowboy feel her breasts and tell her she needed more IV antibiotics for Fish Rot, but she spent her savings to do it. Then she spent my nieces' college fund. Then she had to sell two of her three SUVs. Then she was out of money to spend on Fish Rot.

I thought: Good thing my sister, who's rich, is the one who got Fish Rot.

Her husband got the spores on his tongue when they kissed, before they knew she had Fish Rot, and they colonized his head. He woke one day and pus came out of his eyes. My sister sent him to her doctor. Her doctor said, "You have Fish Rot."

Then their bills doubled.

"Your sister makes a big deal about this 'Fish Rot' thing," our father said to me on the phone. "Do you think it's real?"

"I'm not sure," I said.

"She probably needs more rest and to discipline her kids," he said. "Maybe spank them. Nothing wrong with a little spanking when kids throw fits. I spanked you girls and it worked."

"Yeah!" I said.

"Fish Rot is terrible!" my sister bawled on the phone. "I feel weak! I can't breathe!" Her list went on. She woke up at night. She could not concentrate. Her feet were always numb. Or her legs. She was swollen. Her hair fell out. Sometimes she could not think of words she wanted to say, easy words like "apple turn-over," "tax shelter," or "contradict." She hid this from her clients.

"Jesus Christ," I said, thinking, It's permanent brain damage! Thank god I'll never get Fish Rot!

My accountant sister was a cunty bitch.

When our parents said to her, "We don't mean to denigrate your symptoms, but a lot of people can't concentrate, that's called stress. We've never heard of this 'Fish Rot.'"

She said, "It's real. Do some research. Use the internet."

And when they said that they *had* done research, and they'd learned that "Fish Rot" was largely an imaginary disease, she said, "You're wrong." She was a tough cunt.

At that time, my life was good. I wasn't in debt. I had a job, a three-year, full-time teaching gig at Pegasus University, with hope of renewal if the job I did was good. I took the job for granted, showed up, did the work. Didn't love it or hate it. I had a boyfriend named Scottish Pony. I met him on a Jewish dating site. I wasn't Jewish and neither was he. We both settled. I should speak for myself. Scottish Pony had profiles on sixty-six sites, he cast a wide net. He was tall, he was awkward, I liked that about him, he wrote poetry, he liked to have a few nightcaps before bed, and he loved books, his job cataloging books, and me. Blah blah. My favorite thing in life, even though I didn't know it at the time, was still going to my sister's mansion in Idaho, during Christmas, and in the summer, and it was still fun, in summer and winter, even though my sister and her husband had Fish Rot.

The activities we did were pretty much the same. When we arrived, my mother would say my sister's house smelled bad. She'd say that my sister's carpets had mold, her sink contained grimy scum, and her dog was drinking out of the toilet. My sister would say she knew the dog drank out of the toilet and that they let him do that. My mother would say that custom was gross, and get a bowl from my sister's cupboard and put down water for the dog and try to make the dog drink from it, and the dog would frown, and my sister would get upset, and our father would say, "Now, now, you're criticizing," to our mother, "let's all get along." Then we went to the five-dollar bowling alley so we could all bowl, my mother would say that my nieces were too skinny, and didn't my sister feed them? and ask who wanted corn dogs from the snack shack, and our father would tell my nieces that Grandpa would help them take their sneakers off, and my sister would say, No, no, she and her husband would do that, and then they'd hustle over on their crutches to my nieces and use their one arm that didn't have a PICC line attached to help the girls undo their sneakers and put their bowling shoes on. Later we'd order in Thai food and all watch a movie, something kid-friendly like *Goblin Weirdos* or *Escape from Witch Mountain*.

It was harder, in retrospect, to keep an eye on things at my sister's house; my sister would set up her IV pole and drip medicine into her arm in a comfy chair in the living room, and her husband would do the same in another comfy chair, and it was up to me to spray our father with water when he found my nieces in the yard and started rubbing them. My father also moved away slower, I noticed, and gave me nasty looks when I sprayed. I sometimes had to spray two or three times. You were supposed to be able to train them, I thought, I'd hoped he'd learn that the word "no" meant water was coming, but whenever I found him rubbing a niece and said "no" without the bottle in my hand he just stared at me, and his hand kept squeezing the niece's calf or shoulder or whatever. My sister, being sick, couldn't keep a good eye on it, and when I complained to her about that she said, "Just keep the water bottle *with* you, just spritz him," and when I said, "But what if I'm not *there* sometime, what if you're not, either?" she rolled her eyes and stared at the IV line in her arm and said, "Leah, we both keep an eye on him. We both spray him. I'm doing everything I can. I'm working even though I'm sick. I'm struggling."

I miss those days, in retrospect, I even miss Scottish Pony, even though he was on a lot of psychotropic medications, had to shower four times a day to keep calm, and his favorite thing was for me to wear pigtails and plaid. He didn't like twelve-year-olds, just for me to dress up like one. I was thirty-five. He was a good egg. He liked being "Uncle Pony-Scott," going to my sister's and soaking in her hot spring, and he wasn't put off that my sister had Fish Rot. I set him up with a spray bottle and we both kept an eye on my dad. "It's cool," Scottish Pony said, "every family has their thing. My dad used to beat the shit out of me every day after school when I was twelve." Scottish Pony ratted his dad out, told his mother and his little brother about the beatings, but neither one of them ever believed him. When I called him, years after I dumped him, to tell him that I might have inadvertently given him Fish Rot, he said, "Are you kidding me? That's nothing. Sorry I didn't tell you. I've had Fish Rot for years."

I never considered myself lazy or slutty. But after I dumped Scottish Pony, my sister told me that I couldn't tell my nieces that my boyfriends were "uncles" anymore, because I was a ho-bag. "Uncles are permanent," my sister said. "You've brought twenty different uncles here in ten years. It's making the girls confused. You're a ho-bag." She wanted them to learn moral behavior. And one time, when I complained to her that I wasn't rich, she said kindly, "Leah, do you know why I work? Why I work full-time even though I have Fish Rot?"

"No," I said. I didn't.

"I do it for my daughters," she said. "So that they can have everything that I didn't have. Like annual tours of Europe. I do it for them. I get up early every morning and I work. I do what I have to do. This life is not about pleasure, it's about doing what you have to do. I do what I have to do for my daughters. And that's that. I do a helpful job that helps people and helps the world. In this way, I do my good. I take care of me and I take care of my kids. I pray the earth mother enables me to take care of them. I want them to have every opportunity, and I want them to know their family." She paused.

"And I want them," she said softly, "to know their grandparents, too." She paused. "And you have to be responsible and take care of you."

I knew she was right, pretty much. My sister worked hard. She was a good person. She was beautiful, tall, and blond. I knew my sister didn't believe in Jesus, but she murdered a pine tree every Christmas for my nieces' sake, she said, she killed a healthy pine tree because she liked Christmas, and decked it in tinsel and thousands of expensive miniature yachts, and when Easter came around she pretended a bunny had brought five enormous baskets of milk-chocolate candies shaped like rabbits and chickens to their house. She didn't believe in Jesus, but she believed in distinctions between good, bad, evil, and slutty, and she liked tradition.

No one I knew believed in God except my mother. She believed in the Holy Spirit, the angels, and Satan. She said, "Jesus died for us, Jesus enables us to be loved and saved." "Satan," she said, "appeals to our greedy side, to our vices, he encourages us to stay angry at people we're angry at, to eat a second piece of chocolate cake, and to go shopping." She was angry at many people, she ate chocolate cake often, she shopped all the time. She went to church. She was a prayer warrior. She prayed for President Hubs's health. She and a couple hundred other prayer warriors knelt down for two hours in Our Lady of the Lakes every morning and took donations and requests from the local populace. They got a lot of requests, of all kinds, to pray for a sick child's health, to pray a family's finances would improve, to pray America would win wars in the Middle East, to pray for President Hubs. She'd heard a rumor, put out by a tabloid, that President Hubs had Fish Rot. The article said that for several months Hubs had secretly been receiving intravenous meds at a Washington clinic to kill the infection. It made sense. He loved fish. He was always taking seaport vacations to eat clams. And he'd never been good with words. But now he was worse. Verbally, he stumbled a lot.

People with Fish Rot knew the signs. They saw him speak on TV and nodded and said, "Fish Rot." My mother, who by then knew that Fish Rot was real, prayed that Hubs would recover. She prayed that good would prevail in the world, that all souls would convert to Christianity and be saved from eternal damnation, and that American soldiers would beat the Iraqi rebels in Iraq, would slay them.

My sister came to me when at her worst. Her gallbladder had burst from the IV antibiotics. Her colon had rotted, most of her hair had fallen out, and she couldn't walk. She saw clients in a wheelchair. Fungus had invaded her nervous system and her knees jerked uncontrollably. My sister had no more money to buy antibiotics. She was a careful cunt who never cried. But she called me on the phone and mentioned, in a neutral voice, her situation. If she didn't get more antibiotics, the infection would root into her bones. She might be in a wheelchair forever; she might die.

I expressed horror, concern; I had no money to lend or help.

"Yes, yes," she said. "I just called to ask your opinion of what I should do.

"Purely academic, of course," she said. "But I value your opinion and I wanted to get your input."

"Well," I said. "It's obvious. There's no question."

"You think so?" she said.

"Of course," I said. "You have to do what we always said."

What we'd said we'd do, if either one of us truly needed money, was to finally accept the parcel of ten acres of land that our father had offered each of us, should we ever want a bit of our inheritance early, and sell it. We were quite aware that we had an inheritance, and that the family land was a gold mine. It was beautiful land, in the most exclusive part of Maine: wooded mountain land with a lake view. Every family has this story. Historically, our family owned a mountain. The mountain and its road bore our surname. Our great-grandfather sold half the mountain to a local millionaire, in a moment when farming was bad and he felt blue. Our grandfather, during our lifetime, occasionally sold bits to tasteless people who moved up north from Massachusetts. He'd give them four acres at the top of the hill, gorgeous land amid blueberry fields, and say, "It's enough for you to piss on." He'd sell four acres like a gentleman for $50,000. The new-money people would build on two of the acres and sell two acres to more new-money people for $100,000. Those people, more tasteless, would build on one single acre, and sell the second acre for $100,000 to people *more* tasteless. Those people would build on a mere half acre and sell the extra half acre for $75,000. All these people built tacky mansions on their land bits and bought large motorboats to disturb wildlife and pollute the lake. At Christmas every year they made cookies and brought us down platefuls to thank us for letting them ruin our mountain. Our father's greatest wish in life was for none of our family to sell any more land.

My sister and I had done calculations. We'd each failed calculus in high school, but we weren't math slouches. Twenty-and-a-half acres times $75,000 each was $1,500,000.

My sister and I felt the family land was cursed, what with our father's compulsive illness and the plague of sick deer that drank from streams in our woods and roamed our backyard, their skin falling off in patches from Fish Rot, and we'd always agreed that if we were ever in dire financial need, we'd accept a ten-acre parcel from our father and sell it.

"You have to take your ten acres that Dad offered you," I said, "and sell it."

She sounded unsure. "You think?"

"Of course."

"But if I ask for my land," she said, "he'll want to know what I want it for. And if I tell him I'm going to sell it, he won't give it to me. So what should I do?"

She was silent, expectant. I didn't see her confusion. "Just lie," I said. "Tell him you want the land so you can build a summer-house right next to him so he can spend a lot more time with his granddaughters!"

She was silent. "But that's not true," she said. "I'm never go-ing to build a house right next to him, and I don't want him to spend more time with his granddaughters."

"I know," I said. "That's why it's a lie! Just *lie!*"

"Dad won't be happy."

I guessed my sister meant that if she fooled our dad by pre-tending she wanted ten acres now so she could build by him, and then grabbed the land and sold it, our father would be so peeved that he might not give *me my* early-partial-inheritance if I asked. But what did I care? I didn't have Fish Rot. I knew I'd never get it. And I didn't want any favors from our dad. I thought about how my sister's hair was all gone and she couldn't eat food be-cause her colon had rotted.

Her husband wasn't doing well, either. First, butterscotch-colored patches appeared all over his legs and groin, then his nuts shriveled like figs and had to be cut off. A surgeon offered to make him new ones, but the cost was $20,000 a sack.

I said, "You need the money, right?"

"Right."

"Then too bad," I said.

"Okay," she said. "I just wanted to know what you thought."

So my sister told our father she'd take her early-partial-inheritance of ten acres and then she sold it off in tiny parcels to eager people who showed up from Massachusetts, and then she was set for a long time, as far as I could see.

My sister took the land-money and hired a lawyer who made Black Sword, Black Visor, her insurance company, pay her $300,000 for ten months of intravenous antibiotics for Fish Rot. Black Sword, Black Visor denied coverage the whole time, but my sister's lawyer took them to court and used the Two Standards of Care law that says that when two standards, a shitty one and a good one, have been established for treating a disease, an insurance company must cover both. My sister's lawyer said that their win would break ground, that a favorable ruling would establish a national precedent that would force Black Sword, Black Visor and megacompanies like it to pay out billions to provide proper treatment for millions of Americans with Fish Rot, and he might have been right, because as soon as my sister's suit began, she started receiving checks from Black Sword for $30,000 each month, and when my sister and her lawyer got to court a scrawny guy with big teeth from Black Sword told the judge that the judge could not rule on the controversial case because through a clerical error, the scrawny guy said, my sister-cunt had been paid. Clerical error, the scrawny guy said, cunt was paid. Must dismiss. Don't dismiss, my sister said, but she'd cashed all those checks, and the gavel came down. The judge didn't say anything, he just sneezed.

When I remember all the great times, the best in my life, that I had hanging out at my sister's, I also remember one mishap, really Scottish Pony's fault, that happened the last visit before I got sick. It was no big deal, really. It happened a few days before Christmas. We'd all gone skiing, then ordered in Thai food which was particularly delicious, and then we made spiked hot chocolates, and virgin ones for my nieces, and watched *Rise of the Gook Goblins* in my sister's living room, and then we decided, since it was a nice night, we'd all go for a quick dunk in the hot spring in the yard, the whole family except our father, who hated water, and I put on my suit, and was cuddled next to Scottish Pony in my sister's hot spring, next to my sister and family, looking at the stars, and Scottish Pony rubbed my leg under the water and whispered, "Let's go inside," and he went first, to make things seem subtle, like we weren't going to our room to do nooky, and I followed a minute later, and entered the house and saw him standing frozen and stiff in the door to the living room, where we'd watched the movie, and he didn't turn around to look at me, he squeaked, "Water, water, water!" Then I saw we'd forgotten my oldest niece, who was six, she'd fallen asleep on the couch on her tummy watching *Gook Goblins* and never made it to the hot spring with the rest of us and my father was leaning over her in the dark in his boxers and he'd pulled her pajamas down and was methodically rubbing, with both hands, her butt. Scottish Pony stared at me and shouted, "Water, water!" so I ran to get the water, thinking, "Christ," Scottish Pony wasn't the type of boyfriend to grab an iron lamp and hit my father on the head with it, and I wasn't the type of daughter to do it either, we were both wusses, plus I felt bad for my father because he was head-sick, so I ran faster than ever and got the bottle and strode forward and sprayed my father in the face with it three times, and eventually—it took a lot of spraying—he took his hands off my niece's butt.

I looked at him.

I sprayed him again in the face.

He backed away a little.

I pulled my niece's pants up.

My niece looked at me.

She had a pale round face, wide-set brown eyes, and was alert. She looked scared. It was clear she'd been awake the whole time, at least once the rubbing began.

"Run to your room," I said. "Bad, bad, bad!"

I wasn't sure whether I meant *she'd* been bad, or that what had happened was bad, or that I was bad, and she wasn't sure, either. She sure fucking ran.

When I told my sister about the incident, she looked unhappy.

I said, "Maybe we should do something?"

She said, "What do you want me to *do?*" She still had the PICC line in her arm. She was bloated. She smelled like trout.

"I don't know," I said. "Maybe we should use a gun and not water?"

"Jesus," she said. "He's our *father*."

Later that visit, Scottish Pony looked at me and said, "Your house is fucked up." That's when I decided to dump him.

When I got the signs of Fish Rot I ignored it for one full year because I didn't frigging want to have it. I am strong and smart. Also a writer, a professor, I teach at Pegasus University, one of the best universities in America. A fever was first, then some eye things—gook coming out of them, swollen up at night, very dry. I bought eyedrops. After that my hands went numb. I broke a lot of drinking glasses. I was thirty-six. I yelled at my roommates, "Who the fig is breaking all the glasses?!" It was hard to remember names. I heard my roommate come home once, I was lying in bed, I yelled, "Yay, Tonyella's home!" but my roommate's name was Stacy. I did that because Stacy was black and spunky and I liked her, and I had a graduate student at Pegasus named Tonyella who was black and spunky who I liked, too. Stacy said, "Are you okay?"

"Yeah," I said. "Sorry. White person thing."

After that I grew smarter.

I kept a map in front of me, hidden behind some books, when I taught. The "map" had all my students' names. I called on students by name to show I could. Sometimes I couldn't think of the vice president's name, I'd say, "That vice president guy, ha!"

They'd say, "Pullwool?"

I'd say, "Ya! Haha!"

It was witty, I thought. I thought, Smart people can overcome anything.

But I started talking bad. It got worse. I saw things, too. Things that weren't really there. Everywhere I looked, kitchen drawer, coat closet, trash bin, I saw snakes, or silverfish, thousands of them sliding together over the tops of things. Bats flapped in dark corners when I looked in my closets, it sounds cliché but it's true, I saw bats in my closets, stuff like that.

My cunty sister saved me. "It's Fish Rot," she said. "The earlier you hit it, the better off you'll be."

So I saw five doctors my insurance liked. I saw doctors my insurance liked because they were cheaper. When I saw them, my insurance paid.

"You could lose weight," they said. "But that's about it. Also get the ugly look off your face."

"Okay," I said. I thought: Maybe Botox?

"You don't have Fish Rot," an infectious disease specialist

who purported to specialize in Fish Rot said. "But I'll check you for celiac." He peered at me. "And lupus."

"You're over thirty-five," an in-network neurologist said. "And not married. And all the symptoms you're describing—peripheral neuropathy, brain fog, headaches, hallucinations, memory and word loss—are signs of depression." He offered me a prescription for Happizap.

"See *my* doctor," my cunty sister said. "You should have hit it six months ago, when you had a chance of kicking it." She'd been cured. "There are doctors who know how it works," my sister said, "and who'll treat it. Don't be a rube. If you ever want to recover from an illness, you have to see an out-of-network doctor. You have to pay to be cured. I know the Cowboy's out-of-network, but he'll help you, so it's worth the money."

That was the beginning of my great depression.

Also my awakening.

I realized that I'd do anything to get money.

I vowed to get cured, and not get the permanent brain damage.

At my sister's urging, I flew to Idaho to see my sister's medical doctor, the Cowboy, and also, eventually, her naturopathic doctor, the Ivory Witch, and later, the Ivory Witch's nutritionist, and later, her nutritionist's chiropractor. I spent my book advance and my savings. Then I started in on my credit cards. When I started, I had a zero balance on my credit cards.

Soon I was near broke.

"You're not getting better," the Cowboy said, "I'm not sure why. It's like you're retarded. I guess you need heavy-metal chelation and a lot more expensive treatments."

I told him I was near broke.

He shrugged. "Got someone who can help ya? Or something you can sell?"

I thought—for two seconds—about asking my father for my land. I didn't think he might say no. I just thought, Eff that. Not asking him for jack. Nohellno.

I cashed out my retirement account.

Eventually, the Cowboy took pity on me. He said, "You don't have to fly to Idaho to see me, you know. Go see Dr. Cerebus, at the Cerebus Center. It's in New York, where you live. It's an exclusive clientele. But on my word, he will let you in and chelate you. He's kind of an expert at it."

I hadn't known there was anywhere in New York that treated Fish Rot. Neither had anyone else in New York, or at least, neither had most people. The Cerebus Center was a secret—for the lucky and rich.

"The *Cerebus* Center?" my sister said. "What the frig?"

I told her that her doctor had recommended it.

"Well, I recommend my doctor," she said, "and no one else. The Cerebus Center sounds weird."

At the Cerebus Center they put me on oral antibiotics, then IV antibiotics, and a lot of pills. My cunt sister wrote my insurance a letter saying, "You'll pay for intravenous antibiotics for my sister for Fish Rot, or else she'll sue using the Two Standards of Care law," and she cited, for why they should pay for my antibiotics, how I'd become retarded, getting the tremors at night, and not knowing my students' names, hallucinating, and pretending all through teaching my classes that I was just kooky when really I could not think straight.

She was right that I was not professional. Sometimes I did not write the comments for my students' stories, instead I made gingerbread cookies in the shapes of characters from my students' stories, and when I got to class I arranged the cookies in a tableau on our discussion table and said, "These cookies constitute my response." One time I tried to write the notes all teachers at

Pegasus were required to write for their students, but it hurt my head and I could not narrowize my thoughts, so my typed comments turned out to be sixteen pages and single-spaced. In that case I thought the student would be angry, because sixteen pages of me blah-blah-blahing is not helpful to a young Manhattanite who wants to be a writer and is paying fifty grand a year to learn the keys and the tricks. I had not told this student the keys and the tricks, because I knew if I did he would kill me. Or hate me. Or both. So instead I blahblahblah. But the sixteen-pages kid, he was fifty-six years old, was not mad, during our conference about his story he said, "You are the nicest teacher ever, I can't believe you wrote me sixteen pages of comments, no one has ever done that!"

I was scared of this student. Not only was he fifty-six, he was a trust-fund journalist. His father went to Yale and so did he. When he said this, we were sitting in my office. Really it was the office of a Genius Prize–winning, Diet Coke–addicted, Iraq War–veteran poet, but the poet was not around school much, so twenty of us non-tenure-track teachers had "hours" when we could squat in his enormous book-lined, sun-filled office. The scary journalist was sitting in a wicker chair with a green velvet seat. I leaned forward. I was sweaty. I'd stopped using deodorant long ago, when the Ivory Witch told me it was toxic. The journalist's story was set in the future. It was about two women. They were fat, fatter than most, half-tonners. The women in the story did not do anything. They rode around in a car being fat. I blushed.

"Listen, Ajax," I said. "I am going to tell you something that I am sort of nervous to say."

The journalist blunk. Was he used to women making confessions? I thought.

He had that average, chubby-cheeked, pink-skin confide-in-me look that some men who went to Yale have.

"The reason I wrote sixteen pages," I said, "is because your story is so good."

He liked that, and from then on, when I was not able to read or type comments for students' stories because of my head hurting and Fish Rot, I just came to class anyway and said, "I did not type comments for the stories this week because they were so good." I told my students that their stories were so dense and sophisticated that I needed more time.

My evaluations that year said, "Leah is strange. Her comments are late. She is also late. She tries hard and is enthusiastic, that's true. She smells bad. It is difficult to concentrate when she smells like salmon. She makes good cookies. Her discussions are not at a graduate level. She says weird things. What level are they at? Is it kindergarten?"

I had a boss. His name was Dad Cloud. One day he said, "I read the evaluations."

"I'm sorry," I said. "I'm sorry, I'm sorry, I'm sorry, I'm sorry."

I blubbered a bit. Just out of one eye, which had stuff coming out of it anyway, because of Fish Rot.

"Don't be sorry," he said. "Your evals are okay. We don't care much what students say around here. They can suck it."

I felt hopeful. "Really?" I said.

"No," he said. "Not really. You better not be late anymore. Do you KNOW what those kids pay per YEAR? Get their comments to them on time from now on, or else. I know ninety people offhand who want your job."

"Okay," I said. "No problem. I'll make sure I do that from now on."

My boss smiled. "Just kidding," he said. "We honestly don't

take student evals that seriously." He grinned. "Students bitch and carp about every little thing."

"Thank god," I said. "I've been longing to tell you. I have Fish Rot."

"Sorry to hear that," my boss said. "I heard that sucks. By the way. Have you been writing?"

I blunk. "No," I said. "I have Fish Rot."

"Listen," my boss said. "People get Fish Rot and get better all the time. My cousin had it. Most people at Yaddo had it. They recovered in a month. I hired you because you were writing. If you're not writing now, you'll be gone. And if you think we don't care about student evals here at Pegasus, you're a moron. We love our students, we treat them like gold, we do our best by them, and we honor what they say. We're here to serve them."

"Fig," I said. "Fudge, fig, fuck."

So my sister-cunt put all that in the letter to my insurance company. She said, "If you don't obey the Two Standards of Care law, she will sue because of the big damage to her mental abilities, which are, or once were, worth a lot." That was a lie. My mental abilities were never worth much.

But they paid. My sister was good at scaring insurance.

I got a PICC line and a port, a tube went into my arm and spit out in my heart. Every day I dripped a pound of liquid Azithromycin into my heart. It was awesome. I gained ninety pounds. That's when I stopped having lovers. I was already "curvy." I bought, using my credit cards, whatever my doctors told me I needed to buy to be cured. I bought a $20,000 nano-molecular oxygen box, $2,000 worth of plant stem cells in vials, I bought resveratrol, cat's claw, devil's root, CoQ10, fish oil, turmeric, artemisia, B-12 shots, cholestyramine, garlic pills, yucca extract, mushroom powders, hundreds of bottles of pills made from rain forest plants, all sorts of tinctures, amino acids in tubs, digestive enzymes from the stomachs of silkworms, dozens of tiny $100 vials of ozonated antifungal oils, an electricity machine with ear clips that sends jolts through your head to make you think straight, I bought bags of $1,000 red clay from New Mexico that, if swallowed, absorbs all toxins, I bought chlorella, I bought doxycycline, Mepron, Rifampin, Malarone, Alinia, Trental, blood thinners, vasodilators, Levaquin, I turned yellow from Alinia, I tried to buy Vivi-Dick for use as a vasodilator but was refused coverage because I'm a girl, and I bought and drank wheatgrass juice every day. But in all that time, fat as a cow, sweating at night, digesting food only if I ate ten capsules of digestive enzymes, I never met a guy who wanted to help me recover from Fish Rot.

I didn't think I was lonely, but I was. I tried to follow my sister's advice and work hard. I hoped work would cure me. By telling my creative writing students they were very good writers, I was able to convince them I had no dementia. I did not tell them the tricks and the secrets. I blabbed clichés, told them, "Writing is like juggling," "Set up three threads in the first chapter of a novel," "To write hot, write cold," "Use tertiary characters to beat the shit out of your main character," and things like that.

I wrote some things myself, thinking, So what if I have worms, bad diarrhea, and fungal yeast, I can still tell a story. Boy, did I write, thirty thousand words at least, three different times. Whenever I wrote, I knew I was writing the best I'd ever written. Political, universal, important, heartbreaking. When I went to type it up, it was gibberish. I typed it up anyway, sent it to my agent.

"I don't think you want me to send this out," he said.

"Okay," I said. "I take your word."

"Feel better," he said. "Heard you got herpes."

"No," I said. "Fish Rot."

"Ah . . . whatever," he said.

"Thank you for keeping me as your client," I said.

"Goodbye," he said.

When I emailed my boss at Pegasus to ask him what class I should teach that spring, a seminar or a workshop, he said, "I think we filled all our classes for next semester," and when I said, "But what about the next semester?" he said, "We will not be requiring your services."

I moved in to a cheap place with nine roommates. I went to a guy I knew who gave out tutoring gigs, asked if he could get me tutoring. "Do you know math?" he said. "Economics? French?" I shook my head. I sold my books, my extra clothes, and my dead grandma's diamond ring. I applied to work at LilPrincessCafé. I got rejected. Then I prayed. "Dear Jesus," I said. "I know I've been a bad person . . . all my life . . . plus I never believed in you . . . Now I do . . . Please help me recover from Fish Rot." I waited for an answer. "Jesus . . . ?" I said. I called my sister and asked for money. "I'll give you some," she said. "I love you very much. You know I'll always do what I can to help. I'll always do what I can."

"Thank you so much," I said.

"But we'll have to keep track, and you'll have to pay me back," she said. "My finances are tight, too."

"I know," I said. "I'm fine with that."

"By the way," she said, "I know you're a writer. But I value my privacy and don't want you to write about me. And if you ever write about my daughters, and how we have to spray our father with water, then my Mama Bear instincts will really come out."

I was confused, probably mostly because I had Fish Rot. I thought, Mama Bear. Mama, I thought. Mama Bear? Mama? Bear? I thought how in Idaho, where my sister lives, you can see the stars. From her hot spring at night, you could see thousands, but I never could tell where the bear constellation was. I could definitely see the soup ladle and the archer. Was there a mother constellation? I didn't think so. If there was, I couldn't tell where that was, either.

Sometimes, when patients sat around the Cerebus Center, we wondered how we got Fish Rot.

"I've always been sick ever since I was a child," one woman who'd run marathons before getting Fish Rot said. "If it wasn't one thing, it was another. Allergies, pneumonia, bronchitis, mono, you name it. My whole family's crazy. My parents divorced when I was young. It probably affected my immune system. I'm sure it's connected to my getting Fish Rot."

"My family's crazy, too," a divorce lawyer said.

"My family's crazy," a hotel chain owner said. "But I don't think that's why I got Fish Rot."

"How do you think you got Fish Rot?" the former marathon runner asked.

The hotel chain owner blunk. He was a big tall guy who always wore Wrangler jeans and leather boots and made business calls while dripping.

He yelled, "I got it because I ate fish!"

A housewife nodded.

"I used to eat fish," she said. "Sushi every day. Crab. Lobster. If I'd only known. Sashimi! I LOVED sushi. Mussels. Oysters! Now I NEVER eat fish. I made my whole family stop, too. But it's too late." She looked down at her bloated body and the tube attached to her arm. She added, "What is this world coming to?"

"You don't *always* get it from fish," a young woman who had Fish Rot and lupus said. "I *never* ate fish, but I still got Fish Rot."

"How do you think you got it, then?" the hotel chain owner asked.

The girl with lupus looked down.

"The microbes are everywhere," she said. "I mean, I drink water, and the water comes from the ocean, it's sanitized with toxic chemicals by the city, of course, but the ocean gets in the air, and makes the rain that goes in the reservoirs. I used to not have a good water filter."

Someone said that the disease was a result of industrial contamination coming from China. Someone else said the virus came from Haiti. Someone else said the disease was a judgment upon earth and society.

"Well, I got it from my wife," an accountant said. "I told her she smelled fishy. She didn't believe me. She said I was being a jerk. Now I got Fish Rot."

"Are you still married?" the girl with lupus asked.

He nodded.

"I love her," he said. "It's not her fault. She just has a terrible sense of smell."

"I didn't know it was transmittable," someone said.

Several people looked down and nodded.

"It doesn't matter *how* you got it," the accountant said. "Anyone can get it. Especially if your immune system's down. If you're stressed. The important thing is to take the medicine and get rid of it. That's what matters."

"Who's *not* stressed?" the hotel chain owner said. "Is anyone in New York not stressed?" His phone buzzed. He put his hand on his phone. "Jesus," he said.

Time went fast when I was sick. An hour passed, or what seemed like an hour, but it was three; a month passed, or what seemed a month, but it was six. The problem was I missed my own subway stop, then got off the car, reversed direction, then missed my stop, then got off, reversed direction, and missed my stop again. It slowed time. Once I got a brain scan my doctor told me to get that required fasting then drinking sweet orange liquid, and when I entered the test room I told the technician, while looking at the silver, body-length tubular machine, that I was nervous, and the technician said, "Yer fine, all you neurotic bitches are, I see you, yer fine," and I got into the machine and it scanned my head for an hour and when I got out I passed the technician at his desk watching his computer and the screen showed a bar graph beneath a picture of a brain and the bar was filled less than half-way and the screen said "38 percent," and the technician looked at me and blushed. He said in a low voice, "Get better." I taught classes here and there, got antibiotics, iron infusions, intravenous hydrogen peroxide drips. How did I get Fish Rot? I wasn't sure. It was perhaps two years after I dumped Scottish Pony that my sister called me with her request and I'd almost forgotten who she was, she was familiar, of course, I knew her, but she felt strange to me, and her request seemed out of the blue.

"We've gone on a few family vacations without you," she said— places I wouldn't want to go, she explained, Hawaii, Scotland/

London/Paris/Madrid—they knew I wasn't well enough and couldn't afford it—they'd invited me, of course, she said, I must have received the invitations—they'd doubtless been lost in my mail—and, she said, she and her husband had been particularly vigilant about watching our father to ensure he didn't do any inappropriate rubbing; but unfortunately, there'd been several incidents . . .

In short, she said, she was about to take action. She would, she said, lay down a No Unsolicited Touching rule that would protect my nieces forever, she felt, and make the spray bottles superfluous . . . Great, I said . . . I adjusted the valve on my home drip line . . . and to lay down this rule, she said, all she needed me to do was write a letter to my father and say what he was, and tell him that I thought my sister's rule was good.

"Uh," I said.

"You're the one who's always been bothered by it," she said. I guessed she meant his touching my nieces.

"Yuh," I said.

"And you and Scottish Pony saw that thing."

"True," I said.

I felt confused. Since my sister had seen several "incidents," I wondered why she needed me to write the letter. She was my big sister, after all, and they were her kids. I didn't want to be the only one to write a letter. I wanted to be part of a team.

"Why can't *you* write a letter?" I said.

She *would* also write a letter, my sister assured me. In her letter, she'd say that because of my letter, she supported my letter. Of course, she'd announce the guideline, too.

I paused. I wasn't thinking much. I was thinking: Antifungal pill time. Three, or two?

I counted my antifungal pills.

"It would really help me if you'd do this," my sister said. "I'm going to write my letter carefully, so I don't piss them off. Even though they're not perfect, I love our parents, and you can say things I can't, so your letter will be stronger than mine."

I had fifteen antifungal pills. They made five neat piles of three.

"Why can't you say things?" I said.

I heard her breathe, like *hhhhn hhhn hhhn*.

I heard a six-year-old voice say, "I'm scared."

I ate two of the piles.

"It's for your nieces," my sister's normal voice said.

"Of course!" I said.

I felt glad she was taking action. I was happy to support her.

She said, "You won't regret it, you're not afraid?"

Another call flashed on my phone. I glanced at the bills on my table. I didn't recognize the phone number but guessed it was my student loan company, a debt collection company, or the prerecorded voice of the woman who called me nine times each day from one of my credit cards.

"Afraid of what?" I said.

I wrote the letter. I said, "Yer a molester." Things like that. I said, "Not cool to rub my nieces." "Cut it out, you." "I support my sister's big new guideline." Stuff like that.

I didn't think twice.

It was much later that I found out they'd gone on lots more family vacations without me, my parents, my sister, her husband, my nieces, my little sister and her husband, their new twin babies, New Zealand, Thailand, Europe. I was glad the guideline had worked.

•

Breaking News ran a special on Fish Rot. An epidemic of fungus-infected fish, the reporter said, largely coming in off the eastern seaboard, particularly around the areas off Connecticut, Massachusetts, and New York, were spreading a bacterial disease called Fish Rot. You could get it from eating infected fish, the reporter said—which might taste like ordinary fish—from intimate contact, i.e., exchange of any bodily fluid, with a person who already had Fish Rot, or, if your immune system was down, from breathing the air in the Hamptons.

If the disease was treated within three weeks of contraction, the reporter said, then the virus would not yet have morphed into a shape undetectable by the body's immune system or invaded its bone marrow, and all that was needed for complete eradication was a one-month course of oral antibiotics.

To stay healthy, the reporter said, all East Coasters needed to do was to (1) make sure to eat only nice fish from reputable establishments, (2) avoid intimate contact with anyone who showed signs of Fish Rot, and (3) avoid stress.

Also, the reporter said, all East Coasters should keep an eye out for Fish Rot's early warning signs:

migraines
blurry vision
fungus, especially mouth, hand, crotch, toe
memory loss
difficulty recalling words, especially movie titles and
    celebrities' names
sleeplessness
stiff neck
dry eye or conjunctivitis
back pain

fatigue

loss of libido or surge in libido (which, scientists specu-
    lated, might be how the disease spread itself)

unusual thirst

cravings for salt, seaweed, fish, or iodine

bulging eyes

sore throat

a slightly enlarged neck, and/or nodules on the thyroid

"Nodules on the thyroid!" the hotel chain owner at the Cerebus Center said when discussing the report, "Ha! I got my thyroid removed decades ago! Still I got Fish Rot!"

"Maybe you *had* it decades ago," the accountant said. "And
that's why you got a bum thyroid."

"*Everybody* has a bum thyroid," a yoga instructor said. She had
long blond hair, a high, beautiful forehead, creamy alabaster skin,
and wide-set gray eyes. "My doctor told me that fifty percent of
Americans over age thirty have nodules!"

"That's right," the divorce lawyer said. "They look at your thyroid, they tell you that you have nodules, or else 'suspicious cells,'
and that the cells *might* be cancer, but that they can't know for
certain unless they take a look, and that to do that, they have to
take the whole thyroid out! Then they cut you!!" He leaned forward and wiped sweat off his mustache. "The key is to never let
them *look* at your thyroid in the first place."

"But what if you're tired . . ." the yoga instructor asked plain-
tively. She rubbed her hands along her pink leggings. "And suspect you're hypothyroid?"

The divorce lawyer shrugged. "Don't know," he said. "Just
know you should never let 'em look, because then they'll see
your nodules and take the whole kit out. Then you'll have to

take Sim-Thy-Thy forever and your metabolism will never be the same."

"Well, I'm glad," a housewife said, "they're spreading the news about Fish Rot. It's a national epidemic. Finally it's getting attention."

"But people still won't know they have it," the yoga instructor said, "because the insurance companies design the diagnostic tests, and the tests always come out negative."

"*And* they're saying all you need to cure it is one month of antibiotics," the hotel chain owner said. His cell phone buzzed.

"If my *dog* got Fish Rot," the hotel chain owner said, "I'd give it three months of antibiotics."

"Can you get Fish Rot *from* your dog?" someone asked.

"Sure," the hotel chain owner said. "All you have to do is exchange bodily fluids."

"I probably got Fish Rot from my dog," the divorce lawyer said.

We looked at him.

He shrugged. "My dog's the only one I kiss," he said.

The conversation devolved into dog jokes.

The world changes, it does, it morphs, it turns upside down flip flip flip when you're not watching. One minute, people calling each other by picking up phone receivers that hang on the wall, and the next minute, everyone's texting on cell phones. One minute, friends with Saddam Hussein, and the next minute, enemies! One minute, receiving letters in envelopes in the mail, and the next, no more letters, and instead of books on the subway, pale faces peer into tiny machines.

I did get a letter from my parents, in my mother's handwriting, in response to mine, and it said, "Yer no more daughter of ours . . . We're sorry you have Fish Rot . . . You've always been disturbed . . . We're excellent parents . . . nothing but love . . . excellent loving Christian household . . . You were a slutty teenager . . . also disturbed . . . Yer still slutty now . . . We'll speak to you again one day when you are ready to be truthful . . . By the way we know you convinced your sister she should fib about why she wanted her ten acres, then sell them, she regrets doing that and from now on will implement her own ideas, not yours . . . We've decided to give your sisters all the land when we die, because unlike you they are truthful and still part of this family . . . Keep writing your stories . . . that's very artistic of you . . . you have a wild imagination . . . You lied and told your sister that your father did things he would NEVER do . . . We spoke with her and she understands now that yer deceitful . . . We also know you told your sister that Dad can stuff it . . . that was not respectful . . . now *you* stuff it . . . We pray that you prosper and find your way to the LIGHT . . . Jesus loves everyone, even you . . . you are full of lies . . . XOXO Mom and [in Dad's handwriting] DAD."

I did send one shameless text to my mother. I tried to buy a soy latte at LilPrincessCafé and my credit card bounced. I texted: "Can I have my ten acres?"

The text back said, "Who are you?"

Then I got mad. I thought, Christ! All I did was tell the truth! So I texted my father: "Can I get my ten acres?"

He texted back: "I don't think so."

I texted my sister, and it turned out her cell phone number had changed. I texted her office, and it turned out that my sister had stopped using phones entirely. "Your sister moved actually," they said. "She switched universes. She's not in this universe anymore at all. A new technology has developed . . . She's not in Alpha Centauri!"

"What?" I said. "That's ridiculous!"

"Yes, I'm sorry," they said. "It's a very new technology. Yer sister's gone. She's just not in this universe anymore at all. Try Galactum Trifatta or Gigaboo Gobla. Good day!"

It's odd that I never met Prince Horndrak before I did, because according to Subnurse at the Cerebus Center, he'd been coming to the center forever.

I was sure I had room for one drip on my credit cards. I flew over the Sleeping East River on the Q, in what I knew would be my final visit to the center, because for two years I'd extended my Pegasus University insurance through the national "Python— Gotcha Covered!" plan, but the extension only had one day left. In reception, the nurses told me that the drip room might be full, because they'd given the last seat to Prince Horndrak. I asked who that was.

"You've never met *Prince Horndrak*???" they said.

Subnurse's eyes went wide. "He's here every day. He practically lives here."

She touched her shiny bunned black hair and smiled, and her arm went around her belly. "I've gained ten pounds since he started coming, and I blame Prince Horndrak," she said. "He brings these sprouted-spelt-flour milk-chocolate-chip cookies . . . the flour's sprouted so they digest like a vegetable. They're so delicious . . . guilt-free . . . he uses healthy clarified butter . . . bakes them himself!

"By the way," Subnurse said. She'd moved to the register. "Dr. Cerebus wants you to make an appointment with him because you're not getting any better. Also, your credit card was denied last week. You owe $6,666." Her lip curled. "Have another?"

My brain was so foggy that I guessed I could easily have bought medications I'd forgotten buying, or used the card to pay debts I'd forgotten I had.

I gave her another card.

Her hands moved behind the computer. She put on her glasses.

"No," she said. "No, no. Not going through. Sorry."

Subnurse looked at me sadly.

"I'm high," she said. "It's from the sugar. Why don't you drip today. We'll pretend this didn't happen. But after today . . ." She smiled. "That's it for you."

Her hand steered my elbow to the drip room. It was full of sick people reclining in leather loungers and receiving intravenous antibiotics.

"The room's full," she said. "But there's one seat . . ." She pointed toward a very old, very fat, wheezy, white-haired man. He looked down at his immense chest. His cheeks were filled with liver spots. Six or seven attractive women, all tall and with long lustrous hair, and all wearing skirts and high heels, clustered around him, put their manicured hands on his chest and thighs and talked to him excitedly, even though they were attached by plastic tubes to IV poles, which they'd rolled over from their own seats to his.

"There's one seat," Subnurse repeated loudly, and the women looked at Subnurse and frowned. Slowly, they rolled their poles toward their own chairs. Then I saw the empty seat beside the old man. "There," Subnurse said. "By Prince Horndrak."

•

As the reader can guess, given that we had to sit next to each other while we dripped our medicines, Prince Horndrak and I got to talking. Being a bad girl, pretty soon I asked him what he did for a living.

"Oh," he sighed. "I do several different things."

His eyes widened and he smiled.

"I work for a hedge fund," he said. "Sold my soul, I guess. But it's a good group, actually, a very small one. We mostly invest in ecofriendly projects. We invest in small businesses with big potential to help the world." He paused. "You know those 'Fair Trade' Organic Chocolate Bars, that give fair pay to short farmers in tiny countries?"

I nodded.

"I invest in that." His arm gestured.

He smiled in a friendly way. "One thing I do is, I'm a sculptor. I love to sculpt, and I own a company that sells sculpting supplies, also therapy for sculptors, to sculptors all over the world."

"Therapy?" I asked.

"Well," he said, "when I sell the sculptors the materials for their projects, we often get to talking on the phone. And you know sculptors, artists, they're often blocked . . . so sometimes I offer ideas for new materials or designs, and ask questions." He paused. "It's kind of like therapy," he said.

His name, originally, he said, was Lord Kradnroh. His people were from Bulgaria, although they weren't "Bulgarian" per se. When they came to America, the pronunciation was too hard. The name changed to Draknohr, then Nohrdrak, then Horndrak. "I have many different names," Prince Horndrak said. He shrugged. He smiled. "Some people just call me Bob Helman." He had dimples when he smiled. He said, "Some people call me Buck Singer."

It was then that I looked at him and realized that he didn't look as old as I'd thought. In fact, he was not old but only middle-aged, at the top of young, perhaps forty-five, and very attractive, and he resembled, to a T, one of my favorite ex-boyfriends, a muscular, tawny-colored forty-five-year-old Jewish-American Sagittarian investment banker with a high, large forehead, piercing hazel gold-flecked eyes, a strong nose, dimpled cheeks, and a nice wide jaw who was called, for various reasons, Buck Clydesdale-Singer.

"Are you . . ." I said. "Wait . . . do I know you?"

The man . . . Lord Horndrak . . . or whoever he was, shrugged. He still had a PICC line in his arm, and vitamin C dripping into it through a tube.

"I think so," he said, "yes, but on some subcellular, nanomolecular-particle level, everyone really knows everyone, don't they?"

His hand was on my knee. I must say his hand felt good on my knee, and even though his hand's being there was inappropriate, no one had touched me in a long time and I was loath to move my knee.

He looked at his hand.

"Do you mind?"

I shook my head.

"Are you hungry?" he said.

I said, "We're at a detox center!"

He shrugged. "Why can't someone be hungry at a detox center?"

I was still looking at my favorite ex-boyfriend, Buck Singer.

"Buck?" I said.

Subnurse swung by.

"Lord Horndrak?" she said. "Do you have any more of those cookies?"

He smiled, took a Tupperware container out of his leather briefcase, and gave it to her. She giggled.

I felt so happy, happier than I'd felt in a long, long time, maybe ever, because I was looking at a beautiful man, my ex-boyfriend, one in a long line who "hadn't been ready for a relationship."

"Who are you?" I said. "Whatdyou want?"

His hand moved onto my thigh.

"Not much," he said. "To get to know you . . ." He smiled modestly. "I've worked hard in my life and I've done well . . . you're a pretty girl . . . I'm at that . . . well . . . stage . . ." He smiled embarrassedly.

Subnurse swung by eating a cookie.

His hands spread in the air. "Since you know me you probably know . . ." His hands fell to his sides. "I'm Satan. Actually, I've had a crush on you for a long time. I like you. You're a nice girl and you're a little bit bad, let's be frank, you're a bad girl."

"BAD?"

He looked down. "You want me to list?"

"I'm *good*," I said.

"I'm sure you are . . . but . . . really, should I?"

I nodded.

"Well," he said, "remember that time you took twenty dollars from your roommate's wallet?" I nodded. He shrugged. "Tax evasion," he said. "Every year since you've been paying taxes. Not patriotic. Selfish, maybe. Stealing money from your mother's purse, we won't count that. Wearing her underwear when she wasn't around . . . Teasing, that doesn't count. But insurance fraud? Using illegal narcotics? Lifting filing cabinets, potted plants, and reams of paper from your workplace?" I blushed. He tsked. "Sleeping with married men." I blushed. "Married women," he added. "Sexual partners, I won't say the number, this is not bad in my eyes, but in the *world's*." He shrugged. "Remember the time you practiced voodoo on your enemies?"

I nodded.

"It's considered bad. We can stop. You don't want to do this, do you?"

I shook my head.

"We don't have to. You're bad. I like that. I know what I like and I've made up my mind. I've dated you for a long time."

Satan, in the guise of my ex-boyfriend Buck Singer, looked at me. "I was Buck Singer," he said. "I was Goatboy Lewis, Scottish Pony, Tyrone Foster, Christian Millford, Meatloaf Lebut, Marc Stroffoloni, Musad Sherif, Bobby Chung, Konyo Sakimoto, Jose Fuente . . ." He named a hundred names.

I said, "ALL of them?"

"Well," he said, "not totally. I just went inside them for a while when they dated you . . . borrowed them."

I thought: Oh! Well!

"You're Satan," I said.

He nodded.

Satan looked disparagingly at his arm. "Unfortunately, I'm dying of cancer."

Subnurse walked by and patted him affectionately on the head.

"I don't have much time left. But I have a lot of support to give, to take care of someone who could desperately use the help . . . and what time I have, I'd like to spend with you if you'll let me . . ."

I was still looking at what appeared to be my favorite hot ex-boyfriend, Buck Clydesdale-Singer. His outline shimmered a bit, but maybe it was the Fish Rot.

"I want someone to have my baby."

"A baby!" Subnurse said. She smiled. So did everyone in the center. Main Nurse carried in organic Thai food in cartons and distributed it to everyone. "On Lord Horndrak," she said.

I looked at the six or seven beautiful women who'd been clustered around Lord Horndrak when I came in. They were all dipping forks into ginger chicken and shrimp pad thai. I said, "What about them?"

"Oh, well." Lord Horndrak blushed. "Those are friends."

"Really?" I asked.

He nodded. "I have a lot of friends," he said. "I like people. I hope that's okay. When you came in, we were talking about water filters." His eyes widened. "It's an interesting topic."

Several of the women glanced over, lifted their forks, and waved them at Lord Horndrak. He waved back.

Reader, I won't make a short story long. I quizzed Lord Horndrak—Satan—about the nature of good and evil and his intentions.

"Evil?" he laughed. "Evil? Did I cause Fish Rot? Please. I did not cause Fish Rot." His voice lowered. "People's immune systems lowered because of eating too much processed food. And I think they did something weird to wheat . . . bioengineered it or something. That wasn't *me*." The Holocaust? he said. Of course not! Just think, he asked, what religion were the Nazis? I shrugged. Christian? I said. His shoulders lifted. Extreme weather? Not him, he told me—he loved Earth, because unlike God, he spent time on it. So he supported only companies that supported the environment—ecofriendly! I asked why people said he was evil. He held his hands out palms up.

He said, "I'm a libertarian."

I blanched.

He added: "I think some people are worth more than others."

I felt horrified.

"I support free trade and homosexual marriage."

"Well, that's fine," I said.

"I like chocolate cake," he said, "salsa, spicy food, and extreme sports adventures. I like contemporary art. I enjoy rap music, sometimes I'm profane, and okay, I like sex backward. Forward, too, also upside down, I've never had it that way, but I think I'd like it. I enjoy urban planning and systems design, I want to improve the world, I applaud human initiative."

"Okay," I said.

"Plus I dislike God."

He explained, in a nutshell, that all religions advocate surrender to God's will. He shrugged. "I don't like God," he said. "I'll admit that. Fine. You got me. I don't believe in surrender to God's will. God's a fucker."

He looked at me. "I like bad girls," he said. "So did . . ." He named a few of my ex-boyfriends.

"Stop!" I said. "I admit I'm a ho-bag!"

"That's the thing!" he said. "I like that! Have my baby!"

"No!" I said. "Jesus! You're Satan!"

He told me to be realistic. He pointed out that I was forty-three. "You're very cute," he said, "and you could pass for forty-two. But . . . you're broke. And you have Fish Rot. I like you . . . I want to take care of you . . . if you agree to be my girl . . . you'll have a house in Paris, and one in Madrid, and one in Senegal . . ." His eyes widened. "Your sister will love you again . . . Your whole family will welcome you back . . . I can cure your father . . . if you want . . ." He paused. Added, "Yes. I can probably do that."

"Really?" I said.

He rubbed his forehead. "I'm not Jesus and I can't do magic," he said. "But what if . . ." Satan gazed at me with Buck Singer's earnest, inward-tilted gold-hazel eyes. "He'll get laid off from his current job, get a new job as a meatpacking inspector, and have a small accident in a hot-dog factory."

He watched my face.

"That's violent," I said.

"He'll be the same, but better," he added.

"Okay," I said.

He put his hand on my thigh. "You ask a lot of your sister, by the way," he said. "She did everything she could for you. She warned you that she couldn't do it all. You can't change anyone else, you know, just yourself. And honestly?" He leaned forward. "If you're going to take a stand about something, it's not taking a stand unless you're prepared to stand alone."

I thought about that. "Right."

He tucked my hair behind my ear.

So reader, there was still one problem, an existential problem that I guess we all come to eventually. I was looking at Satan, who looked, felt, and spoke exactly like my most beautiful, sexy, funny, and talented ex-boyfriend, and he was finally, as he never had before, saying he was ready for a relationship and wanted me to have his child . . . It was a dream come true.

I whispered, "But you're dying of cancer."

"Hahaha," he said. "True. Dr. Cerebus is good but even he can't do much about that."

He looked at his watch.

"Twelve thirty," he said. "We got an afternoon. Whadya say? Catch the swan boats in Central Park? Maybe after we can hit the sex museum?"

I must have flinched.

"The Neue Galerie!" he said. "Then maybe shopping in SoHo. Yes?"

I froze. I wanted it. But having Satan's baby?

"You'll be damned." He shrugged. "But, by the way, I can cure you."

Reader, may you never know what it is to have Fish Rot.

"Let's get out of here," I said.

(2013)

THE INTELLECTUAL SITUATION (CHATHEXIS)

The Editors

Someone who wanted to know how we live might ask how we talk. Madame de Rambouillet talked in bed, stretched out on a mattress, draped in furs, while her visitors remained standing. Blue velvet lined the walls of the room, which became known as "the French Parnassus": a model for the seventeenth- and eighteenth-century salons, where aristocratic women led male philosophes in polite and lively discussion.

Talking, of course, is nothing new. But conversation, in the seventeenth century, was a novel ideal of speech: not utilitarian instructions or religious catechism, but an exchange of ideas, a free play of wit. Thus the hostesses of the Enlightenment received visitors in a new kind of furniture. In 1667, the Gobelins tapestry-weaving workshop became Louis XIV's official furniture supplier. Previously, fabric—like Madame de Rambouillet's velvet—had been confined to walls and clothing. The Gobelins were the first to apply it to chairs, which for many long, uncomfortable centuries had been small and hard. Now they were wide and soft—more like beds. The *fauteuil confessionnal*, for instance, had wraparound wings against which the listener might rest her cheek, as the priest had done behind his screen. Listening and talking became even easier in the 1680s, with the introduction of the sofa. Seating for two! For the first time in history, people could sit comfortably together indoors for long stretches—thereby making it easier for them to speak comfortably together for long stretches. Thus was conversation enshrined—encouched—as a vehicle of Enlightenment, fundamental to the self-improvement of civilization.

Face-to-face exchanges continued in the exchange of letters. As the salon had the sofa, "written conversation"—as one style manual called it—had the desk, another invention of the seventeenth century. For men, there was the bureau—a big, heavy table for conducting official correspondence. (From bureau comes "bureaucracy.") For women, there was the secretaire. Unlike the flat bureau, the light, portable secretaire featured stacks of shelves and cubbyholes, which were kept locked. Some writing surfaces slid outward, like drawers. Others opened from the top, as if the desk were a jewelry box—or a laptop.

If talking is one thing, and conversation another, then what is chat?

In the early days of the internet, chatting was something that happened between strangers. "Wanna cyber?" millions of people asked, and millions answered: "Yes!" On AOL—as of 1994, the most popular internet service provider in the United States—half the member-created chat rooms were for sex. AOL also launched the first mass IM interface, which was where the real action happened. Each conversation appeared as a flat white square on your screen—it was like having sex on a tiled floor. But at least it was someone else's floor. Signing off was like walking out of a public bathroom. Nobody knew where anybody went: answers to "a/s/l?" were likely lies, screen names universally inscrutable. Because AOL permitted five screen names per account, it was possible to use one for strangers, another for friends. Before the introduction of the Buddy List—in 1996, dubbed the "stalker feature" by AOL employees—you could come and go without anyone noticing.

Eventually, AOL's dominance waned as people signed up for free web-based email and downloaded desktop-based chat clients, like AOL's own Instant Messenger (1997). In AIM, all that remained of the original AOL was the AOL Buddy List, which hung in the corner of our screen. (Chat rooms were still out there, but mostly for terrorists and pedophiles.) Chatting now required constant tabbing between applications: browser for email, IM window, browser for search. Like hermit crabs outgrowing their shells, people kept shucking their old screen names for new ones.

Gmail changed all this. We signed up using our real name. So did our friends, and one day those names appeared in a column on the left side of our inbox. This was Gchat, and whenever we signed in, up came the gray, ghostly list of Gchattable names. And what names! Previously, we'd *decided* which screen names to include on our "Buddy Lists" (poor AOL: it came first and had to name the animals, and it named them in a corporate-midwestern way that couldn't help but become comically creepy). Gmail made the choices for us, pulling names from our email contacts. It was like standing outside the door of a party that all your friends had been invited to. Maybe they had already arrived!

Gmail began "in beta" and by invitation only in 2004 and remained technically in beta for the next five years; it continued to feel exclusive long after everyone was using it. (Registration opened to the public in 2007.) Being new, it was also youthful: you could tell when a person signed up for email by the client they used—AOL between 1994 and 1999; Hotmail or Yahoo! between 1999 and 2004; after 2004, only Gmail. When Gmail automatically added Gchat to every user's inbox in 2006, it was like a conspiracy of the young against the old. We would chat while they thought we were working; they would grow old and die; we would inherit the earth and chat forever.

So what do we chat about? Not sex. Our real name is right there, and anyway the mood is all wrong. AOL was a series of semiprivate suites; Gmail is an open loft, wallpapered with distractions. "PROTEST HYDROFRACKING!" says one email. Another is from our grandmother (grams31@aol.com): she misses us. Hard to picture anything less erotic than the inbox, that cluttered room whose door can never be locked. Imagine having sex and someone from the alumni association bursts in to ask for a donation. Everywhere the professional intrudes: a former coworker signs in; a friend's status message links to his latest article (Congrats, dude!). And as the virtual setting is all wrong for eros, so, too, is the actual one, because most of our Gchats happen at the office. We chat all day as we work, several windows open at once—windows into all the offices in all the cities where our friends spend their days Gchatting. Or we chat with coworkers, carrying on an endless conversation that sounds, to the half-aware ears of our superiors, like the soft tip-tapping clatter of real industry.

Our banalities are more shameful than any fantasy or confession. Gmail saves the histories of our chats, should we ever care to look. It turns out we use the internet to talk about what other people are talking about on the internet: "Oh god please look at what she just tweeted." "Hang on I'll find the link." And then there are the tactical chats—"I guess I am not that in the mood for Thai food?"—that would be harmless enough on their own. Mixed in with the rest, and preserved for all eternity, they assemble further evidence of our gross mortal wastefulness. Time is misspent twice: we talk about life as thoughtlessly as we live it. And the server farms know this.

In contrast to chat rooms, where we talked to many people in public, in Gchat we talk to many people *in private and simultaneously.* (We could gather our friends together—group chat has been around since 2007—but mostly we don't.) "As long as one is in society," said eighteenth-century salon hostess Suzanne Necker, "one must occupy oneself with others, never keeping silent out of laziness or from distraction." But distraction is endemic to daytime Gchatting, especially at work. The medium creates the illusion of intimacy—of giving and receiving undivided attention—when in fact our attention is quite literally divided, apportioned among up to six small boxes at a time. The boxes contain staccato, telegraphic exchanges, with which we are partially and intermittently engaged. Together the many chats divert us from work, speeding up time—yet look closely and you see time break down and stop. The clusters of text are followed by time stamps, which Google inserts whenever the conversation lags. For David Hume, increased conversation between men and women corresponded to "an increase of humanity, from the very habit of conversing together." But Hume didn't know about Gchat, which offers us so many opportunities for conversation that conversation becomes impossible. We are distracted from chatting by chatting itself.

Eventually, we apologize for dropping the ball, invoking a more pressing technology: "Sorry, on the phone." But now it is our friend who doesn't respond! Is he really gone, or has the sneak downloaded that add-on that allows users to appear idle when they're chatting? Like a shield, the round orange icon affords protection—to the person behind it, who is permitted to ignore any unwanted chat, and to the sender of the unwanted chat, who can tell herself, *I guess he's not there.* The way we chat now—using plug-ins or hidden behind Gchat's own invisibility feature—suggests that what we really want is a way out of chat. Consider chat's entry in the OED, which includes what must be the most melancholy example sentence in the history of example sentences: *"I keep getting messages popping up on my screen from people wanting to chat."* What anguish, when the definition of chat implies the desire not to chat! We, too, keep getting messages from people wanting to chat. And we keep being those people, too.

One good thing about work Gchats: they can't be videochats. The videochat is too eye-catching, too attention-getting—although the attention it gets would be other people's, not ours. For even when we maximize the video—when our friend's face swims into view, as large as our own, eclipsing our MacBook's starry default desktop—it still seems small and insignificant. Videochat—introduced to Gchat in 2008, and before that one of the major selling points of the popular chat client Skype—is a medium that, except for the way it allows you to display cats and babies to distant friends, is every bit as alienating as techno-phobes predicted. The built-in camera tends to cast everyone in the same gray pallor. Revealed to us in videochat, our friends are all nostril and no heart. Our interlocutor looks lonely, bored. Tired. We feel the same. Every relationship is reduced by video-chat to two properties: (1) the inability to touch and (2) the lack of desire to.

There is something so *literal* about video. It reminds you of a world that can't imagine anything but itself. It's almost as bad as walking down the street. Our friends are made over into evasive strangers: just try making eye contact in videochat. You can't.* It's as bad as a first date, or a job interview—you sit there, face-to-face with another human being, and feel unseen. Videochat's promise of intimacy—friends on the other side of the world, looking at us in our homes!—makes us forget the conditions in which actual intimacy occurs. Where have we had our best conversations? When we were sharing a booth with someone in the back of a dark bar, or lying in bed, or walking somewhere, or nowhere at all, our faces turned in the same direction: outward, toward the world, into which we moved forward together. We arrive at a shared perspective when we do, actually, share a perspective—when we take, quite literally, the same view of things. Then, turning away from that view—and toward each other—can mark a moment of surpassing agreement or sympathy. There are no such moments in videochat.

No, there's nothing erotic about videochat, despite what the experts keep telling us. According to a study commissioned by the hotel chain Travelodge, in twenty years we will be having "virtual sex" with whoever is waiting for us back home. In the old days, the traveler might have seized the opportunity to sleep with someone else; or, more adventurously still, deployed the noble and fading, video-menaced art of phone sex. In the motels of the future, a guest will simply conjure her partner via Travelodge's

---

* It's now possible not to make eye contact with up to ten people at once, thanks to Google's new social networking platform. Google+'s stated purpose is to make "sharing on the web more like sharing in real life," which is true only if "in real life" is understood to mean "on the rest of the internet." Instead of occurring in our inbox, group videochats—called Hangouts—open in separate windows, like pop-up ads. Each face moves inside its own rectangle, forming together a mosaic of talking heads. What sadist would take cable news as a model for conversation? It's like building a hotel using the blueprints for a prison.

"active skin electronics," which will be to sex what Gchat is to work: a way of making the dull endurable, a way to forget the fear that, stuck in the wrong office or the wrong relationship, we are *wasting our lives*.

It's already in our Gmail calendar: no Travelodge after 2030.

There is hope, but not for videochat. All we really need, to know love, is a plain old wireless connection and somewhere to lie down: the best Gchat conversations take place, like those of the salon, with one or both participants in repose, stretched out on a couch or in bed. Tucked beneath our covers, laptops propped on our knees—is this not the posture most conducive to meaningful Gchatting? In addition to being comfortable, our beds are private; on Gchat, we must be by ourselves to best be with others. Night affords another degree of solitude: like the lights in the apartment building across the street, Gchat's bright bulbs go out, one by one, until a single circle glows hopefully. Like Gatsby's green light, it is the promise of happiness.

For if, as Necker wrote, "the secret of conversation is continual attention," the enduring romance and appeal of Gchat can perhaps be explained by the way certain nighttime Gchats so effortlessly hold and reward our attention. Gchat returns philosophy to the bedroom as, late at night, we find ourselves in a state of rapturous focus. Which perhaps is why so many of us feel our best selves in Gchat. Silent, we are unable to talk over our friends, and so we become better and deeper listeners, as well as better speakers—or writers. (To be articulate—but not alone! To be with another person—but not inarticulate! When else does this happen?) We have time to express ourselves precisely, without breaking the rhythm. It's like the description of letter writing in

Françoise de Graffigny's 1747 novel *Lettres d'une Péruvienne*: "I feel myself being brought back to life by this tender occupation. Restored to myself, I feel as if I am beginning to live again." Chat's immediacy emphasizes response, reminding us that we do not simply create and express ourselves in writing, but also create and express our relationships. Gmail—simultaneously salon sofa and locked secretaire—stores the proof forever.

And whom do we Gchat with, when it counts? Friends, past boyfriends, future boyfriends, other people's boyfriends. But rarely our actual boyfriend, who's next to us in bed, looking for something to watch on Hulu. (Unless he's out of town, in which case we chat with him, and are reminded why we fell for him in the first place.) Gchat is for friendship, and affairs. It's for allowing into the home everyone who isn't supposed to be there, who's supposed to be at home in their own bedroom. It offers a temporary escape from the prison of the family—a reversal of what Engels called "the great historical defeat of women"—and patriarchy, which depends on monogamy and its enforcement. When we sign into Gchat, we do not enter utopia, but sometimes we catch a glimpse of it. We initiate a conversation and, some nights later, resume it. Meanwhile we initiate another. These exchanges are not exactly casual, but they're not unique, either. In Gchat, as in life, we are happiest when paying attention—when we belong completely to a conversation that continues. Might this be a model of commitment: truly felt on both sides, mutually desired, without exclusivity? These conversations don't occur at the exact same time—if we wanted threesomes, we'd be in group chat—but the long view is the one to be taken here, and the beginning of one chat does not mean the end of another.

At the very least, Gchat holds out the promise of "free commerce between the sexes" (Hume), which will surely be a feature of any utopia worth the name. Listen to people on first dates, old married couples, or anyone in transit between infatuation and resignation: mostly you hear the following of a tedious script. People say the things they always say, that they're supposed to say, that other people say. And we say these things, too! Yet Gchat has at times liberated us from this dialogue of the deaf, and provided us with a template for another way of talking. If, as Madame de Staël (Necker's daughter and the most famous salon hostess of all) put it, "the spoken word . . . is an instrument that is enjoyable to play," then chat—these broken lines, these misspelled words, this transliterated laughter, this long, unpunctuated scroll—has tempted us to compare it, at times, to the musical language that is poetry. But what it is, of course, is conversation. And that is compliment enough.

(2011)

SLICKHEADS

Lawrence Jackson

Around my way we really tripped over two things: the beef with them Woodlawn whores in '85; then four years later, when stick-up boys shot Sonny.

In high school, me, Charm Sawyer, and Piccolo Breaks got up a social club called the Oxfords. More or less just the little guys with round glasses from our block, plus an off-brand or two from the Avenue—North or Wabash—or from the Heights—Liberty or Park.

I pimped in the fine honey from church to the jam. Tanya, Carla, Kim, Lisa, Stacy, all of them dying to get out of the house. I was about fifteen when I booked out, and it took every bit of two years to get snug. But it had started in middle school with me and Rodney Glide freaking the white girl in the basement and him working her skirt up.

I wasn't really built like that. Check it out. Back in the day I loaded dirt and wood chips at a garden supply store on Wabash. One time, a church girl gave me a ride home after work and I told her wait while I caught a quick shower. Since the old-school play was to answer the Jehovah Witness knock at the door in a towel, any girl at your house was supposed to get open-fly treatment. Church girl called her mother telling her why she was hold up. Her old mother, an ex–opera contralto, started fussing. "Kim, use common sense. Even little Lair's trying to get some!" I took it as a compliment. Her mother didn't think I was gay the way her unafraid daughter did when I stepped from the shower, still in a towel. That's when I started liking older women, because they always act like, given the chance, you might knock them down. And I got it backwards, since all what she said really did was start me on eating out.

The Oxford clique came together for an obvious reason. When we still footed it to parties and up Rhythm Skate, we needed a whole crew or a connect to get by in the world of yo boys and slickheads. As time went on, the Oxfords put it together for real. Even though all us from out the row house—a snatch of grass in front and the #51 bus chugging by, floods and bugs in the basement, alleyways of blackness out back—all us little men had turned out the next Timex Social Club.

Woodlawn niggers called us the Pajama Crew for spite, because we draped our fathers' old trench coats, that winter of '85. Them County slickheads wore tight their Adidas nylon sweat suits, silk BVDs, and herringbone gold chains, flexing power. But the real Oxford contribution to the B-More scene was the D.C. Go-Go haircut—the flattop—or sometimes just faded, Jerseyed, Phillied. Bear in mind that your average yo boy from off the corner cut his naps down to the scalp. That's why we called them unremarkable niggers slickheads.

To me, slickheads lacked imagination, and their haircut was only the beginning of that emptiness. When I was first learning about it, slickhead behavior seemed inhibited, closed down, and reactionary. Like when I was prancing at the Harbor with my merry-go-round honey Sade, me ragging in a cycling cap, moccasins, bleached jeans, and an Ocean Pacific tee of a man surfing on a beach I had never seen, and some slickhead called to her, "A yo, drop that prep and get with this slick." They had no class, and if I hadn't thought he would have shot me I might have banged him in his mouth. Then again, he wasn't talking to me, and I was into women's lib, eating out and everything.

The Oxfords went for exhibition and fullness, the whole way, and took it straight to those break-dancing older slickhead clowns from Woodlawn. Yeah, they was popping and breaking, helicopter and all that, but that shit is for tourists. Our thing was the leg dances, speeded-up jigs. I copped our step from this old head who rocked coach's shorts and a touring cap, and who gave up the flow downtown every summer. At the Inner Harbor, near the water-taxi line, seven or eight of us would break into the Oxford Bop, a crisscross reel, while we shouted the lyrics to Status IV's "You Ain't Really Down."

"Said you were my lady . . . And your love was true . . ."

More attention than pulling your thing out.

The Oxfords liked a Roman holiday. Pretty Ricky brother crashed through the top of the telephone booth at the Harbor. Charm jumped from the second-floor balcony onto the reception desk in the Comfort Inn lobby. James Brown leapt through a car windshield, hind parts first. But mainly we threw cranking jams and released our boredom into the laps of the Oxford Pearls. All them was getting down, especially the girls from Catholic school. Even though we modeled ourselves on the old-time Negro fraternities, chanting "O-X!" through dim basement corridors pulsating with Chip E. Inc. stutter-singing "Like This," the Oxfords

could also function like that—like a gang. Coming up in
21215—Bodymore, Murderland—attending public schools, we
only did what we had to do. Anyway, a homeboy of a homeboy
kicked some slickhead in the chest over a girl at a high school
party at a fraternity house on Liberty Heights, and the war against
Woodlawn jumped off.

The jam was a cranker, Darrin Ebron spinning "Al Naafiysh,"
"Set It Off," and "Din Da Da" over and over; naturally it was
honey heaven. I was wedging my knees between so many willing
thighs that I never saw Pretty Ricky cousin Jerome and Ron J
guff. First thing I knew the music cut off and Pretty Ricky and
Mighty Joe Young were shuttling back and forth from the Kappa
House to the phone booth in the 7-Eleven parking lot and
Charm Sawyer was popping cash shit. I looked out into the mild
May night, and it was enough shell-toes and silk BVDs to stop
four lanes of traffic. Me and my homeboys were wearing moccasins
and corduroy shorts. I had a pound of Dax in my hair, dripping
like Shabba Doo's, but faded like a prep's.

I loaded all of my men into the car and left the scrum thinking I was just helping out, like Jesus would do. I had a Monte
Carlo, an orange EXP, an IROC-Z, and a Cressida on my ass—a
slickhead caravan in hot pursuit. Then I thought I got lucky.

Northwest Baltimore's finest had been called about the scrap
and I braked when the blue lights spun behind me. I pulled over
and I told the police everything I knew, which was that some
grown men were following me and I was scared. But you know
how Five-O handled his bit.

"I want you out my ju-risdiction! Get your ass out of my sight!"

You know how Five-O cuss you when he through with you.
Then he drove off.

It was six of us in the AMC Sportabout, a car about as good

for driving as open-toed shoes for running ball. Besides the fact that the starter on my people's car was iffy, the windows didn't operate, and the door handle on the driver's side was broke. That night I put that old yellow wagon to the test. I headed down Liberty Heights back to Garrison Boulevard, and I learned what Pretty Ricky had been doing on the telephone. He had reached out to his wild cousins, some hoppers who ain't mind popping tool. I took Garrison and that baby right turn by the firehouse to Chelsea Terrace, to fetch some gun-slinging boy from out his house. After Five-O shammed on me, I was needing Ricky's cousin to appear with that .357 Magnum that Hawk carried on *Spenser: For Hire*. Instead a jive compact cat hopped into the old station wagon with barely a .25 in his dip.

Now, I had seen some young boys around my way with tool. I think one of them even got into *Time* for showing up strapped at Garrison or Pimlico, the local junior high schools. In fact, it had been the cats from my year at middle school, the twins from Whitelock Street now going up Walbrook with Charm, who had brought tool to #66, setting the trend right at the beginning of the 1980s. They had got put out for a couple of days for that stunt. The next year, at Harlem Park Middle, them boys had burned up a cat for his Sixers jacket. I had seen a couple niggers pulled off of a public bus and beaten before. I held my ground standing next to a boy from Cherry Hill who had got his head opened up with a Gatorade bottle at a track meet, and I had gone with Charm to square off at some boys' houses who had been running their mouths too much. And of course I had fought with everybody in my crew except Ricky, who was getting too much ass to fight, because if he won he could double destroy your ego. The best one to fight was Sawyer's brother Chester, who was always threatening you with a nut session or worse. I hoped that the beef would get squashed, but I thought that it would take a big-time older head to do it, and I thought he would have needed a .12 gauge or something with some heat. Because on that night, Woodlawn was coming thick.

We were just idling in the middle of the street, nigger shit, everybody talking at once, planning to fail, when the IROC-Z came up from behind, and the Monte Carlo and the EXP drove up from the other direction. The motherfuckers had some kind of CB or headphone communications. A crabapple-head big boy marched out of the Monte Carlo shouting, got up to my face and started yanking on the door handle. I know it: I had that plead-ing, begging look on my face. He swung on me anyway and then tried to rip me out from the AMC Sportabout, but the broken door handle saved me. My people, my people. Mighty Joe Young was riding shotgun, and he shouted at me, "Drive!" I hit the gas and thread a needle through the IROC-Z–Cressida–EXP posse, racing my way down Chelsea Terrace. It was ride-or-die down the hill to Gwynns Falls Trail, Walbrook Junction, the briar patch for Charm, Pretty Ricky, and Knuckles.

Knowing the Junction better than our foes, we got back to our block unscathed. I let out Ricky and his cousins, and then we cooled out in an alley. First the slickheads got Ricky's ad-dress from some girl and tried to raid his people's house, but they were in the middle of the block and Woodlawn couldn't get to a window or through the front door. I thought I had made a safe passage until the next morning my father woke me up and asked did anything happen. I told him no, and he walked me outside to the ride. Late that night, them damn County yos had chucked a wedge of concrete through the windshield of the wagon.

A couple of days later a homeboy who worked at the McDonald's on Liberty Heights, just over the line in the County, got banked. Charm and Knuckles stopped going up the 'Brook because Simon, the concrete thrower, had promised them a bullet. A week after that Pretty Ricky fought the cruelest of the host, Carlos Gallilee and Dante Rogers, in the middle of Reisterstown Road. For a cat known throughout the city as a gigolo, a guy with slanted eyes and a Puerto Rican look, Rick had a whole lot of heart. He knocked the knees out of his jeans beating those dogs off and he stayed with his cousins in Philadelphia for a couple of weeks after that.

The war went on at high schools, parties, football games, festivals, and public events. About two weeks after the chase, in the parking lot of the all-girls public senior high school where Muhammad, Dern, and I chilled out every day after track practice, this boy Meechee was sitting in the back of a green Thunderbird steady loading a .38 while his homeboys, a lanky bastard about six foot nine and some other culprit, leaned on us. They cornered Muhammad on the hood of his Sentra.

"Where Ricky at? Where your boy at?"

I was wanting to run away with my whole body, but my feet got so heavy in the quicksand of his pistol that I could only look longingly in the direction of the administration building. My heart was pumping Cherry Coke the whole way, but I was proud of Muhammad for how he kept the fear out of his voice. The next day Muhammad and Dern got their family arms and we went all tooled up to high school. They took it as far as slinging iron in their sport coats. The day after that, we cut school altogether for marksmanship class in Leakin Park, an abandoned grassland just west of the Junction that had become a desolate zone. The Pearls were jive giddy. I just blasted into the creek, but I had to stop Sawyer, who never had a whole lot of sense, from shooting the pistol right behind my ear. To my mind, nothing is as loud as the roar of that .38.

The war changed the landmarks of our scene. Up to that time I had been keen to play in the County, and I could have cared less about my grimy, down-on-its-heels hometown. Now that we had to go everywhere in groups for safety, Reisterstown Road Plaza Mall and Security Mall in the County, the places where we used to flock to scoop out the honey, were less inviting. Our neighborhood mall, Mondawmin, became safe—if we toned our flamboyance down a little—and we started falling through Mondawmin, the Harbor, even Old Town Mall on the East Side. We kept linking up with city cats we'd gone to school with or had been in summer programs with, guys I had known from church at Lafayette Square, or the Druid Hill Avenue YMCA, where my father had been the director. Plus the girls I knew from those parts of town were slinging enough iron to take care of a boy. We went to our cousins and neighbors from around our way to get our back, to hustlers I had worked with at minimum-wage jobs all over the city, who came from tiny-ass streets crammed with thousands of brick row houses. The kind of music a cat listened to, or how he cut his fade, became unimportant compared to if he was from the city, how good he was with his hands, and, especially, if he had heart. That was how Sonny got down with the clique, because even though he was a young boy, he had all of the above.

Heads from around my way cut their teeth on the Woodlawn beef. The hoppers, the young boys we never had room for in the car, they headed straight up to Bell and Garrison to build themselves up. The hustle on Garrison, or, even more big-time, Park Heights and Woodland, was strictly Fila and Russell. Man, them cats bumped. From then to now it must be something like three

thousand cats shot on Garrison between the Junction and
Pimlico—that's one boulevard in one section of one chocolate
American city. Plus, ain't nobody ever see a bustling swaggering
yipping corner like Park Heights and Woodland in its prime.
Serving 'em well, boy and girl, serving 'em well. Knuckles and
Mighty Joe Young knew how to get by around there. I never
caught on and only went up to the Lot, the neighborhood
McDonald's on Reisterstown Road, a couple of times. I wouldn't
throw quarters away on Pac-Man or Space Invaders. I was spending my money on rugged-sole Timberlands and 12-inch records
so I could become a club dancer. Same as slick, the corner was
insular and monotonous, unless you had a taste for street fighting and raw booty. Anyway, the hoppers wound up getting tight
with cats who the corner was all they had. Like Ringfrail's
brother Clyde, who wore brass jewelry, or Taiwan, an adolescent
beggar who graduated to being a teenage beggar. Or Little Toby,
who had started smoking too early and would always be short
and skinny. I think (and was glad) Wookie was already gone by
then. I know, and was sad, that Monty was. Every time I go home
and walk to the Korean store to get some Utz or Tastykake, I run
into them all.

The young boys of course had to take it serious. I only had a
year left of high school, but they were going to be in this thing
for a long time. Pretty Ricky's younger brother Maceo started
going to war on his own, against anybody at all. At the corner
store on Wabash and Sequoia he stabbed Richard Franklin, who
then followed Maceo back to his house and sent him three-
quarters of the way to their family's funeral home with the same
knife. Some vet's old bayonet. Kind of intimate, being punctured
with the same steel that still has your victim's blood on it. When
Five-O locked up Chucky Blue that same night, Chucky, on

something like love boat, almost turned the paddy wagon over. That was pure dee Chuck Blue, living out the Myth. I'd never seen a motor vehicle rock from side to side on two wheels like that before.

It was curious. I found out a lot more about my neighborhood, and was surprised to know that I had a place in it. Slickheads from around the way, cats known for hanging on the corner, mad ill dynamite-style cats like Darius, who rode his Honda Elite scooter in Fila slippers—they respected preps from the city, as long as us cats carried that thing original, which was to say never perpetrated no fraud. It meant taking pride in where you're from. And we did. The Oxfords off Wabash were gaudy preps: pink shirts, green pants, bright-colored track shoes, and Gumby haircuts. Plus, there was no bourgeoisie contingent at the schools we mainly attended. Loyola, Walbrook, City College, Carver, Cardinal Gibbons, and Forest Park. To go to school there, you couldn't stand out more than to be an African American prep from the city. I might have eaten humble pie on a bus ride or two, but plenty of times I strutted the city like the word "Hero" was stitched on my chest. And the best-known cat in the clique for that air of confidence was Sonny.

But then our style became a casualty in the war that went off and on for years. On account of the Woodlawn beef, everybody began to ease on down the road to slick, Russell sweats and Filas, bald head and sullen, gold in your mouth, pass the reefer. All of a sudden, it seemed like slick had something serene you needed to get through life, a good way to not mind being an outlaw. I didn't like it on a number of levels. And I was always the historian—the identity "yo" was too much connected to the "yo-ski" thing from the 1970s, when the kids ran "What's up, yo-ski?" into the fucking ground. And as I got more black and proud, the "ski" part of it sounded too close to the Polack-Johnny level, the city-wide hot dog stand. Corny for us to follow the hick klan from Dundalk and Highlandtown.

I never even knew all of exactly how we survived. I had a play cousin from Edmondson Village, slick as a wax floor and known throughout the city as the Ninja. He had jumped with the air-borne in Grenada. One story went that he jogged up at a park on Woodlawn with an Uzi and told them to lay off. Another tale had it that the big-time boys from up the top of our street, who owned Yummy's at North and Gold, took an arsenal up to the courts at Bedford, where everybody from the county ran ball, and said they was holding so-and-so personally responsible for whatever went down. I admit, a couple of years later, one night we did have Carlos Gallilee all by himself up at Club 4604 on Liberty Heights. Darius, who had the distinction of having popped tool at the LL Cool J concert, wild Chuck Blue, and the ill James brothers were there, really wanting to hurt somebody. I just talked to Carlos, not feeling it was sporting to bring all of that wrath down on him on a night he was acting humble. But then again, he was an actor and today he's set himself up in Hollywood.

Funny how the slickheads didn't fare well in the end. Rocky, the mastermind—who had said up the Kappa House, not to me, just in my general direction, "You and your homeboys is just fucked!"—shot in the head. Muscleman Dante, whose girl I stole, ended up strung-out after sitting down for ten at Jessup. Simon, the lunatic concrete-block man, gunned down at a police roadblock. I think pistol-loading Meechee fell into the dirt, too— and, if he did, then that's too much like right.

Then again, now that I think of it, these were mainly city guys, who had hung strong with Woodlawn, eighteen and nineteen and, like me, trying anything to get out to the suburbs. Slickheads and their expensive tennis did win the style war; but, really, it was just that the city guys lost.

That summer, about ten weeks after the beef got under way, I learned that the police was the slave patrol and the Confederate Army extended. I had been surprised when they refused to protect me from the Woodlawn slickheads, but I hadn't known that my category was on their assassination list.

My father replaced the yellow wagon with a Japanese compact car, used, but with a tape deck and a sunroof, a real surprise. Somehow I had the car in the early afternoon, and me, Charm, and Mighty Joe Young were skylarking around the neighborhood, telling lies about the fine honey, bumping "The Dominatrix Sleeps Tonight." I noticed two white guys and a brother in a Chevrolet Cavalier near the library on Garrison, but I wasn't on the corner so it only seemed odd, not a personal threat. We stared them down and, three deep, drove off to the Plaza, doubling back and through, around Garrison Boulevard and Wabash Avenue.

At Reisterstown Road and Fords Lane I reached the traffic light. All of the sudden it seemed like a car was smashing into the side of me. A Highlandtown cracker pushed a heavy revolver through the sunroof and up to my head, his other hand reaching for the steering wheel. I could count the bullets in the chambers, and see the tiny indentations in the cones of the soft lead. I wet my lap. For real. I was preparing to die. The angry man was shouting, "Move over!" and "Git out the car! Git the fuck out the car!" Then, with some time, I thought to myself that he must

be a damn bold car thief. It was broad daylight. And even though
we had just bought the sporty little Toyota, I couldn't see why
he'd be so amped up for a $7,890 car. In a minor key, I thought
that a cool hustler would probably find some way to drive off.

I tried to throw the car in park and slide away from the gun at
the same time, but I couldn't get past Charm Sawyer's legs in the
passenger seat. Charm had been yoked halfway out of the window
by the black gloved hand of . . . Five-O? I heard commotion in
the back, and next thing I knew Mighty Joe Young had his teeth
on the asphalt. Then I noticed a silvery patch swinging from the
chest of the man from Highlandtown with the dirty beard,
and he demanded my license and registration. After about fifteen
minutes the dirty white man came back to the car.

"You ran a red light back there, but my buddy doesn't have
enough time to write you a ticket. Beat it."

I looked around, fumbling, with my mouth open and managed to get the Toyota away from the intersection. We got to
the next block and pulled over, me and Charm shaking and crying from relief and shame and Mighty Joe Young mouthing
Who-Struck-John. Never will get that dirty white man and that
giant .38 from my mind.

When I told my father about it, I could see in his face and his
demeanor that there was no authority to appeal to. When I was
just a kid, I had been robbed by some bullies and had reluctantly
confessed that humiliation to my dad. In his house shoes he
stalked out into the middle of the avenue, attempting to find the
boys who had wronged his child. But this new violation was just
a new burden to shoulder. I knew enough to sense him crying on
the inside. We were father and son inside of our house, but outside we were black males in America, with the same honor and
respect as number-one crabs in season.

I guess prep or slick wasn't all that.

The Pell Grants and the Maryland scholarships got cut off around this time, and all of a sudden nobody was going to college out of state. The money went out as fast as the dope came in. That ride to Edwin Waters or Cheney or Widener, that had been wish fulfillment in the past. By the second half of the eighties, if you went to school, it was either down the street to the community college or up to Morgan, the old state college for Negroes where my parents and Charm's parents had been sent, at the end of the #33 bus line. Most of my homeboys, their parents would let them try it out for a semester. Our people believed in control. In our neighborhood fathers would brag to each other, "I'm never letting that nigger drive my car," meaning their own sons. Young boys like Dan Redd and Darryl and Mark were smart, but they couldn't get to school out of state and get that big jump on life from out the neighborhood. I got into college three hundred miles away—and those last weeks when the beef was running fast and furious, I tried not to be so simpleminded as to jeopardize a chance.

About two weeks before I was supposed to go off to Connecticut, a year now after the chase, the fellas wanted me to drive the brigade down to the Inner Harbor to square off against Woodlawn one last time. Remembering how my father's car had got kissed by the concrete block, I chilled. I heard that when it went down, it wasn't like a Murphy Homes versus Lexington Terrace scrap. Woodlawn had sent mainly the little boys. The police got into the fight before anybody got stomped, or thrown into the water. Still, everybody began their adult criminal record that night in '86, and later it helped me that I wasn't there. But I saved the car one night and burned it up the next. When I got back after my freshman year in college, still dropping off into sleep after six weeks on line for Kappa, I passed out at the wheel and hit a neighbor head-on. I never drove again until I was on my own.

They were dog years between the end of high school and the end of college. Time folded every summer: scrapping in '86, macking in '87, bent in '88, and banging a gun in '89. I wouldn't want to live through '89 again, bringing all of that time together. We weren't Oxfords so much anymore—just homeboys now—and only rocking the prep style as a kind of occasional comment on the absurdity of our condition. The world had turned Slick with a capital S. To me the hi-top fade had its funeral rites when the cornball Toms at Duke started wearing it. I even stopped collecting house music and let the Blastmaster speak for me with that record *Ghetto Music.*

We knew what time it was, but used the powerful narcotics to keep ourselves from the numbers. Heroin was flowing like water that summer, and Saddlehead and Jidda, Paris and Los, all of them good ole North and Poplar Grove boys could get it. Poplar Grove. Longwood. Bloomingdale. The Junction. Then we started falling further down. In the wee hours we used to slumber outside some spot at Lombard and Arlington, not far from ole H. L. Mencken's, blunted, waiting for Troy and Stanley to finish sniffing that dope. The world of joogy. Around my way they call it "boy" or "joogy." "Girl" is "Shirl" caine—after Shirley Avenue where you go get nice. If you live in a town with a lot of joogy, everything else, like girl, seems real regular, jive legal. Joogy got me down from the psychedelics that they pumped up at college. Put it like this: in a world of disarray, joogy helps you to carry that thing.

That summer, back from college, every time I left out the house I saw somebody with tool, and one time I'm making eye contact with this lean slickhead, shooting a .45 into the air to keep street fighters tearing up a park festival from scratching his Benz. When I caught his eye I thought he was going to finish me. No question, joogy helps keep that begging, crying look off of your face. It got to the point where the police would be detaining me for walking down the street, and I'm getting ill to handle the stress, which everybody say is imaginary. That summer of '89 people was cross and fussing and we used to wear our Africa medallions at these problack rallies organized by Public Enemy. The next summer, all the music was about killing each other over colored rags.

The summer Sonny got shot my right hand Charm Sawyer had to hit a boy who was holding a pistol on him, and even though I was making speed toward a degree, I doubted it was fast enough. Hanging out with Sawyer was scrapping every night, which wasn't really my style, especially after he busted my head on Muhammad's basement floor. Plus it's tough on your gear, my main way to get notice from the ladies. "A yo, Lair, hold my glasses," he'd say as he sized up someone for a scrap. "Imma piece that nigger." I would take them. Then he'd smirk and start throwing the dogs. He started out with skinny light-skin boys, but he was working his way up to short, wiry, dark-skin men. When we went out, he would always say that he would either get some pussy, beat a nigger, or get blind ill by the time the sun came up. I didn't understand his rage at the ceiling of possibility until a little later.

Charm got took over by the Myth, which had a couple of ingredients. The Myth meant crazy outrageous athleticism in every activity. It helped the style of it if the head of your thing went past your navel, but it all came together in an attitude of defiant obdurateness that we called Hard. I would try to cool him out, because I was being taught something different at school, but every time I wasn't around, he would trip the fuck out. At a party he shucked off all his gear and swung around ill until he got what he was looking for. One night Charm fouled a catatonic girl's mouth to stop niggers from running a train on her, but she still had to leave the city. He was getting known and some people were afraid of him. He had mastered the art of drilling any girl, no matter her look, no matter her size, at any time. Like, Pretty Ricky had written a book on the art of seduction. He had this snakelike way of peering into the eyes of the slinkiest, the trickiest, the flyest—the LaShawns, Letitias, Sheilas, and Keishas—the girls who had had so much exposure to slick that I didn't even know what to say to them. I only tried to win by light touch. But Charm didn't work in a whole lot of small talk or eye contact or hand holding. He went on the Mandingo principle. He knocked down big China up against the freezer in my basement and she clawed grooves into his back. It took years for me to know what he did to make her cry out and lose control like that. She was so wide open every time we went with armloads of Guess apparel to the department store counter where she worked, it was like cashing a check.

I got a strong dose of the Myth, too, the dreamworld life of supernigger. One night of the dream me and Charm drank a couple of quarts of Mad Dog and picked up some wild ill broads from the Brook down at the Harbor. I only had one condom, used it on the girl I knew was out there, and ran raw in Sheba, thinking the odds were better because it was her time of the month. I thought another threshold of existence was at hand. Even the girls laughed about it, lil Lair happy cause he trimmed twice.

The ill vibe kept clicking, though. At a party in the Junction Charm hit this boy in the face and broke his nose, and the jam was at the house of the broke-nose boy cousin. We had to fight Charm to get him out of there. Then, sitting five deep in a two-door Sentra trying to cool out, two hoppers came up on us. One skinny boy was on the street side, and a bald-headed light-skin boy with a shimmer in his mouth stood in the back. Skinny boy tapped the window with something metal. I heard a crack and the glass breaking, and we were all shouting to Pretty Ricky, "Drive!" "I'm hit!" I was pushing Charm and Knuckles so hard to peel away from that hot one searching for my ass. Decades of nightmares about that gunman.

About a week later, Sawyer and Sonny were throwing a cranker on Maryland Avenue, the little club district anchored by old-school Odell's (*YOU'LL KNOW IF YOU BELONG*, the T-shirt used to say), house music Cignel's, and citywide Godfrey's Famous Ballroom. All the young hustlers and fly girls hung out in that zone. I was a little late getting to the jam.

I'd get the feeling of supreme confidence and contentment, just walking up the street and wading into a real players' crowd. Hundreds deep with hustlers and fly girls—herb bumping—passing quarts of Mad Dog and Red Bull malt liquor. Knowing my hair was faded right and I was getting dap from the players and intimate touches from Sheila, Kim, Lisa, and Tanya. "The Sound" by Reese and Santonio filling the air with our versions of the djembe, dundun, kenkeni, and sangban. Taking everybody way back. It's better than caine. Demerara. Ouagadougou.

Mighty Joe Young and me was nice, dipping up Murlin Avenue, near the bridge, gandering over to the zone from the Armory subway stop. All of a sudden, Ed from Bloomingdale drove by us and shouted, "Sonny got shot!" Old school, we ran

the mile or two down the street. Ten minutes later we're outside
the operating room at University Shock Trauma, screaming on the
state trooper and the young Asian lady doctor who said, "Your
friend didn't make it." She spat out that shit to me like I put the
gun on Sonny.

I felt like the hospital was run by people with the slickhead
mentality, that mentality that claims a nigger ain't shit. Me, I
always wanted to redeem a nigger. The state trooper, a brother
who understood, saved that bitch's Chinese ass. I wanted to do
something. Sonny's parents came in a few minutes later. Crushed.
Crying scene. Me and Mighty Joe Young walked down to the
central police station where they were taking Sawyer's statement.
We were amped up, spreading the word at hangouts like Crazy
John's and El Dorado's, where we ran into some of our people.

Sawyer had been standing next to Sonny when they got stuck
up. Sawyer's antsy brother Chester had a few dollars on him and
gated up the alley, so Sawyer and Sonny, on the other side of the
car, booked for it, too. Rodney, Birdman, Dern, and Rock could
only stand with their hands in the air while the runners gave it
up. Sonny and a guy sitting on some steps got shot by a .22 rifle.

A lot of people blamed Sawyer for Sonny's murder, but I told
him I was happy he had made it. He was my boy. We had been
lightweight wilding up until then. No QP, no Z, no eight ball, no
stickup, no home invasion, no pop-tool, no cold-blooded train.
Sawyer, James Brown, and Rock had taken a white boy for bad
once. And Sawyer had been seen running down the street with a
television, which had kind of got the police looking. Omar had
taken a girl's telephone and her father's horse pistol. Sawyer and I
had run a couple of gees on some wild young girls, and one time
a grown woman did start fussing, but it was his cousin. I remember, because I left my high school graduation watch at her house.

I thought if you were going to do the do, you had to take off everything. One night a little boy who had connections had tried to kill James Brown with a bat down at Cignel's, and we beefed over our heads, but James Brown let the thing go. I don't know how many times I got in a car with folk I ain't really know, on their way from or to do I don't know what. It was all right there. Rock, Darius, Worly, Chucky, Taft, Fats, Paris, Wood, Flip, Yippy, Champ, Ringfrail, Hondo, Reds. A whole lot of people got caught up in the mix.

What really hurt everybody was that Sonny had a whole lot of heart. He was a stand-up cat who had the will to make a difference. Shirt-off-his-back type of cat. Break a bottle over a big nigger's head for you cat. If the police looked for the killers, three men and a woman, they never found anybody. I had been in the Five-O palace on Baltimore Street and seen them lounging like they were on the whites-only floors. I had seen an office with a Confederate flag in it and some other of that old-timey, Frederick County shit. They always acted like Sonny's murder was "drug-related," like half of three hundred other murders that year. It hurts to think about his unsolved killing, twenty years later.

After Sonny's funeral, we started linking with cats who had hurt people, hoping to luck up onto that stick-up boy with the letter *G* on his hat who had gunned him down. The night after they shot Sonny we ganged into a dark room lit by the dutchy going around. A powerfully muscled old head addressed the mourning circle. "I gits a nut every time I pull the trigger." None of us ever forgot his sincerity. He said it to us like he was confessing something deep and personal, something that came out of the soul. I believed him.

Since Sonny had finished a year at Morehouse, the less stand-up guys figured that life wasn't worth struggling for. They started to get ill after the funeral like it was a paying job. I knew I didn't have as much heart as Sonny, so I did my share in the dim rooms. The morning after the funeral me and Clifton tried to run a gee on a young girl with a glass eye, not knowing she was five seconds from tricking on the corner—and Clifton months away hisself from the cemetery. Sometimes you would even pity a cat and bip half that bag of dope so that they wouldn't get hooked. One reason I stopped getting high was that Rock, my man from the bus stop days, pulled me up strong about looking weak, chasing. Sometimes you need to see yourself through the eyes of someone who has looked up to you. Then he got caught with a package and sat down at the department of corrections at Jessup, so I really tried to pull my pants up. After about eighteen months, overdoses began and cats started heading out of state to get away. Then there were the guys among us who thought that joogy wouldn't get to them, since they weren't shooting it up. But next thing, they started flashing pistols to the countergirl at Roy Rogers. That gets you a seven-year bit at Hagerstown, or you could get lucky and go to Jessup where people at least can visit you.

A couple of the cats really tried to make a fortune. If Sawyer was my right hand, then Muhammad was my heart. When I decided to make a break for school in 1990, after my father went back to Guinea, Muhammad told me soberly, "Lair. Imma make a million dollars this year." The hustler thing was in the air. All of the rap music was trying to help you know the I Ching of Rayful and Alpo and our hometown man Peanut King. We all knew by heart the D.C. anthem "Stone Cold Hustler" and G Rap's "Road to the Riches." But I was so deep into reading about the COINTELPRO thing and what they did to Dr. Martin Luther King Jr. that none of the stories about stacking chips could reach me. Besides the fact that all the New York cats at school would be flipping out over the Bodymore stories I was telling, or the time my homeboys fell through for a visit, joogy-deep. Anyway, Muhammad acted hurt when I looked away from him.

For about two years, we didn't have that much rap for each other, a homeboy blood problem. Meanwhile, Muhammad tried to get water from the rock with Rodney Glide. They stretched out until they tripped. Eventually, the state of Pennsylvania took the wind out of Glide's sails for eight years, twenty-nine miles west of Philly at Graterford. I remember reading the newspapers about the old crew when I was in graduate school in California, a million miles away.

Sawyer turned the Myth in a new direction. He laid up with a Jamaican sister, got back in school, and earned a degree. He won an internship with a congressman from the streets who knew where he was coming from. He started working with the hoppers at George B. Murphy Homes high-rises, before it got blown up to make way for condos and the university hospital, where they work on getting the bug out. Just going down to Murphy Homes was a trip to us back in the day, where life and death, crime and punishment was wide open, like at my cousin's house on Myrtle Avenue, where Carmello's from. "Fat Boy's out! Fat Boy's out! Girl on green. Girl on green," is how the touts would run it down.

Sonny dying like he did definitely motivated me to finish graduate school and teach at the university level. But going to college for eleven years was, no doubt, the most sterile experience I had known. It was feeling all balled up like an English walnut. An experience that seemed designed to make me question who I was, if I was a man or not, if I was doing something worthwhile or not. On top of it all, it trained you to appreciate everything about old master and them, right down to studying their trifling distinctions, which is why I guess not that many brothers, when they know this thing about the war, bother with school.

After some years in the trenches, Sawyer got hooked up by George Soros. Now he has a company trying to help "at risk" young people. I guess he helped himself. Sawyer stood for one thing, and I got down with him on it. "Just put it out there. No matter who it hurts, whether it's a lie or not, right or wrong, good or bad. Never stop putting it out there."

(2013)

MONEY

Keith Gessen

How much money does a writer need? In New York, a young writer can get by on $25,000, give or take $5,000, depending on thriftiness. A slightly older younger writer—a thirty-year-old—will need another $10,000 to keep up appearances. But that's New York. There are parts of this country where a person can live on twelve or thirteen thousand a year—figures so small they can be written out. Of course it depends.

My wife and I moved to New York after college, at twenty-two. We lived in Queens and paid $714 for a one-bedroom apartment (inherited, complete with artist's installation, from my friend, a poet and the founder of Ugly Duckling Presse, Matvei Yankelevich). That year, the two of us combined made $24,000. But we had a car, and on weekends we visited my father on Cape Cod. I wrote stories; she organized an art exhibit. We were young.

We moved to Boston. Our rent rose to $900, but it was 1999, even a doorpost could create "content," and I was more than a doorpost. I wrote long book reviews for an online magazine that paid fifty cents a word. Our combined income rose to $34,000. I failed to write stories, though; journalism took all my time.

The magazine collapsed with the NASDAQ. We moved to Syracuse and broke up. I stayed on at the MFA program, from which I received $15,000, then $12,000, then $15,000. I wrote stories again. My rent for a two-bedroom apartment was $435.

But I hated Syracuse. I moved back to New York; another friend, a novelist, sublet me his apartment. My rent was $550! That year, with what was left on my graduate stipend, plus some journalism and a book translation ($1,500), I made $20,000. I put $2,000 of it into *n+1*.

I turned thirty. Things had to change. I moved to Brooklyn and signed a one-year contract for $40,000 to review books for *New York* magazine. This seemed like so much money that I immediately sent some to my ex-wife, who was back in Boston, with those high rents.

There are four ways to survive as a writer in the United States in 2006: the university; journalism; odd jobs; and independent wealth. I have tried the first three. Each has its costs.

Practically no writer exists now who does not intersect at some point with the university system—this is unquestionably the chief sociological fact of modern American literature. Writers began moving into the university around 1940, at the tail end of the Federal Writers' Project, which paid them to produce tour guides of the United States. The first university-sustained writers mostly taught English and composition; in the 1960s and especially the 1970s, however, universities began to grant graduate degrees in creative writing. Now vast regiments of accredited writers are dispatched in waves to the universities of Tucson and Houston, Iowa City and Irvine. George Saunders, the great short story writer and my adviser at Syracuse, told me he knew only two nonteaching writers in his generation (born around 1960): Donald Antrim was one and I forgot the other.

The literary historian Richard Ohmann has argued that the rise of English departments in the 1890s, and their immediate bifurcation into literature on the one hand and composition on the other, emerged from a new economy's demand for educated managers. Our own age—born around 1960, and variously called postindustrial, informational, service/consumer—demanded copywriters and "knowledge workers" and, with the breakdown of traditional social arrangements, behavior manualists (*He's Just Not Texting You*). With the rise of communications came the rise of creative writing, and the new split of English departments into literature, creative writing, and (still) composition. It's pretty clear by now where this is tending, and which hundred-year-old discipline will become less and less relevant from here on out. We do not have a reading crisis in this country, but we do have a reading comprehension crisis, and with the collapse of literary studies it will get much worse.

For now, the university buys the writer off with patronage, even as it destroys the fundamental preconditions for his being. A full-time tenure-track position will start at something like $40,000, increasing to full professorial salary—between $60,000 and $100,000—if the writer receives tenure. That's good money, plus campuses have lawns and workout facilities and health insurance, and there are summer vacations during which the writer can earn extra as a counselor at one of those writing camps for adults.

On the minus side, he must attend departmental meetings and fight off departmental intrigues. Worse, he must teach workshop, which means responding intelligently and at length to manuscripts. A writer who ignores his teaching duties in favor of his own writing will spend an inordinate amount of time feeling guilty; one who scrupulously reads and comments on student manuscripts will have a clearer conscience. But he will be spending all his time with children.

Journalism's pitfalls are well-known. Bad magazines vulgarize your ideas and literally spray your pages with cologne. Good magazines are even worse: they do style editing, copyediting, query editing, bulletproofing—and as you emerge from the subway with your trash bag of books (a burnt offering to the fact-checker), you suddenly realize that you have landed a $6-an-hour job, featuring heavy lifting.

Yet the biggest pitfall of journalism is not penury but vanity. Your name is in print; it is even, perhaps, in print in the most august possible venue. But you are still serving someone else's idea of their readership—and their idea of you. You are still just doing journalism—or, worse, book reviewing. "What lice will do, when they have no more blood to suck," as the nineteenth century put it.

Odd jobs—usually copyediting, tutoring, PowerPoint, graphic design; I don't know any writers who wait tables but probably some exist—seem like a better idea in terms of one's intellectual independence. But these can lead to a kind of desperation. What if your writing doesn't make it? How long can you keep this up? You have no social position outside the artistic community; you have limited funds; you call yourself a writer but your name does not appear anywhere in print. Worst of all, for every one of *you*, there are five or ten or fifteen others, also working on novels, who are just total fakers—they have to be, statistically speaking. Journalism at least binds you to the world of publishing in some palpable way; the odd jobs leave you indefinitely in exile. It would take a great deal of strength not to grow bitter under these circumstances, and demoralized. Your success, if it comes, might still come too late.

And then, of course, a writer can make money by publishing a book. But if it is depressing to lack social status and copyedit *Us Weekly*, it is even more depressing to talk about publishing—because *this* in fact is what you've worked for your entire life. Except now you will learn about the way of things. That book you wrote has sales figures to shoot for; it has a sales force to help it. And you are in debt. Publishers have always used anemic sales to bully their writers—Malcolm Cowley speaks of their claim that only after ten thousand copies sold could they break even; of course, says the good-natured Cowley, "they may have been displaying a human weakness for exaggeration." Now publishers come to lunch armed with Nielsen BookScan—to the same effect. The comical thing about this up-to-the-minute point-of-sale technology is how inaccurate everyone agrees it to be—"522 copies trade cloth" sold might mean 800 or 1,000 or 1,200 because so many bookstores don't participate. The less comical thing is that, as a measure of short-term popularity, it is all too accurate—*Everything Is Illuminated*, a work of Jewish kitsch, has sold, according to BookScan, 271,433 copies since it came out in 2002; meanwhile, Sam Lipsyte's *Home Land*, a scabrous work of Jewish humor, has sold 13,503 copies; Michael Walzer's *Arguing About War*, a work of political philosophy in the skeptical Jewish tradition, has sold 3,136. Of course, one knew this; of course, one was not a fool; yet it's still hard to believe.

The very precision of the numbers numbs the publishers into

a false sense of their finality. They cannot imagine a book good enough to have its sales in the future. Publishers wish things were otherwise, they will tell you; they would rather publish better books; *but the numbers don't lie.* The chief impression one gets of publishers these days is not of greed or corporatism but demoralization and confusion. They have acquired a manuscript; they know how they feel about it; they probably even know how reviewers will feel about it; but what about the public? Those people are animals. Over lunch the publisher tells his writer what it's like out there—"You have no idea." In fact, the writer does have an idea: he lives "out there." But the publisher can't hear him; he is like an online poker player, always checking the computer. Nielsen BookScan rules.

"That equivocal figure," Pierre Bourdieu calls the publisher, "through whom the logic of the economy is brought to the heart of the sub-field of production." Yes, but he's all the writer's got. Is he looking tired? Poor publisher—last week he became so discombobulated by the "realities of the publishing industry" that he paid $400,000 for the first novel of a blogger. "He'll be promoting the book on his blog!" the publisher tells his writer over seared ahi tuna. "Which, you see, is read by *other bloggers*!" He is like Major McLaughlin, the cursed, hapless owner of the Chicago Blackhawks, who once became so frustrated with his team's play, and successive coaches' failure to mend it, that he hired a man who'd sent him a letter about the team in the mail.

Once the book is published it only gets worse: the writer proceeds to the calvary of publicity. Advances on first books vary— about $20,000 to $60,000 for a book of stories, though sometimes higher; between $50,000 and $250,000 for a "literary" novel, though also, sometimes, higher. Even the top figure—$250,000— which seems like so much, and is so much, still represents on both sides of the writing and rewriting, the prepublication and postpublication, about four years of work—$60,000 a year, the same as a hack lifestyle journalist in New York. But the costs! The humiliations! No one will ever forgive a writer for getting so much money in one lump—not the press, not other writers, and his publisher least of all. He will make certain the phrase "advance against royalties" is not forgotten, and insist the writer bleed and mortify himself to make it back.

Our forefathers the Puritans used to have, in addition to days of thanksgiving, "days of humiliation," when they prostrated themselves before God and begged for an end to their afflictions. "Before long," the intellectual historian Perry Miller wrote, "it became apparent that there were more causes for humiliation than for rejoicing." And so it is for the published author. The recent dress-down of James Frey and his publisher by Oprah was an event that people at publishing houses gathered to watch on their office televisions as if it were the *Challenger* disaster. But this was just karmic revenge on publishers and their authors, who spend every day prostituting themselves: with photographs, interviews, readings with accordions, live blogs on Amazon. ("In the desert, it probably doesn't matter if the groundhog sees his shadow," went a recent entry by the novelist Rick Moody, a man who for all his sins is still the author of *The Ice Storm*, and deserves better than this. "Oh, by the way, the film *Groundhog Day* is one of my favorites!") Henry James complained about writers being dragooned into "the periodical prattle about the future of fiction." If only that were the worst of it. Consider the blurb: how humiliating that younger writers should spend so much time soliciting endorsements from more established writers, and how absurd that established writers should have to apologize for not providing them. If they'd wanted to be ad copywriters, they'd have done that, and been paid for it. But they once asked for those blurbs, too.

In the age of BookScan, only an unpublished writer is allowed to keep his dignity.

Most writers lived as before, on crumbs from a dozen different tables. Meanwhile a few dozen or even a hundred of the most popular writers were earning money about at the rate of war contractors.

—Malcolm Cowley on the
Book-of-the-Month-Club era, 1946

Not long ago I found a very interesting letter, a letter of advice, folded into one of my mother's old books. It was from the Russian émigré writer Sergei Dovlatov, to another writer, apparently newly arrived. My mother was a literary critic, but I don't know how that letter got into that book; in any case, it describes literary life here in the States—the two clashing editors of the émigré journals, in particular, one of whom is pleasant and never pays, while the other is unpleasant and does. And so on.

Dovlatov had done his Soviet army service as a guard in a labor camp and wrote dark, funny stories about camp life—"Solzhenitsyn believes that the camps are hell," he wrote, explaining the difference between himself and the master. "Whereas I believe that hell is us." In 1979, he emigrated to Forest Hills, Queens, and began writing about the Russians there. He published some stories in *The New Yorker*, met often with his good friend Joseph Brodsky, and died, mostly of alcoholism, at the age of forty-eight. He had liked it here. "America's an interesting place," Dovlatov concluded the letter that was folded, for some reason, into one of my mother's books. "Eventually you find someone to publish you. And you earn some money. You even find a wife. Things work out."

It's true. It's mostly true. And when you think of the long-standing idea of art in opposition to the dominant culture, if only by keeping its autonomy from the pursuit of money—the only common value great writers from right to left have acknowledged—you begin to sense what we have lost. Capitalism as a system for the equitable distribution of goods is troublesome enough; as a way of measuring success it is useless. When you begin to think the advances doled out to writers by major corporations possess anything but an accidental correlation to artistic worth, you are finished. Everything becomes publicity. How many writers now refuse to be photographed? How many refuse to sit for idiotic "lifestyle" pieces? Or to write supplemental reading group "guides" for their paperbacks? Everyone along the chain of production compromises a tiny bit and suddenly Jay McInerney is a guest judge on *Iron Chef*.

Publicity is not everything; money, also. Émile Zola was so concerned that he would lose his position in French artistic circles because of his incredible popularity that he formulated an aesthetic theory to explain his art. As recently as 2001, Jonathan Franzen, too, worried lest his *Corrections* might seem to have fallen outside the main development of the American art novel, justified his work in aesthetic terms. (For doing so, for letting his guard down in public in tortured meditations on aesthetic value, Franzen has been made to pay, and pay again, by inferiors whose idea of good literature is German film.) Now writers simply point to their sales figures and accuse other writers of jealousy. Well, it's true. Everyone wants money, and needs it ("a woman must have money and a room of her own"). The only relevant question is what you are willing to do for it.

As for me and my $40,000, I recently went off contract at *New York* so I could finish a book of stories. My last article for the magazine, written as a freelancer, was about the New York Rangers. I received $7,000—a lot. Two weeks later I hurt my finger playing football on a muddy field in Prospect Park.

Sitting in New York Methodist, my finger worrisomely bent and swollen, I watched a man in scrubs yell into his cell phone: "One-point-two million! Yeah! We put down four hundred!" The doctor had bought a condo.

This was the hand surgeon. After glancing briefly at my X-rays, the hand surgeon declared I needed surgery.

"How about a splint?" I said.

"No way."

I decided to negotiate. "I can afford three thousand," I said.

"I'm not a financial adviser."

"Well, how much will it be?"

"Seven thousand."

Ha ha. It was like an O. Henry story: I wrote the article, they fixed my finger.

Except it wasn't like that, because I declined the surgery and kept the money. At my current rate of spending, it will last me three months. That should be enough. I hope that's enough.

2014

And then I sold my book. I finished it, I sent it to my agent, and she sent it to publishers. It was fall 2006; the weather was nice. I was dating a Columbia grad student and spending a lot of time uptown. I remember, about a week after the book went out, sitting on the steps of the Cathedral of St. John the Divine, across the street from the Hungarian Pastry Shop, talking on my cell phone with my agent, Sarah Chalfant, as she ran through the offers. There were two good ones and a few bad ones. We decided to go with a good one, from Viking. At that point I had $1,000 in the bank, and was grateful for the free coffee refills at the Pastry Shop. The book sold for $160,000, and Sarah proceeded to sell translation rights for about as much in sum to several European publishers. After discussing Viking's offer with her that day, I closed my phone, looked up at the Cathedral of St. John the Divine, then crossed the street and went back into the Pastry Shop, a rich man.

What was it like to be rich? It was fun. I paid for dinner a few times. I went to my college roommate's wedding in Brazil without worrying about it. It was as if a great stone—*economy*—that had lain on my mind, dictating what I could and could not do, what stores or cafés I could or could not enter, had suddenly been removed. I remember leaving the *n+1* office late one night with my roommate and coeditor, Chad, and Anne, the grad student. We were in production, and Chad had been spending entire days proofreading. The office was on Chrystie Street, on the Lower East Side, and to get to our apartment in Brooklyn we'd have to take two trains, neither of which ran very often so late at night. It would take about an hour. Or we could take a cab, which would take ten minutes. But a cab would cost $15. We discussed it. "Chad is very, very tired," Anne summed up the arguments. "And Keith is rich!" We took the cab.

Almost exactly six years later, in fall 2012, I was again sitting outside, talking on my phone about a moneymaking proposition. Anne and I had broken up. I had been together with Emily, a writer, for nearly five years, and we'd been living together in Brooklyn for a year. We were broke. In fact, a few weeks earlier we'd received a perplexed phone call from our Jamaican landlord, saying that our rent check had bounced and his bank had charged him $50. It was a screwup—we did, barely, have enough money for that month's rent, and had written the check from the wrong account. But it wasn't like the right account held $100,000: it held $3,000, minus that month's rent, now minus $50, and there was no money coming in. I sat talking on my phone on a bench next to the parking lot of a ShopRite off I-84 in Connecticut while Emily tried to keep her cat Raffles from running under a car.

How had I managed to squander all that money? Sometimes it seems unbelievable to me, something out of Dostoevsky; other times I can see pretty clearly how it happened. In the past five years I've translated two books and edited two others; the payments I received totaled $8,250. It's certainly easier to translate or edit a book than to write one—I could never have *written* four books in that many years—but it still takes time. In those years I also wrote articles and book reviews for several magazines, but not that many—about two or three a year. All in all I made $100,000 from my journalism in the period between the two phone calls. That, plus my book advances, minus commissions, amounted to about $330,000 of pretax income over six years. This is pretty good money for a thrifty male with no children, and going into 2011 I had a $60,000 nest egg in my checking account. I liked keeping it there, where I could see it. Then two close friends got into financial trouble and asked me to bail them out. I was liquid and I didn't really think twice about it. Suddenly I was down to $10,000. And then $7,000. And then $3,000. Then we bounced that rent check.

The person calling me with a financial proposition was an old friend; years before, he had sublet his apartment to me for very little money, allowing me to move to New York while I was still in graduate school. He was also one of my first editors, at *Dissent*. Now he was the head of the creative writing department at a college near the city. They had just learned that more students had enrolled in creative writing classes than expected. The college could turn back some students, but not this many; they wanted to hire an extra teacher to do a fiction workshop. Today was Friday; the semester started Monday. Would I be willing to teach a fiction workshop? They would pay me. I had to create a syllabus; I had to meet every student for conference every other week; I had to read and comment on their work. But I did not have to attend departmental meetings, or any meetings. That was the deal.

I had never wanted to teach. Part of it was that I'd been unhappy in college, and in grad school, and was glad to be out of reach of the university. Part of it was me teaching: I'm not friendly enough. And part of it was teaching writing: it seemed fraudulent, more fraudulent than other kinds of teaching, and bound up in a more fraught dynamic. Students don't take French or history classes because they want to become French or history professors; they take them because they want to learn about French and history. Whereas writing students take writing classes because they want to become writers—at least, I always did. In fact, what I most wanted was to be told, by a writer, that I was myself a writer, that I had it. And so by teaching such a class, weren't you taking part in that deception, in the deception that all these students might become writers? And weren't you also forced, all the time, to lie to them, in effect, whether mildly or baldly, about their work?

In short, I had hoped to avoid it. But I looked now at our car parked in the ShopRite parking lot. It was a 1995 Honda Civic with more than 180,000 miles on it, and for the last hundred miles it had been making a funny noise. I looked at Emily, who was still working on her novel, the completion of which might or might not get us out of our financial rut. I had just completed a reporting trip for a magazine, during which I'd grown a dramatic beard, but it would be months before the article was finished and I got paid. I looked at our cat, Raffles, whose recent illnesses had drained the last of our resources. In the past six months I had written an introduction and given several paid lectures—on translation, long-form journalism, and the writing life—at universities. But it was barely enough, and I *still* didn't have health insurance. I said I'd be happy to teach a fiction workshop.

Later that day, as we were pulling into Emily's parents' driveway, the back left wheel collapsed. That's what the funny noise had been. Interestingly, about fifty miles after that, as we headed up 95 to New York, the front hood of the car suddenly popped up, smashing the windshield and remaining there as we pulled over into the breakdown lane. I sold the car to the auto body shop we got towed to, and used the money to rent a car to get us home to New York.

The college was small and bucolic, a thirty-minute train ride from the city through leafy Westchester County. It was a fifteen-minute walk through town to campus; on my first day and on subsequent days, I bought a bagel with veggie cream cheese for $2.99 at Bagel Town. The campus was on a hill, just like in *White Noise*, and so I tended to arrive at my office a little out of breath. The office was tiny, one desk and two chairs, and I split it with another creative writing teacher: she had it on Mondays and Tuesdays, I had it on Thursdays and Fridays. Still, it was nice to have an office. I checked my email there and prepared for class.

I had fifteen students, ranging from first-years to seniors. Some had taken workshops before, others had not. There would be, according to my reading of the class list, eleven girls and three boys, with one wild card (Mackenzie). But then it turned out that Logan and Sameer and Mackenzie were all girls, which made fourteen. At least Tyler was a boy. He was rail-thin and had green hair, but at least he was a boy. Not that it mattered. I could teach writing to anyone.

The first class did not go as well as I had hoped. My plan was to begin at the beginning. After briefly introducing myself and scheduling everyone's workshops for the semester, I asked the students to list their favorite authors. I wrote them on the board.

Aimee Bender
Michael Ondaatje
Carl Hiaasen
George R. R. Martin
Orson Scott Card (this was Tyler)

Okay. Well, okay. I then asked the students to name some *old* writers they liked. Jane Austen, they said, and Tolstoy. That was more like it. My next question was this: Why write? Why—when there is so much writing in the world, so much great writing, some of it listed now on the board, and so much of it unread— would we continue to produce more?

I was hoping, I think, that someone would say, "You're right. There is no reason. This is hopeless." And then slowly, together, we would feel our way toward some arguments for why—maybe—a person could justify attempting to write. I figured it would take up most of the two hours.

In fact, no one even blinked. "Values have changed," said one student. "There is new technology," said another. "That's right. Cell phones. The internet." "We have a different vocabulary, new words." "You want to intervene in contemporary political debates," Tyler put in.

These were all correct answers. I just hadn't expected to get to them so quickly. I was reeling. I bought myself time by writing the answers on the board. But I didn't know what to say.

"It's a profound question," I concluded, lamely. "We'll keep thinking about it as the semester goes on."

We moved to my next profound question: What do you know that no one else knows? My premise was that good writing depends on a kind of specialized knowledge—whether of some process, or some relationship, or some situation or event. If people would just tell us what actually happened! We would know so much; we would learn so much. Of Kafka's commitment to telling the whole truth about himself and his life, Elias Canetti wrote: "A human being who offers himself to knowledge so completely is, under any circumstances, an incomparable stroke of luck." We do not have to be Kafka—but we can at least tell one truth, or two, about our lives. As the editor of a literary magazine, I had read so many "stories"—fiction or nonfiction, it didn't matter. They were made-up, and the more made-up they were, the more conventional. Where truth was left out or kept general, cliché filled the void. The mistake made over and over was to search for the "universal," when (this is itself a cliché, maybe, but still) it was the specific stuff that readers wanted to know. But, of course, it's not so easy to figure out what the specific stuff is. One's life contains so many things; how are you to know which of these things is distinctive?

In some form, I put this question to the class, and the answers were again disappointing, though in a different way. The answers to the first question had come too quickly, like the class had been asked the question before. The answers to this question came too slowly, like the question made no sense to them, like they were hostile to it. "Experiences of culture," someone said. "Your childhood," someone else said. Eventually someone said: "Your family." (An answer that can be right or wrong. "My crazy Jewish family"—bad, because conventional. "My repressed Jewish family"—interesting.) But no one said something so simple as "What I did last weekend." Or "How I lost my virginity." Or: "Why I no longer speak to my former best friend."

"It's something we're going to keep thinking about as we go through the semester," I said again, hopefully. "It's okay to use your experiences in your fiction. Your life is interesting and contains drama. The trick is figuring out where the drama is and what it means." The stories I liked best, I said, were ones that made you think they were true, even though they may not be.

The first student I lost was a first-year who'd never been in a workshop before. She emailed me the day after class to ask if I would let her out. I wrote to her adviser and said that of course she could drop the class if she wanted, but she was also welcome to stay. "Thank you for being so understanding," the adviser replied. The student, he said, had been intimidated by the pace of the first class; she felt like she'd been air-dropped onto an alien planet.

Maybe I had plunged into things too quickly. But more experienced students were also thinking of leaving. One student dropped the class without explanation. Two others, a self-identified "magical realist" and an "experimenter with language," came to discuss with me the question of whether my approach—too realist, they said—was right for their particular unique styles of writing. "I've had a happy and normal life," one of them claimed. She didn't think she would have anything too interesting to write about, if she had to write from her own experience.

I assured both the magical realist and the language experimenter that we could work together. I wasn't *prejudiced* against their styles of writing. All styles are great. Kafka was a magical realist! I said. Joyce was an experimenter with language! We could read those writers and learn from them together. And surely I had things to learn about their approaches. We could learn from each other, I said.

I was lying. In fact, I had no idea what to say to these students. I had read their first exercises and they were not for me. They were obscure; rather than being less self-involved than traditional first-person writing, they were *more* self-involved. I should have said: "You are not ready to do this sort of work. You need first to figure out what you are trying to say to the world, and only then go about finding the means adequate to the saying. I can help you figure out the first thing. If you're not interested in that, this class will not be useful." But I didn't say that.* I didn't want to put my friend, who'd hired me, in a bad spot. He had brought me in because too many students were being rejected from the classes, but now students were rejecting me. What kind of teacher loses 25 percent of his students *after one class*?

---

*"And furthermore," I should have said, "Joyce and Kafka were realists, obviously. They were not fleeing experience—they were trying to describe it. And they especially did not do this because they had happy, uneventful lives—though Joyce at least was a happy person, through it all." Anyway, I didn't say this.

•

The second class went better than the first. We discussed a terrific short story by Chris Kraus called "Trick," about a young woman who moves to New York to become an artist and ends up working as a stripper, and Philip Roth's *Goodbye, Columbus*, which struck me as less interesting than I'd remembered it: certainly a very good long story, but formulaic. You wouldn't have known, necessarily, that this guy was going to write *Sabbath's Theater*. Maybe Roth didn't know, either. During the discussion, one of the students, Charlotte, made a brilliant observation about Brenda Patimkin: she has very bad vision, and yet in the first scene she jumps off the diving board, despite the fact that she might not be able to see the pool—that's how confident Brenda is that the pool will be there.

That second Friday, before class, I held my first conferences. Conferences last thirty minutes. That may not sound like much, but you'd be surprised. What is there to talk about? The students had written short exercises, but these were slim reeds on which to sustain a half-hour discussion. My first conference was with Mackenzie, a first-year from Wisconsin. She hadn't done much writing before. For the assignment—which was to describe something that only you knew about—she'd written about a visit from a boy to her house in the middle of the night. This was her secret, and not a very interesting one. But during conference it emerged that she'd grown up in a town of four thousand people. That her high school had three hundred students. That she'd worked at the Dairy Queen, which was owned by a scary Norwegian guy named Otto. In fact there were a lot of Norwegians in town. They had celebrations, and Mackenzie, not herself a Norwegian, was left out. As she described all this, a whole social world appeared before our eyes in that small office. "Is this interesting to you?" I said. "Usually I think it's boring," she said. "But it's interesting to talk to someone who finds it interesting." I was feeling pretty good—a person who was not entirely a fraud—as Mackenzie left.

Then came Julie, the magical realist. I had been unable to make head or tail of her writing exercise. It appeared to be a ghost story of some kind, with the ghost possessing erotic potential. Did the narrator have sex with the ghost? This is what I wanted to know. But Julie wouldn't say. Magical realism was her thing. In fact, continued Julie, she had written a novel. Would I be willing to read it and discuss it with her in conference?

Well, I said. What about workshopping it in class?

"I want to workshop other things in class," said Julie.

I was stumped. I hadn't expected this. The tuition at this college was very high—in fact, it regularly ranked as the most expensive college in America. So these students should get good service. On the other hand, I was just one person. A person who did not want to read Julie's novel. Not only did I not want to read it, I didn't *believe* in reading it. Who would benefit from this? Already she had read it with her previous semester's writing teacher. And now she was going to read it with me? She was going to drag this novel from class to class, from teacher to teacher—in hope of what? The whole point of a workshop was to put your work in front of your peers, to see what it feels like to have a readership, to see how they react. I said we'd see about the novel. In the meantime, I wanted Julie to consider that there is realism in magical realism. But I knew that a more experienced teacher would have handled all this better.

It was time for class. After class, I returned to my office for the next set of conferences, and there again was Julie. Had she forgotten something? No; she was holding an Add/Drop form. I signed the form. The conferences rolled on.

I met with Vanessa, my chattiest student—her chattiness was bad for class, but it was good for conference. The half hour flew by. Next up was Charlotte, who had made the penetrating remark about Brenda in *Goodbye, Columbus*. Charlotte was working in the fantasy genre. This seemed to mark her as yet another student who had nothing to learn from me. And maybe that was true. But unlike the magical realist Julie and the language experimenter Leslie (who also dropped the class), Charlotte didn't think I was an idiot. She explained the ways in which her deployment of orcs and elves in her work differed from and in fact subverted the tropes of ordinary fantasy fiction. I didn't mind discussing all this, even as I found it surreal. These were the times we were living in. I was on a college campus. I was a visiting professor. And I was sitting in my office, bearded and wise-looking and, in all serious- ness, with one of my brightest students, discussing orcs.

We settled into the semester. There were, it soon emerged, three types of student in the workshop. There were three upperclass- men who had taken several workshops already. They were not necessarily the best writers in the class—not at all—but they were used to classroom discussion of literature, and brought to it some maturity and poise. There were some first-years who had done a lot of writing in high school and were genuinely talented. In fact one of them, Allison, was so talented I didn't know what to say to her. And then there was the rest of the class, music and theater majors for the most part, who had never done much writ- ing. These turned out to be the students to whom I had the most to say, and who were the most eager to listen.

The question of criticism, and of lying to students about their work, continued to trouble me. I am by nature a critical person—but I know that people need positive reinforcement about their writing. I have always needed it, for example, and still need it today. So how critical should one be? The school was so expensive. It seemed to violate some law of capitalism that someone should pay so much to attend a college and then be told that her work is no good.

My first encounter with this, after the departure of the experimental faction, was with Logan. She was a jazz singing major; she hadn't done much writing before. Her first exercise was an unpromising and brief account of her parents' divorce, told mostly in cliché. Then, nervous about the story she was going to hand in for workshop, Logan sent it to me in advance. It was a highly conventional story about a girl who lives alone in Manhattan (on what money?!), goes to a museum, meets a boy, and then goes home with him. They stay up the whole night talking. They don't even sleep together.

I did not know what to do. I had no suggestions for how to improve the story. And it wasn't the world's worst story. I just knew that I found it boring, and not just because they didn't sleep together.

I told Logan, as gently as I could but probably not gently enough, to try something else. There had been a hint, I thought, in one of her exercises, of a slightly angrier person than the one she was presenting in this story. During conference I suggested that this would be interesting to hear more about; her anger at one of her friends, who treated her badly. With examples. Logan nodded and left conference. Then I didn't hear from her. I spent several days worrying that I'd shut her down entirely, that by rejecting her first story attempt I'd rendered her unable to write.

Finally she handed in her story: it was a funny and angry mono-
logue about her Mexican grandmother, a model and a man-eater.
It wasn't a masterpiece, but it was entertaining and new. The
class liked it. I liked it.

The low point of the semester may have been the workshop of
Carrie's first story. Carrie was one of my talented first-years. She
was also a devout Christian who had missed class—very apolo-
getically—to go on a retreat with fellow students. She wrote
several exercises about her Korean family in San Diego—sharp,
observant, funny, very sweet. But for her workshopped story
she'd decided to write about teenage Japanese prostitutes. Why?!
Carrie wasn't even Japanese! I spent the days before class thinking about what to say. Then it came time for workshop. The
students, it turned out, loved the story. Charlotte said that she
had cried at the end. When they were done praising it I mumbled
a few elliptically derogatory remarks. Carrie looked pained—less
for herself, I thought, than for me. The students left class thinking that I was not only a fraud, but also an asshole who had no
sympathy for Japanese girls who'd decided to sell their bodies for
a few extra yen.

Objectively speaking, the classes were getting better. We
read and discussed George Saunders's "Sea Oak"; an excerpt from
Sheila Heti's *How Should a Person Be?*; several stories by Ludmilla
Petrushevskaya; a section of *The Corrections*; and Curtis White's
great story "Combat" from *Memories of My Father Watching TV*, to
name the most popular pieces. In addition to workshop stories, I
assigned exercises to be discussed during conference, and some of
these turned out really well. An exercise for which the students
simply recorded a conversation they had and transcribed it yielded
a series of extraordinary transcripts. (The follow-up exercise, to
create a short narrative around the transcript, was less successful.)

Still, I could not shake the feeling that the whole thing was a sham. The fact that students had to pay so much to attend school; the entire process of teaching writing; and most of all, me. I was a fake. Tyler, who in his understated, green-haired way had emerged as one of the more thoughtful students in the class—at the end of a discussion he would ask, "Why did you assign this story? Do *you* like it?"—always pulled up his chair to face mine when he came for conference. One day he pulled it up and asked, quietly, what sort of fiction I wrote. I admitted I'd only written one book of fiction—and not very recently, at that. Tyler took this in stride, but what was I doing? What did I know about fiction? I knew more than my students. That didn't seem like enough.

Still, it was a pretty good way to make a living. It took me two full days to prepare for class—and I learned quickly that the more I prepared, the better the class—but that was because I'd never taught before; the syllabus I was developing could be used again, and I'd only get better at discussing those stories and novel excerpts. I wrote years ago, in the predecessor to this essay, that the problem with teaching writing was that the writer spent his time hanging out with children, but, in fact, it was fun to hang out with these kids. They came from all over the country, and I could see glimpses of what they would, or could, become. And as they began to write more along the lines that I was encouraging, I learned more about them, and it was interesting. It was genuinely interesting.

I'll say another thing for the job: it was nice to have a job. I'd spent fifteen years—too long—as a freelance writer. I was the (unpaid) editor of a magazine few people had heard of, and though

I wrote articles for much larger magazines, which people *had* heard of, I did this irregularly. I did not go into an office or draw a salary. Much of the time, when someone asked what I was working on, I didn't have anything substantial to say. I was always working on this or that; I was always working. But it felt precarious. It was precarious.

About halfway through the semester, I had drinks with friends from college. We saw each other about once a year. Two of them had gone into finance; two had gone into law. All of them earned a fair amount of money and owned their homes. I, meanwhile, always had little to show for what I'd done. This time around, however, I was a college professor. I was teaching students. We met on a Friday, and I came straight from Grand Central, in my suit.

I felt like a person. I wasn't making very much money, but I was only teaching one class. A full course load would be four classes; if you multiplied my salary by four, you'd have a decent salary. Plus benefits. Plus you got to hang out with kids all day—and talk about fiction. I never entirely shook the sense of my personal fraudulence as a teacher of fiction, but the enterprise of teaching fiction began to seem a little less ridiculous as the semester went on. It wasn't something "real," something applicable, it wasn't math—but it's not as if I daily apply the math I learned in high school, or even remember it. And learning fiction may not be difficult in the way that, for example, learning critical theory can be difficult—but, looking back on the critical theory I studied in college, what a lot of mumbo jumbo! Very few of my professors were equipped to present it in an accessible way, free of incomprehensible terminology (and ideology). At least my students were studying actual literature. And, in fact, after we read the opening section of *The Corrections*, and the students didn't seem as familiar as I'd expected with the theory that Chip spouts while standing in the street with his sister Denise—"I'm saying that I personally am losing the battle with a commercialized, medicalized, totalitarian modernity right this instant"—we read Foucault's "What Is an Author?" which was lots of fun.

I even began to feel, in a way I'd never felt as a student, that the old saw about how you can't teach writing was possibly untrue. My attempts to teach grammar failed; no matter how many times I put various examples of speech attribution on the board, showing when to capitalize "He said" and when not to, the next set of stories would feature the same mistakes. Nor was I able to do much for Allison, my most talented student. After reading a few of her exercises, in which the use of figurative language was nothing short of astonishing, I became convinced that there was very little about writing that she could learn from me. Perhaps I could give her some books to read? For conference I suggested we go to the library—where it turned out that she had, in fact, already read everything. Of course she had; you don't just wake up one morning writing like that. But what did happen, as the semester progressed, was that the students began to write more about their own lives, to find the interest, the drama, in their own lives. Not the things that were obviously dramatic—family illness, divorce, death, et cetera—but the little things that made life interesting, and specific, and unlike the lives of others. Whether this holds up as a theory of fiction more generally, I don't know. I do know that it made the stories interesting to *me*.

So what's the problem?

There's no problem. For the most part, I liked my students; I liked going in to talk to them about fiction; I usually felt I could be honest with them. When I could not be honest, I enjoyed meeting up with my friend and supervisor to complain—mostly about the dismissive things students had said about works of fiction I really liked. I loved getting up in the morning, dressing, and catching a train from Grand Central. I loved having access to a decent university library. As I learned when I returned a DVD a week late, faculty don't pay fines.

I did sometimes think of what a publishing executive said to me when I came to the realization that a book editor had to perform two very separate functions—an editorial function and a sales function; the shaping of a manuscript and the convincing of other people to read it—and that an aptitude for both was probably quite rare. Weren't these actually two separate jobs?

"Yes," said the publishing executive. "But it's more convenient when they're combined in one person."

It's more convenient for a writing teacher to be both a writer and a teacher—but these are separate things. I was an okay teacher; I did my best. But someone who had trained to be a teacher would have done a better job. And when you are teaching it is not easy to be a writer. I had written the bulk of the magazine article for which I'd traveled over the summer before the semester began, but the issue it was in closed near the end of the semester. During the final week and a half of closing, you go through fact-checking, which amounts to a full-time job, and also last-minute editing, which adds to that. Usually I just stay on the phone for five or six straight days. But this time around I was busy: I had my students' stories to read and mark up and prepare. I did less for the fact-checkers than I would have liked, and they noticed. One Friday after class I found a rare voice message on my phone; it was from the head of the magazine's fact-checking department, and he was not happy. Meanwhile, I went back to being the lousy teacher I had been at the beginning of the semester. How some people manage to do a lot of writing while also teaching well is, frankly, beyond me.

If the students noticed that I was slacking off, they didn't show any sign. A lot of them were leaving a day early for break, and so would be missing the last class. As a result, there were only six of us at the end. And we had to workshop four stories. We ran through them quickly, too quickly, and then held our final conferences. Mackenzie, from Wisconsin, had been through a lot in her first semester—a love affair, a class in film history that made a deep impression on her—and she was going to be taking the train home to Wisconsin with some of the books we hadn't gotten a chance to read. Logan, the jazz singer, had learned that anger could be a positive element in art. Carrie had forgiven me for my comments on her Japanese teen prostitutes story and written her next story about her family. "Will I ever see you again?" she asked after her last conference. I didn't know! Charlotte did not stop writing about orcs, but she did start trying to inject some real-world details into her fantasy stories. Some of her exercises—nonfantasy—were terrific.

Allison, my best student, had the last conference of the semester. She asked me, very humbly, the question I had carried around unceasingly my first year of college, and especially during my first writing class. I'd wanted to know if I was a writer. When my first writing teacher said, "Yes, you're definitely a writer," I thought I'd won the lottery. I relaxed. It wasn't my teacher's fault, but it probably cost me a couple of years, years I should have spent working and developing, instead of basking in the fact that someone had acknowledged me.

Allison asked the question more gently: Did I think she could someday be published?

The answer to me was obviously yes. She could probably be published tomorrow. But I tried to be careful. I told Allison she was extraordinarily talented, and that I really looked forward to reading what she wrote. But I also said that whether or not you became a writer, in the end, depended on a lot more than talent. Many talented people I knew in college decided to pursue other things—they became academics, or screenwriters, or rabbis. Being a writer required you to make the decision, over and over and over again, to write. No one would care if you stopped doing it, even if they noticed. So there would be many moments in the future at which to decide to stop; or to decide not to stop, and to keep going.

With that, the semester ended. The students went back, by bus, train, and plane, to Michigan, Wisconsin, Texas, North Carolina, Colorado, and California. I cleaned out my desk; returned my library books; and caught the 8:22 back to Grand Central, and from there to Brooklyn.

(2006, 2014)

HOW TO QUIT

Kristin Dombek

We do not know how to renounce anything, Freud once observed. This type of relation to the object indicates an inability to mourn. The addict is a non-renouncer par excellence.   —Avital Ronell, *Crack Wars*

The way of life is wonderful; it is by abandonment.
                              —Ralph Waldo Emerson, "Circles"

Two blocks east of the river, beside the Williamsburg Bridge, stands a white factory building, seven stories tall, whose windows look onto the bridge and across the river to Manhattan and over the neighborhood's low rooftops and famous water towers. It is 2011, but this building hasn't yet been cubed up into condos. Inside, it still looks like 1994, each floor a maze of ad hoc lofts, studios, galleries, and workshops, the stained hallways thick with strange smells and years of dust. A couple of years ago during a party a kid from some band jammed the freight elevator between floors, tried to jump out, fell, and died; the elevator still isn't working. So to get into the building, you climb steep factory flights of gray stairs up away from the basement, where a giant machine rumbles. By the fifth or sixth floor, it is hard to breathe. It is winter, and the rumbling is a steam heater. Every few hours, it blows scalding-hot, wet air up through clanking pipes into the lofts. All over the building tenants open windows, and long white curtains flutter in the hissing steam. Outside, people are climbing up the steep slope of the bridge's pedestrian walkway, on foot or skateboard or bicycle. Only a few look at the building, and even fewer try to glimpse inside. I am in here, watching the bridge and chain-smoking.

The sun sinks down behind the bridge, filling this big white room with warm red light. When a J, M, or Z train passes, the room darkens and then flushes red again. The sky turns red, then orange, then indigo, then starless, like every Brooklyn night. It's happy hour. Half the neighborhood is already drunk on two-for-one drafts or shot-and-PBR deals. All week, the kids in lofts and storefronts who do under-the-radar marketing for creative agencies in other lofts and storefronts have been chasing Oxy with Adderall and Adderall with Oxy. Now they're pulling bottles of tequila from their desk drawers and texting their dealers. A country band is carrying banjos into the Rod & Gun club. They're sound-checking at Trash Bar and lighting the fire at Union Pool. The Shabbos siren sounds across the south side. It's almost time to go out.

Snow came on Halloween weekend this year, fat slow flakes falling on the bridge, turning the scene outside the windows all industrial Currier & Ives, the Gretsch Building just a wide gray ghost beyond the trains. There was a cold wind blowing the slush around, and I watched people breaking their umbrellas against it and struggling to walk, sliding carefully on the sidewalk. This was the day the heat turned on. First, a clanking from below and up through the walls, then the sound of rushing water, and then, in the large sculptor's studio that I've turned into my writing room, a sound like a teapot ready to blow. Steam shot upward from the end of one of the pipes, and water poured and pooled on the floor. I braced for an explosion, but it turns out this happens every time the building warms up. It only sounds catastrophic.

That afternoon a guitar player on a dead-mother bender was walking over from Bushwick in the snow to fuck me, his feet wrapped in plastic bags inside his Converse because he's too broke to buy boots. I walked down six flights to let him in. I hadn't seen him sober before, which was why I'd requested the afternoon appointment, but I'd stashed a fresh liter of Jack Daniel's above the fridge. The lighting in the stairway was pulsing and dim. Snow from the roof was melting down the yellowed walls and pooling on the landings. We didn't kiss in the entryway. We made small talk as we wound our way up around the puddles, through the industrial waterfall. A few minutes later I was on my knees. The next week I bought new boots myself—short black boots that lace up, boots from the time of coal and steam, but with heels so high they are always sexual.

I am in this building, but I am thinking of another white factory building, ten blocks behind me, beside the river. In 1999 I was living with a friend in a railroad apartment on North Seventh by the Brooklyn–Queens Expressway that smelled of cheap floor varnish and mildew, no matter what we did. After we moved in, the upstairs neighbors told us that the landlord had kicked out a

Puerto Rican family with four children and doubled the rent to
$1,200, which was almost too much for us. Then a bike messen-
ger we knew heard some friends of his were building lofts in an
old textile warehouse on North Third. We walked to the river and
up five flights of stairs, into a massive room with a wall of windows looking out onto the river and the whole bright city, a place
as thrilling as a cathedral, as beautiful and sad as the person you
fall in love with when you already know he will break your heart.
We knew we'd be kicked out and priced out, just as we'd kicked
out and priced out the Puerto Ricans. But we had to get into
this building anyway, and to afford it we had to get our deposit
back.

This was our plan: the bike messenger would ride by our
apartment and throw a brick through the window wrapped in a
note that read, *Yuppies go home*. I'd call the cops, file a police report, and then call our landlord crying, saying the neighborhood
was unsafe and could we get our deposit back. But the day before we were to execute this ingenious conspiracy, my boyfriend
at the time, a sweet-eyed punk kid from New Orleans who was a
drug dealer and had some experience with the police, convinced
me that I'd never make it through the report because of what a
bad liar I am, according to him. So we gave up, lost our deposit,
borrowed money from the bike messenger (who somehow always
had more than we did), and moved in.

My share of the rent was $650. I cannot hope to capture for
you the happiness of sitting by those windows and watching
slow barges guided down the river by bright red tugboats, the
buildings of Manhattan transformed every hour by different sunlight, and the mesmerizing plows of the waste transfer station
next door, pushing around piles of garbage among beautiful
brightly colored dumpsters. There were five years of potlucks and

parties, bands and shows, cross-genre multimedia interactive technology performative collaborative art projects. The towers collapsing across the river, military tanks rolling down Bedford Avenue, then all the war protests. A man to fall in love with, a beautiful ex-junkie and sometime pain-reliever addict who moved in next door. All our nights spent in bars, the fucking in bathrooms, the lines snorted in back booths after close, the shouting on sidewalks, fucking all the way up those five flights of stairs as the sun came up. You have been young, or you are young, and you know that story, and you know the story of this neighborhood, or you think you do. The landlords began trying to force us out so they could build multimillion-dollar condos, and I moved east with the ex-junkie, as everyone was having to do, east to the Williamsburg of the Italians, in our case. My rent tripled, and soon the world felt like it was ending. I started dreaming of a quiet garden apartment in Boerum Hill or Prospect Heights, away from twenty-two-year-olds and condo buildings. But when I left him, I moved back here, to the old but now unrecognizable neighborhood, into this building that looks like the building where I met him, or how it used to look.

Beyond the bridge, the Gretsch Building lights up. Inside it rich people are having cocktail hour, or something. I can't see them. The Gretsch was a musical instrument factory, then full of artists. In 1999, the management company began to turn the water and electricity and heat off, then on again, then off. In this way, they drove the tenants out. Now it has a granite lobby, glass elevators, a meditative waterfall, and units with Sub-Zeros and exposed concrete beams and floating fireplaces framed in Pietra Colombino limestone. Some people think Beyoncé lives in there. I haven't seen her, but I've seen the rest of it, thanks to the dullest New Year's Eve party ever. Starting in the late nineties, dozens more loft buildings pushed out their live/work tenants. Our old textile warehouse was one of the latest, in 2006. After the eviction, architects carved out an atrium and built a lobby out of *2001: A Space Odyssey*—glossy white and grand, flanked by strange asymmetrical hallways. They leveled the waste transfer station and built the Edge and then Northside Piers, thirty-some stories each of tacky glassy condos, and in their basements were pools, "golf systems," screening rooms. These buildings gave you the feeling that when the apocalypse came to Williamsburg, they'd float up into space in luminous self-sufficiency and orbit the wrecked planet while their residents gathered in the billiards room, drank complex cocktails, and eyed each other's neoprene skinny jeans.

But gentrification is the opposite of the apocalypse. The apocalypse would pause history, level the built world to a pile of trash, and most likely lower rents considerably. Gentrification churns history forward, takes out the trash, carts away rubble, hides the poor, makes you work more and more to manage your rent, and encrypts the past, when you didn't have to work so many jobs just to fucking live here, behind its glossy surfaces. To distract us from this decimation of the past and the poor it opens restaurants and bars that simulate other pasts. The old beer and liquor outlet on the corner of North Third and Berry, where we used to rent kegs for parties, is now an old-time German beer garden, its waitresses' breasts plumped cartoonishly by little German beer garden corsets. Across the street, where Slick's motorcycle repair shop was for years, there's a gleaming skate and surf store. There are half a dozen speakeasy-type cocktail bars with handlebar-mustached bartenders. There are three diners quaint enough to make your heart ache. There's Marlow & Sons and the rest of the country-living places, where you eat surrounded by animal trophies and decorative farm tools. There are old-time ice cream shops, general stores, old-time down-home barbecue joints, old-time down-home fried chicken joints, and rustic ski lodge–style restaurants. There is every past you could ever imagine, but little you remember.

When a neighborhood changes this much this fast it feels like either the old neighborhood was the real one and this one is some kind of monstrous double, or if this neighborhood is real, then that old one must always have been a lie.

If the old neighborhood was real, this building is a steam-powered time machine. If the new neighborhood is real, this building is a dream, or a crypt.

In other words, all this building makes me want to do is drink and fuck. I'm in here, sipping whiskey to blunt some post-cocaine jitters, and rolling Bali Shag cigarettes to save money.

The music of this winter is the soundtrack to the movie *Drive*. Everyone in the neighborhood is talking about it. The bartender across the street plays it every time he works. I see the movie by myself one afternoon at the Nitehawk on Metropolitan, where the sound is good and you can get food. I order a Bloody Mary, carefully, not sure how my voice sounds or if my face looks right, because I've been fucking the guitar player for the past twenty-four hours. We're on MDMA, which has turned us into a science experiment. We get within a foot of each other and we have to fuck again. He goes down on me indefinitely. At first it's normal, and then he drops down into some deep, quiet place of absolute and perfect concentration. He is patient, he waits, barely moving, but he turns us from two people into liquid, and I come and come. Finally we stop, because he has to go to band practice, and so I go see this movie. In the theater my legs are weak and I keep checking to make sure I'm fully clothed and my face is burning and everyone seems to be looking at me curiously. The ecstasy is tingling out gently; it's not going to be one of those suicidal E hangovers; everything is luscious and precise. When the music starts, I can feel it in the seat. Soft, thumping bass beats, pulsing in and out in waves, sometimes with sweet synthesized little-girl voices singing on top of them. College and Electric Youth's "A Real Hero": "You have proven to be / A real human being and a real hero." Desire's "Under Your Spell": "I don't eat / I don't sleep / I do nothing but think of you."

The driving is perfect. Ryan Gosling's silent maneuvers, his watching, his listening. The first driving scene is remarkable for its pauses—the way he waits, the way he doesn't drive, hiding the car under an overpass, parking on a side street while the cops drive by. He says nearly nothing and he moves only as much as he absolutely has to. He barely speaks to Carey Mulligan, who has the face of a very young girl. But he takes her on a drive and smiles at her and helps her with her groceries and her car and her son and presumably they fall in love. Their scenes pulse with nothing being said, the way the scenes in *Twilight* pulse with nothing being done, when the girl and the vampire can't fuck because he might accidently kill her if they do. It's so hot.

Once Gosling and Mulligan hold hands, or rather she puts her hand on top of his gloved driving hand, which is on the gearshift. That's all we get of sex until finally, two-thirds of the way through the movie, they're in an elevator in their building, the same elevator where they met, and a man beside them is reaching under his coat for a gun. Gosling turns to Mulligan and kisses her for the first time, really deeply kisses her. The lights start to glow and the electronica is soft and pulsing, and the kiss is in super-slow motion and lasts a really long time. Then he pushes her into the corner, smashes the man's head against the elevator buttons, throws him to the floor and stomps on his head until it's muck and blood sprays all over and the man is dead but Gosling keeps stomping anyway, like he wants to cover himself in blood. Then the elevator doors open and Mulligan backs out and just stares at him.

When someone changes that much, that suddenly, it feels like either the old version was the real one and this new one must be some kind of monstrous double, or if the new one is real, then that old version must always have been a lie.

The guitar player starts fucking another girl and suddenly won't speak to me when I see him in the bar across the street.

The tragic reversal makes you ache to turn back the clock.

On the other hand, the tragic reversal is already a time machine. It throws you into the past to see everything again but differently, makes you pose questions you can never answer. In the elevator, Mulligan sees that the man who seemed so different from her temperamental criminal of a husband is the same as him, just as violent or worse. So was she doing something different, in loving someone who seemed so sweet, or just repeating the same thing? She'll never know the answer, but it will probably bother her forever, unless she's the kind of woman who can just forget about things and move on.

My favorite residents of Williamsburg are machines of the tragic reversal, the kinds of people who always turn away and disappear into their secret lives—people who pose certain intense problems of interpretation, in a place where no street stays the same for more than a few weeks at a time.

This building is a question about how you live after a tragic reversal, thrown back into history and wondering what can be recovered by returning to the scene.

It was the loveliest hangover I've ever had, watching *Drive*. Every time I try to do molly again, though, the hangovers are so bad they make me want to hurl myself out these windows onto the Williamsburg Bridge just to make the hangovers stop making me want to die. But every next day I wake up resurrected, because this building is full of joy.

Drunks, drug addicts, sex addicts, compulsive gamblers, and/or people on or recovering from deep, life-threatening benders: these are the only people who really hold my interest, which means that I usually am friends with or fuck and/or love people with a dead parent or two, bipolar or otherwise depressed people, musicians, writers, and/or pathological liars. Even so, I never know when I meet them. They always just seem to me like the best people in the world. At some point, a week or two into the friendship or the affair, I find out, but by then I'm already hooked, because the things these people do to ensure they don't have to live in the straight world are wonderful. They turn ordinary nights into wide electric universes that snap in the head like a new beat, get and give pleasure like they'll otherwise die, make music what music is and art what art is. Because they cannot do all the things it takes to marry, they can bring a whole marriage's worth of intimacy into one night of fucking, and you can let that land square on you, like you're the only girl in the world, to quote Rihanna. You're almost definitely not the only girl in their world, but that's the thing about addicts: they are endlessly optimistic, and they can make you believe anything.

I am not unfamiliar with the reasons it is considered unhealthy to love people who can't get through a day without getting shitfaced. They get in stupid fights in bars with guys they think are hitting on you, and you have to hug them until they calm down and sneak your number to the other guy later. When you start fucking someone else, they come to your house in the middle of the night, wasted, and let all the air out of the new guy's tires. They make you stop being friends with all the friends you fucked before you met them, that's how much they love you. And yet they always turn out to be plagued by focus problems when it comes to you. They'll eye-fuck you all through their set and then sit down right next to you and start making out with your friend. They'll say they're not fucking the girl who fills your shared kitchen with baked goods every time you go out of town, until you make out with her boyfriend and force her to angrily admit they've been having an affair. There is the moodiness, the way they'll suddenly start shouting at you on street corners in foreign cities because they can't handle stress and they're too high to read a map. They'll steal tobacco from your purse on the way out of your apartment and then pretend they didn't know it was yours. They'll leave a stolen wallet by your bed and then break back into your building to retrieve it, and have the nerve, when confronted, to pretend that it's not stolen but theirs, and that it is you who has forgotten their real name and how different faces can look on government-issued ID cards. Not to mention how when you ask why their eyes are half-closed all the time, they keep saying they're just really relaxed and happy to be with you, and all the rifling through their shit to find the Oxycontin they say they don't have, the way that even when they're vomiting and slimy on the floor of the casino hotel on your only vacation of the year, and you're trying for three days to get them to eat even the smallest piece of room-service bagel, they still don't admit they're in withdrawal again, and you still believe they just have a really bad stomach, that they're just so sensitive.

The problem is that I find these ways of behaving charming—infinitely more interesting, somehow, than the things that sober people do.

I go out. In the bar across the street they are playing Kavinsky and Lovefoxxx, from the *Drive* soundtrack, his scratchy metallic synthesized voice singing: "I'm going to show you where it's dark / But have no fear." I can start out arguing about geography with a drunk from South Carolina and fall briefly in love with a floppy-haired cokehead who's straight out of *Winesburg, Ohio* and end up giving a blow job in the bathroom to a French business-man, and I can carry all these people into the next day, each one stretching the regular world just a little bit. I can stay exactly where I am and see what happens, or I can follow some drunk or drug addict to some other bar or party in Bushwick or Bed-Stuy. Even in the hipster bars they are playing Rihanna's song about pill-popping romance, over and over: "We found love in a hopeless place."

There are things you will never know unless you follow these kinds of people around. Here is one of them: you can drink enough whiskey that the hangover feels opiate, and when you fi-nally make it outside at twilight the next day, the world is soft and purple and shifting and the faces of the people on the side-walk are lit up with possibility and mad peace.

It doesn't always work out. I bring home a wild long-bearded drunk who fucks me within an inch of my life and then doesn't call. I pick up a drunk on the street who says he works for the UN, and that he was trained by the FBI to establish perimeters during explosives investigations or something, whom I don't call. I see a dirty strung-out man on the G train platform with a canvas under his arm and the eyes of a pervert or a man on a cross and we share a look I will never forget, of recognition and sex and the exact shining thing I enjoy mistaking for love, but I am on the train, passing, and soon he is out of sight. Another night I try to pick up a drummer in a country band. He looks like Kid Rock, and, if I squint, like David Foster Wallace, and I'm sure he means to come home with me. But something's off about him. I tell him he looks bored while he drums. He says his back hurts because he was recording all day. I don't think drummers should talk like this, especially drummers who look like Kid Rock, and I berate him for being tired and bored. He should be sexy, but he's just not. It's frustrating. Berating him, however, does not turn out to be a good tactic for seducing him. The next day it occurs to me what was so off about him: he must have been sober.

How do sober people get close to one another? No one knows, at least no one I know does. In the movies, they ask each other out on dates. One person says, Do you want to hang out tomorrow night? The other one says, Yeah, eight o'clock? And that's it. They never say what they're going to do, or where they're going to meet. I worry about them wandering around the city, watches unsynchronized, wishing they'd remembered to make a fucking plan. It's so much easier to get completely wasted and just go home together that very night.

I've been doing this since college, and I'm not just in it for the rapture. I do the other part, too. I'm the friend who will let you crash in my bed for three days and nights when you're ready to go through the shakes, sit with you while you moan, try to get you to eat toast, oatmeal, anything, force water down your throat while you sweat all over my sheets. And a year later, I'll help you buy your week's supply of malt liquor in your New

Orleans grocery store, pretending not to see the people looking at our shopping cart full of clinking forties, and my heart will be breaking, but I'll do it. I'm the friend who will walk with you down Metropolitan Avenue at a pace of a block an hour because you're so doped up and bendy that you have to hold on to each lamppost and mailbox for a while, considering, joking, nodding off, doubling over, until you're ready to move on to the next one. I understand that. I appreciate the way it slows down time. The way there's nothing for me to do but be with you. You make me feel very calm. I'll walk with you when you're so drunk you're screaming at me all the way home. How many times my job has been just to get someone from one street corner to the next, I do not know. I should have been a crossing guard. Because I do not say no, I do not say this is fucking ridiculous. Something in me just goes quiet and I'm right there with you. Later, when I'm sure I've got you, I'll say, Change, please change, but what I really mean is, Look at you, what would you do without me, you're falling apart, you would fucking die without me, I'm the most important person in the world to you. Don't die. Stay with me. Never leave.

Repeating the same words over and over again, claimed Gertrude Stein, is the only way to make sure they will actually mean something different. I've hung a photograph of her in my bathroom to remind me, as I'm putting on my eyeliner and getting ready to go out, that I'm supposed to be fucking girls instead.

I invite home a woman to sleep on my sofa bed. I know she is shy, so I am careful not to flirt with her. I make up the sofa bed, and then I make her an omelet. We drink Miller High Life and she lies down on the bed and curls over on her side and asks me to "cuddle" her, and then I have these perfect, hard-nippled breasts in my mouth. Soon enough, I remember. Sometimes when you are making a woman come it's like you're trying to get her to sound like she's being hurt.

I can see the Gretsch Building and I know what's inside it, but for the most part, when I look out from inside this building, the gentrification is to the north and behind me, like nothing ever happened. I write to the sound of the trains, fast and wholehearted. It's like I'm back in the neighborhood I moved to out of sheer dire love, like I stayed too long at the fair but I keep winning huge stuffed animals at the water-gun game. A loophole. Friends come over whenever they want, in the afternoon or when the bar closes, and we play music and lie on the floor and talk. We dance. I dance when I wake up, and before I go to sleep, and smoke too many cigarettes, and don't care.

It's November when the water turns off for the first time. For years, the building and its tenants have been in a legal battle over an endlessly impending mass eviction. I'm instructed by email to follow the pipes out of the apartment until I find the problem, without drawing management's attention to the fact that I'm in here, instead of my friend. But the pipes are always disappearing into the walls, and I'm too shy to knock on apartment doors. It's easier to work around the problem. In the old loft building where I met my ex, we didn't have a shower or stove for six months once, and we got by. As a child, I spent a month pretending I was Laura Ingalls Wilder. I'd wear a floor-length patchwork skirt my mother made for me and do my chores pioneer-style, the slow way, washing my clothes by hand and beating them with sticks. Sometimes to keep it interesting I imagined I was doing this on television. So I know how to handle this. I bring in buckets of water from the hallway bathroom to flush the toilet, fill up the Brita, line the kitchen and bathroom with glasses and Tupperware containers of water for brushing my teeth and wiping down the kitchen counter. I cart the dirty dishes out to the hallway bathroom and wash them under the faucet in icy water. On days when I might bring someone home, I walk down the stairs and a few blocks to the place where the messenger lives now and take a shower, shave my legs, press warm water on my face, and walk back, my hair wet in the winter air, past the broken elevator, up the six flights. There is less and less time for working and writing, but I don't mind. Soon the bathroom begins to smell awfully of shit, though, and I worry that the sewage is coming up, working its way up these six floors to flood the loft. After two weeks, the super goes down to the basement and turns the water on again, which he must have known how to do all along.

I'm in here getting all pioneer-style with my water, but it's pioneer style they're selling in the form of hand-spun woolen socks for $80 a pair at the general store in Marlow & Sons, across the street from the Gretsch Building. Even so, I cannot resist the happiness of being back here, in the old world, if I am really back, if one can return to the scene.

I buy a fake shearling coat like we used to wear in the nineties, a dark druggie coat with a big collar.

In *Paradise Lost*, it's Satan who thinks the mind can make a heaven of hell, a hell of heaven. He is, famously, the best character in the movie.

I just treat the physical neighborhood itself as if it is on drugs. When I look at it like that, I love it.

In Al-Anon, the doctrine of renouncing addiction to addicts is the same as the doctrine of renouncing addiction: the repetition is a symptom that the disease is beyond your control, that you are powerless in the face of it, that the antidote is to shift your dependence to a higher power, seek forgiveness, develop a moral conscience and some boundaries, put yourself into some abstract category—addict, alcoholic, enabler—and then, because you are powerless, you've got to leave it all behind. You can't go into the bar, you can't go on the internet and even look at the escort ads, you can't try to help your drunk of a husband or your crackhead wife. Instead, you have to weave around yourself this network of strangers who are in your addict category, exit the alternate world you made, go back into the dull real world you were trying to escape, and just take it one day at a time. It's one world or the other—though you get out through one small excruciating step at a time, and you must always and forever, from now on, consider yourself "in recovery."

Programs that reject AA for its puritanical attitude toward intoxicants tend to treat that opposition of worlds as precisely the problem. When you're trying to quit something, this is exactly the double bind: should you view the thing you're addicted to as so powerful that you need to marshal every weapon you can against it, as if it is some overwhelming, apocalyptic force of evil? Should you disavow as false every moment of total transcendence the thing ever gave you? Or would you by means of that disavowal be giving the thing more power than it actually has, and was that exactly the problem in the first place? You thought it was the drug or the person or the place that transported you, subjected you, dominated you, lit you up, disappeared you, raptured you, loved you, but was it really you all along?

The double bind is a fake, too, of course. It's not one or the other. These are the kinds of questions addicts ask, because they are impossible to answer, so we can keep holding on to them forever.

•

Drive isn't playing at the Nitehawk anymore, so I go see it again at Village East. The sound is bad and there are no Bloody Marys. It's just a film noir. The city's shiny surfaces barely contain the violence underneath, and maybe Gosling is like the city, a dissembler and monstrous.

When you know that for the last third of the film he'll be smashing dudes' heads with his boots and drowning them in dark oceans and shoving bullets down their throats in strip clubs and ripping their eyeballs out with hammers or whatever (I had my eyes closed), every early minimalist line, especially the sweet ones, sounds excruciatingly fake, like it's in quotes, like he's just saying whatever everyone wants him to say but just barely. Maybe the kiss is violent in the first place, since Gosling knows he has to steal it before he reveals his secret self. Even worse, maybe the kiss is a cover-up. He uses her, so he can catch his victim off guard. I don't want it to be this, not this interpretation. It seems like a real kiss, a good kiss, but why does he want her to have the taste of his tongue in her mouth while she watches him become a vision of pure brutality, have the feeling of that perfect chest pressed against her (as Emma Stone's character says to Gosling in *Crazy, Stupid, Love* when he takes off his shirt, "Seriously? You look like you're airbrushed!") as she learns everything she believed about him is false?

Trying to figure out whether someone's evil or good is like trying to figure out whether cigarettes are evil or good. It's a way to procrastinate. They're just plants and chemicals wrapped in paper. You're the one smoking them.

Gosling is everyone's favorite male lead these days. He's everywhere. A friend said the other day, I wish Ryan Gosling would just leave me alone. Because he had most of his dialogue taken out of this film, it's easy to project onto his character the Gosling of *Half Nelson* and *Blue Valentine*, working men who teach public school and do construction while wearing impossibly hipsterish clothes. Men who look at their female leads with a kind of searching intimacy that will be shattered or cemented by the secret yet to be revealed: the drug problem, the drinking problem, the brutal temper that we have to decide whether or not to forgive. Is his nameless character in *Drive* also *The Notebook*'s long-suffering workingman romantic hero, quiet 'cause he's sweet, or is he the *Crazy, Stupid, Love* womanizer, sweet 'cause he's about to break your heart? The film's music is about him. Is he a "real hero," as the soundtrack says? Is he a "real human being"?

These are the kinds of questions I'm talking about. Asking them is a way of not renouncing or mourning. This is the way to make the man or the drug or the place uncannily powerful, infused with one's own contradictory interpretations. To love what one has made magical, in this way—at least when it comes to loving addicts and the kinds of drugs that can kill you—is widely considered to be a terrible thing, something to heal from. But our favorite recent romance—100 million copies sold and over one billion dollars at the box office—is about a girl heroic enough to love a vampire who stalks and bosses her around and is addicted to her blood. She keeps wondering: Is he an asshole? But then how can he be so beautiful? Is it possible that he's being an asshole because he loves her so much? In this case, love for the otherworldly addict totally pays off. *Twilight*'s Edward Cullen solves the elevator scene problem, rewinds the tragic reversal: his initial coldness and violence turn out to be totally explained by his own heroic efforts not to kill her. He loves her so much he feigns hating her to protect her. So in this case it's the sweetness that's the secret, the surprise. One reads these books like they're crack, or some women do. Finally, he turns her into a vampire, so that she won't ever have to die.

I keep seeing the dead body of my father in the corner of the studio, naked and blue and cold like a corpse in a morgue. In reality I have never seen his body like that. I've seen him naked and I've seen him dead, but not at the same time. When he died, in a nursing-home bed, I'd been sitting with him for three days, talking to him about our whole lives, not knowing if he could hear me, because he was in a coma, just talking anyway. For twenty years he'd been on a cocktail of drugs for diabetes and epilepsy that made him have moods that were always opposite of one another. My mother and my brother and I were always trying to anticipate whether we'd get the sweet or the brutal, but there was never really any way to know, and it could turn in a second. I couldn't blame him for the bad moods because it was the drugs, or it always might be; there was never any real way to know what was the drugs and what was him. It wasn't really fair to feel things about what he said or did. The most important thing was to keep him from having seizures.

As a child, when I wasn't pretending to be Laura Ingalls Wilder, I was narrating what happened in my head like we were in a novel; after someone spoke I'd say "he said"; after I spoke, I'd say "she said," in my head where no one could hear. It was better not to feel things during the later years, either, when the epilepsy drugs took the meanness away, made him as soft and tearful and wild-smiling as a doped-up bum or a child. I sat with him for the last three days and talked to him about all this, and told him that I'd hated him because he was mean or cold as fuck half the time, and thanked him because the other half he was kind and wise and taught me how to think and how to be.

I was holding his hand when I felt his blood slow. I put my hand on his wrist and felt his heartbeats separate. I put my hands on his legs and felt the blood stop; there was one last thick pulse and then there was none. I put my hands on his neck and there was one last pulse and there was no pulse. As a child, when incomprehensible things happened, I used to panic, and my parents would give me sips of wine to calm me down. But now I was as quiet and calm as could be. I put my hands on his chest and felt him completely still, and I put my forehead against his forehead and cried onto his face. My poor father. What he would be doing back in the corner of the studio looking like a corpse on *Law & Order* I do not know. He's not a metaphor, a reason, or even a clue. He's just a dead body encrypted inside this new life.

I buy a bright red hoodie from fucking American Apparel and wear it every day. On the third day I realize it's yours, the one you were wearing every day under your leather jacket when I met you. I'm the drunk now, when I want to be. I'm the addict. I'm the one to follow around the neighborhood, the one who changes things, over and over again.

The building is getting louder. There's clanking in the eastern wall, sometimes the sound of a small dog inside the western wall. The water goes off, comes on again. Someone is banging on the pipes at four in the morning, but who would do that? Sometimes the clanking sounds like it's right inside the wall beside my bed, but it is not possible that there is anyone in there. Sometimes the steam heater makes the building so hot I'm opening all the windows, leaning out the window looking over the bridge in a tank top and underpants and burning my legs on the pipes. The real tenants are in court with management, fighting to stay, but the building is winning, they're going to build their multimillion-dollar condos, and I stop being able to look out the window without wondering when this will end and where I will go. I would like to decide to leave, myself, before they throw us out, but I don't know how to stop wanting to be here.

The second and only other time it snows this winter, I'm so high that I can't understand why everything is white. I'm taking a walk with friends, everyone alarmingly stoned from pot brownies, arms linked, and finally I announce that we should decide that the whiteness is snow, though I don't believe we have any real evidence for it. The pot had made it so that to believe in and state the obvious required a giant leap of faith.

That same day, on a long car ride, some of us were reading aloud Stanley Cavell's book on film and love and marriage, *Pursuits of Happiness*, where he talks about wrestling with the meaning of films as a practice joined to "checking one's experience," which he describes as "momentarily *stopping*, turning yourself away from whatever your preoccupation and turning your experience away from its expected, habitual track, to find itself, its own track: coming to attention. The moral of this practice is to educate your experience sufficiently so that it is worthy of trust." To have authority in the interpretation of your own experience is a paradox, he says, because "educating" your experience can't come in advance of the trusting.

Loving a place that is always disappearing before your eyes, loving people who are always disappearing into secret lives, and doing this drunk or high—these can be ways of making it extra difficult to learn to trust your own interpretation. You can think that to come to attention means to get sober. This can be a useful thing to think. Or you can think that love and intoxication are themselves ways of stopping, abandoning oneself to the lush and impossible moment between experience and interpretation, where it might be possible to let what is dead be dead.

I bring home a cokehead chef who has to get to his restaurant early in the morning, so we decide to stay up all night. He has the face of a child and at one point he is on top of me and I say, How are you able to do this? And he says, I'm twenty-five. (No one ever says, It's the drugs! They make me feel immortal!) How old are you, he asks. I put my hands on either side of his face and look at him. Older. I put my hands on his neck and I can feel his blood pulse while he fucks me, too gently, but it's okay. I put my hands on his chest, and his skin is warm and smooth. I don't even like him that much, but I put my legs on his shoulders and I put my hands on the back of his thighs and pull him into me and all is well. And then, because he is young and can't say what he wants, I guess, turn over. He puts his hands on my ass and kisses my back. Afterward I put my forehead against his forehead and feel his alien twenty-five-year-old brain, here for the moment and then gone, on its way to work, and I kiss him.

These are the most singular, unrepeatable kisses in the history of kissing, the one in the *Drive* elevator and the ones happening in my bed these days, because they are exactly on the edge of what's already happened and what will happen next, how I have seen things and how I will see them.

It is important to know that there are things that end. Things you can't change with your mind or even your body or even chemicals. As spring draws near, the building wins the lawsuit. We're getting evicted, the tenants who have lived here for ten or twenty years, and the subletters like me hiding out in these labyrinthine halls. "The last of the starving artists who colonized

Williamsburg two decades ago and began its transformation into the hipster capital of New York could soon find themselves out on the street," begins the article about it in the *Post*. It's head-lined, nonsensically, "W'burg Has Art Attack: Hipsters Facing Boot." There's no chance of an appeal. My neighbor makes a ban-ner to hang on the front of the building: TEN HOMES LOST! She's been here since 1994, like most of the residents of the ten lofts. It's not a machine or a dream or a crypt for her, just her home, made impossible by money. Police cars come, sirens wailing, to remove the banner. There will be condos.

This is one way to quit: wait until the bitter end, when you have done all you can to make the time machine keep working. You have learned its inner systems, improvised work-arounds, carted in the water yourself, but it becomes harder to keep it alive than leave it. What they call hitting rock bottom. The final tragic reversal may be slow, boring, and horrible. The time ma-chine has turned into a crypt, but it is not a crypt if you go inside with the body. If you must raise it from the dead again, know the power it has is your own: bend over it like a vampire, fire it up like Dr. Frankenstein. When you are able to stop, there will be a moment when you have to just walk out of the building. It's not that living will be the opposite of addiction now; there can be more life because you know how to stretch out time, more joy because you have practiced the art of reanimation. You are a pro-fessor of transformation; you just need new tools. There is no outside or inside to it, no opposition, no right way to go, just this new way of seeing.

And I do not mean by "seeing" that this is a matter of the mind or the brain or the eyes. The best thing would be if you could figure out what felt good about your particular drug and do it in some other way, with your body, like in your bed.

I am thinking of the Italian. The first time we saw each other, in the East Williamsburg country bar where I was cursing out the home state of the guitar player town by town, he did not ask but told me that I should take him home. Big wild hair. Divorce bender. Massive quantities of whiskey. Naples, where he got very specific and rigorous training in how to boss women around. When I met him I was very scared, and after he came home with me, I couldn't very easily stand or sit for any reasonable period of time. The second time, we began to play a game. I tell him, in the morning or early afternoon, that he has to go home. That I have things to do, I have so much writing to do, so much work. This makes him angry. In anger he stimulates every possible erogenous zone on my body he can at the same time, like a violent scientist of my body, until I'm like some kind of retarded gangbanged cheerleader/Anaïs Nin–type woman, kind of muttering in weird high voices, and he's like, really, you want me to go home, and I'm like, yes, go home, and he hurts me with the pleasure of pretending I have no choice.

But everywhere else I choose things now. The third time there is, at some point before the leaving game begins, a tear coming out of his eye. A tear so singular I just look at him, because I can't help him, I'm just not interested in helping anyone anymore. I say, What's wrong, what is it, and he shakes his head, and I let go of it. It's not my tear. And no longer is the suffering of the benders of others my suffering.

The first drug I took was acid, in an upstairs room in my college house with four girlfriends, all of us naked and wrapped in sheets, because it was a Michigan heat wave—110 degrees and too hot for clothes in Eastown, Grand Rapids, the kind of neighborhood where when it's hot enough you can smell the weed as you walk into that part of town. When the acid slowed everything down, I was watching my friends climb out the window onto a rooftop to smoke cigarettes, and I started crying, terrified that they were trying to get away from me, and that they were going to fall and die. From what I'd heard there were going to be twelve more hours of this, which basically meant the rest of my life. Then a friend put her arm around me. I found my way to some edge, thin as a thread, where the panic turned into laughter.

This is the diamond of the mind, this ability. A lot of people know about it, but I didn't know about it.

From then on when the panic crept in I could just push over the thread-thin edge to the other side, feeling the way to joy.

Joy is the knowledge that the thread is there.

A thread runs through the middle of your life, and if you find it, the second half can be comedy instead.

A place can make you want to die, and then you can turn it over into the sweetest thing. You can do this yourself, if you have found the diamond in your mind.

Addiction is sometimes the attempt to raise the dead by returning to the scene. If you can't yet abandon the dead, at least you can practice abandonment, and will perhaps in that way be on your way to finding the world.

Something like summer comes early to the building by the bridge, seventy restless degrees in early April. The girls are walking up and down the pedestrian walkway in thin retro dresses, the men with their shirtsleeves rolled up, warm air on freshly bare skin. All over the building people have opened their windows and a breeze is fluttering the curtains, scattering projects and stacks of receipts. It's tax time, but there are a few more days to put it off, to walk around instead in the pretty light.

It's Easter morning, and this year it's Passover, too. All week people have gathered to read the story of the liberation of slaves, of plagues that purchase freedom, and to ask, as always, how this night is different from every other night. The occupiers from Zuccotti Park are gathering again in Union Square and so people are walking around the neighborhood in T-shirts that say *STOP EVERYTHING.* Everyone thinks addiction and being addicted to addicts is a terrible thing. Yet most of the people in this country, on this morning, believe in a story about resurrection, about a body that never dies because you put it in your mouth once a week and it takes you higher, beyond death and time. It's the structure of addiction seen as redemptive, and maybe it is. But there are some moments, and this is one of them, when it's only in letting what's dead be dead that you can learn from your body the resurrection of the mind.

I am less interested in zombie stories, though, than I am in this neighborhood's particular light. The thing I most want to tell you is how the sunlight is here, but I don't know how to describe it. It's obviously the same sun that lights the rest of the city, but there is something different about it. Maybe it's our lack of trees, or the reflection of the river, or the lowness of most of the buildings, or the supersaturated colors, deep reds and greens, the bright wild complicated graffiti. We don't have the trees of South Brooklyn, the shady corridors of stoops, the tall stately brownstones of Fort Greene or Park Slope. We don't have cobblestone streets. What we have is this naked golden light. It's a thin, big-sky light, kind of Western, cinematic. Since the first day I saw it, it has alternately flustered and comforted me. Today its particular quality will have half the people in the neighborhood drinking in the afternoon. By five or six, some of the couples will already be fighting on the streets, one of them wrangling the drunker, more belligerent one home, because there is always a drunker, more belligerent one, and one who needs to feel like he or she is taking care of someone.

At the moment, though, a really tall guy on roller skates is coasting down the long steep slope of the pedestrian walkway with his legs and arms spread wide and the wind in his fingers. He has the biggest satisfied grin on his face. There are always a few people a day who roll like this, on bikes or boards or even just running, arms wide, falling down the bridge into Williamsburg, in the pretty light.

(2013)

ACKNOWLEDGMENTS

All the essays in this book were first published in *n+1* magazine:
"Happiness" appeared in Issue Two (Winter 2005). Copyright
© 2005 by n+1 Foundation.
"Torture and Parenting" appeared in Issue Three (Fall 2005).
Copyright © 2005 by Marco Roth.
"Afternoon of the Sex Children" appeared in Issue Four (Spring
2006). Copyright © 2006 by Mark Greif.
"Diana Abbott: A Lesson" appeared in Issue Two (Winter 2005).
Copyright © 2005 by Benjamin Kunkel.
"Gut-Level Legislation, or, Redistribution" appeared in Issue
Four (Spring 2006). Copyright © 2006 by Mark Greif.
"Death Is Not the End" appeared in Issue Two (Winter 2005).
Copyright © 2005 by n+1 Foundation.
"Babel in California" is reprinted from *The Possessed* by Elif
Batuman. Copyright © 2010 by Elif Batuman. Reprinted by
permission of Farrar, Straus and Giroux, LLC. Originally pub-
lished in a different form in 2005 in *n+1* Issue Two.
"An Interruption" appeared in Issue Four (Spring 2006). Copyright
© 2006 by Chad Harbach.

PERMISSIONS ACKNOWLEDGMENTS

Grateful acknowledgment is made for permission to reprint the following material:

"High Windows" from *The Complete Poems of Philip Larkin* by Philip Larkin, edited by Archie Burnett. Copyright © 2012 by The Estate of Philip Larkin. Reprinted by permission of Farrar, Straus and Giroux, LLC, and Faber and Faber, Ltd.

Excerpt of fourteen lines from "The True Import of Present Dialogue, Black vs. Negro (For Peppe, Who Will Ultimately Judge Our Efforts)" from *Black Feeling, Black Talk, Black Judgment* by Nikki Giovanni. Copyright © 1968, 1970 by Nikki Giovanni. Reprinted by permission of HarperCollins Publishers.

Lyrics from "A Real Hero" by College & Electric Youth. Copyright © 2010 by College & Electric Youth. All rights reserved. Reprinted by permission of the artists.